THE AMBASSADOR AND THE COURTESAN

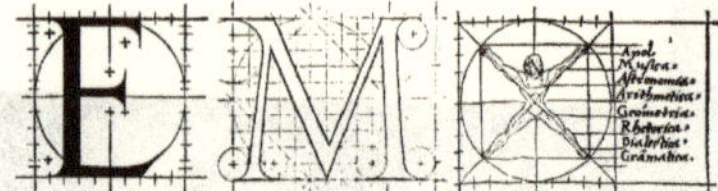

The Early Modern Exchange

SELECTED TITLES

Hagiography in Marguerite de Navarre's Heptaméron: *Saints and Debates in Renaissance France*, Leanna Bridge Rezvani

Widow City: Gender, Emotion, and Community in the Italian Renaissance, Anna Wainwright

The Age of Subtlety: Nature and Rhetorical Conceits in Early Modern Europe, Javier Patiño Loira

Redreaming the Renaissance: Essays on History and Literature in Honor of Guido Ruggiero, edited by Mary Lindemann and Deanna Shemek

Ordering Customs: Ethnographic Thought in Early Modern Venice, Kathryn Taylor

The Waxing of the Middle Ages: Revisiting Late Medieval France, edited by Tracy Adams and Charles-Louis Morand-Métivier

Gendering the Renaissance: Text and Context in Early Modern Italy, edited by Meredith K. Ray and Lynn Lara Westwater

The Ambassador and the Courtesan

Political Bodies in Renaissance Italy

Paola De Santo

Newark

978-1-64453-416-8 (cloth)
978-1-64453-415-1 (paper)
978-1-64453-417-5 (epub)

Cataloging-in-publication data is available from the Library of Congress.
LCCN 2025019360

A British Cataloging-in-Publication record for this book is available from the British Library.

∞ The paper used in this publication meets the requirements of the American National Standard for Information Sciences—Permanence of Paper for Printed Library Materials, ANSI Z39.48-1992.

udpress.udel.edu

Distributed worldwide by Rutgers University Press

Per Alberto ed Emilio

Contents

Acknowledgments

This project has been a long and arduous *viaggio* that would not have been completed without the generosity and support of so many, whom I am honored to thank here. This book started out as a doctoral dissertation at Harvard University under the guidance of Francesco Erspamer, Giuliana Minghelli, and Katharina Piechocki, brilliant and rigorous thinkers, and generous and encouraging mentors. I am also grateful to Lino Pertile, whose capacious intellect and elegant scholarship remain inspirational. The years at Harvard also gave me two dear friends: Caterina Mongiat Farina, with whom it is an honor to collaborate, translate beautifully tortuous quasi-Baroque Italian into English, exchange ideas and offer mutual support; and Samantha Clark, who is a most cherished friend, graceful writer, meticulous editor, and superlative cook—grazie di cuore!

My colleagues and friends at the University of Georgia have offered a supportive and stimulating atmosphere. I am grateful to members of the Romance Languages Department for warm friendship and collegiality, especially: Dana Bultman, our tireless leader, along with Milvet Alonso, Mark Anderson, Alicia Arribas, Nora Benedict, Stacey Casado, Nuño Castellanos, Lesley Feracho, Rachel Gabara, Jonathan Haddad, Cathy Jones, Betina Kaplan, Cris Lira, Nico Lucero, Sharina Maillo-Pozo, Rubén Maillo-Pozo, Diana Ranson, Cecília Rodrigues, Emily Sahakian, and Elizabeth Wright. A heartfelt *grazie* to my colleagues of the Italian section: Barbara Cooper, Lisa Dolasinski, Samantha Gillen, Steven Grossvogel, Jeff Kilpatrick, Thomas Peterson, and Concettina Pizzuti. Beyond Gilbert Hall, I am grateful to Rielle Navitski for her support and astute feedback on this project, and to many other friends here in Athens that have made this town a home.

The generous support granted by the Willson Center Research Fellowship and the honor of the Virginia Mary Macagnoni Prize for Innovative Research were instrumental to the completion of this project.

I am immensely grateful to the University of Delaware Press. Julia Oestreich has been thoughtful, patient, and greatly helpful throughout the publication process; and publication coordinator, Josephine Chaet, provided careful preproduction feedback. I am appreciative of the editors of The Early Modern Exchange series, Meredith Ray, Gary Ferguson, and Julia Domínguez, for their encouragement of this project and support of its publication as part of this series. I also owe a debt of gratitude to the two anonymous peer reviewers for their sharp insights and feedback, both of which helped significantly refine the book.

Finally, my greatest thanks and most profound love go to my family, particularly my son, Emilio, and husband, Alberto. Alberto has always been, when I needed him to be, my bluntest critic, and when I did not, my fiercest champion. He has listened tirelessly to my ideas and generously read every word of this book many times over. I appreciate the mark his vibrant intellect had on all stages of this project, and the sense of order he lent to the oftentimes chaos of my thoughts. Emilio's arrival in the midst of this project significantly lengthened the *viaggio* but ultimately made it much more meaningful. Huge thanks also go to my fiercely loyal, immensely loving, and amazingly fun siblings—Angelo, Juliana, Antoinette, Doriana, Silvana, Marco, and Sabrina—with whom I have shared immense joy and survived much sorrow. I also owe tremendous gratitude to my stepmother, Frances De Santo, for her kindness, boundless generosity, and encouragement throughout these many years. I dedicate this book to the memory of my parents, Vincent Samuel De Santo and Paola Giovanna De Santo née Zanchi.

INTRODUCTION

The Politics of Dual Identity

"What is an ambassador?" (Che cosa sia ambasciatore?) is the fundamental question Gasparo Bragaccia (1566–ca.1632), early seventeenth-century diplomat and diplomatic theorist from Piacenza, posed in one of the dozens of chapters comprising his six-book tome, *L'Ambasciatore* (1626), the first such treatise to be written in the Italian vernacular. Bragaccia contended, by reiterating a false etymology, that, as opposed to other titles that reflect a comparatively inert function, such as "messenger" (messaggiero), or undistinguished status, such as "agent" (agente), the title of "ambassador," "a most beautiful name for this office" (bellissimo nome di questo officio), expressed the diplomatic profession's dignity by connoting the Latin term *ambo*, meaning "both."

> L'Ambasciatore sia come mezzano d'ambe le parti, perché essendo mandato per lo commun bene, & perciò concedutogli tanti privilegi, habbia da unire per quanto possa ambe le parti, & di chi manda, & di quello, à cui si manda, & perciò sia detto Ambasciatore.[1]

> (The ambassador is akin to a mediator between both [ambe] sides, having been sent for the common good and therefore granted many privileges, it is incumbent upon him to unite, to the extent possible, both [ambe] sides, that which sends him, as well the one to which he is sent, and for this reason is called Ambassador).

However, "ambassador" (ambasciatore) is actually from the Latin *ambactus*, which connotes the subordinate vassal or dependent, and derives in turn from the Celtic *andbahts*, meaning "servant."[2]

Bragaccia acknowledged the false etymology of *ambasciatore* yet curiously still privileged it by reproducing and discussing it in his treatise. Bragaccia's reasoning was interesting because, as opposed to the Latinate *legato* (legate) or the religiously inflected *nunzio* (nuncio) and antiquated *araldo* (herald), it speaks directly to the essential mediatory function of the emerging early modern ambassador, which was that of uniting and reconciling opposing sides in a relationship between states, *mezzano d'ambe le parti* (mediator between both sides). However, importantly, Bragaccia also implied that, in addition to this dignified responsibility, the diplomat also has a predicament: The uniting and reconciling function requires inhabiting both sides at the same time, yet neither one fully.

The ambassador, upon election to that office, was "granted many privileges" (concedutogli tanti privilegi); yet, as Bragaccia's treatise suggests, that ostensible benefit was tempered by the demands of ambiguity and hybridity, creating a privileged but alienating space.[3] The ambassador was "required to assume a public identity" (propriamente è persona publica) and "serve the common good" (mandato per lo commun bene), which, beyond the requisite observance of moral and religious virtue, demanded the "subjugating of the appetite to reason, which shall be his guide and moderator" (soggiogando l'appetito alla ragione, la quale gli sia scorta, & moderatrice).[4] Additionally, the ambassador's authority was inherently unstable. The powers conferred upon him were, like the extraterritorial location of his own body, situated outside of his domain, dependent on the whim and/or the existence of his prince, and therefore may shift at a moment's notice from full ("piena potenza") to expired ("essendo spirata la sua potestà").[5] The ambassador's predicament could therefore be understood to derive from a status at once privileged and restrained. Beyond the difficulty of having to appease both his prince as well as the authority he was sent to communicate with, the ambassador existed in a transient authoritative state, the fluctuations of which could result in abrupt shifts in both status and identity, producing a disorientating dynamic that could be detrimental—or even dangerous. The physical danger to which an ambassador might be subjected because of his variable authority or status was compounded by the required disavowal of corporeal appetites, a restriction clearly and understandably meant to ensure the diplomat would prioritize his public office over personal desire, but also to reinforce the mind–body divide, alienating the ambassador from his own body and potentially further complicating and/or confusing his identity.

Just as the ambassador's body ("the appetite") was subjugated to reason, the ambassador himself was subjugated to the prince upon whom his authority fully depended, as Bragaccia explained in this way: "[L'ambasciatore] colui il quale *rappresenti li mandati* d'uno altro *dal qual talmente dependesse,* che non havesse come tale altronde altra potenza, che quella, che dalli predetti mandati gli fosse conceduta" ([The ambassador] *represents the commands of another upon whom he depends* to the extent that he does not have power deriving from anywhere other than from what is granted to him by the aforesaid commands; italics added).[6] In this definition, Bragaccia undermined his more dignified notion that the ambassador occupied "both parts" as a dynamic "uniter" and "mediator." In fact, here the ambassador lacks agency, "represent[ing]" instead a static catalog of "demands." This subservient conception of the ambassador is reflected in the true lexical lineage of *ambasciatore* that Bragaccia ignores or represses in his treatise. This omission suggests Bragaccia's desire to elevate the office of the ambassador to its more noble, conciliatory, and ultimately modern meaning. While the false etymology (from *ambo,* meaning "both") privileged by Bragaccia evokes the hybrid figure of the Renaissance diplomat, this study seeks to prove that the term's original root, the subordinate "vassal" or "servant," also informs the corporeal realities and requisite subjugation that characterized the diplomatic figure and complicated the office in early modernity. The ambassador's body, and its appetites, were to be suppressed, yet the body was precisely the vehicle that facilitated diplomacy, allowing for the ambassador's extraterritorial movement, as well as serving a protective function by shielding the prince's own body, which was not safeguarded by diplomatic immunity and inviolability.

A new diplomatic exigency reflected in the semantic development that led to the creation of a new term in the lexicon (which was really the resuscitation of a very old one, *ambasciatore*) and coincided with the increasing need and desire to define and delineate the office. This is confirmed by the spate of humanist and theoretical treatises on diplomacy and the ambassador, which appeared with increasing frequency from the late fifteenth through the seventeenth centuries, of which Bragaccia's is but one example.[7] Europe was embroiled in near constant war in general, and the Italian Wars devastating the peninsula threatened the few remaining independent Italian states. The role of the ambassador thus became central to the practice of diplomacy, particularly because rulers were excluded from the *ius gentium* (Law of Nations), the customary protections that guaranteed safe conduct, immunity, and inviolability of diplomats.

This period also gave rise to another figure of conciliation, the courtesan. The term "courtesan," like that of "ambassador," came to prominence in the Renaissance, announcing an emerging social actor whose function deviated from that of her predecessor. Moreover, the fluctuating characterization, or ambiguity, common to both ambassadors and courtesans, evidenced by the various terms employed to describe them, reflects the instability of their social status and function, as well as the mobility of their persons. One of the very first appearances[8] of the term *cortegiana* (courtesan)[9] can be found in Marin Sanudo's diary entry of October 16, 1514: "Era dona di tempo tuta coretesana" (She was the consummate courtesan of her day).[10] Additionally, there was the similar sort of lexical fragmentation we saw in relation to "ambassador," including *meretrice* (prostitute), *puttana* (whore), and *cortegiana*.[11] These differences relate superficially to the socioeconomic status of the prostitute herself, as well as that of her clients. However, they also indicate the co-existing compulsions to individuate and circumscribe the multiple, ambiguous identities of the prostitute, often driven by politically charged motivations. For various reasons aimed at the public defamation and legal censure of courtesans, a *cortegiana* was labeled alternately a *meretrice publica* (public prostitute) or *puttana*, erasing, or at least attempting to erase, any potential indication of social, cultural, political, or moral elevation. The purpose was to reduce the courtesan to the social function of her body: a mere prostitute.

On the contrary, the term *cortegiana* referred specifically to the multitalented, cultured prostitute, "neither lady nor whore," as Patricia Fortini Brown noted, whose access to male-dominated spaces of power and culture could also be involved in the seduction of those politically important to the state.[12] Whereas the ambassador represented the body politic outside the "geographical confines of official power," the courtesan embodied the host country, yet at the same time was also unburdened by the expectations that restricted other women.[13] In fact, being situated outside the demands of decorum could also be a space of power, which courtesan poet Veronica Franco (the subject of chapter 5) exploited for her own benefit and that of other women as well as that of society at large. Additionally, courtesans were conspicuously present at court affairs during which the Venetian state entertained visiting dignitaries, a space often indecorous for noble women. Courtesans acted as incarnations of the "feminine splendors of court society" and figured in the practice of early modern diplomacy.[14]

Both the ambassador and the courtesan are products of the Italian Renaissance.[15] The courtesan was "a very distinctive Italian Renaissance social type, with no obvious medieval precedent and no real parallel in other European cultures at this time."[16] Martha Feldman and Bonnie Gordon, in their path-breaking cross-cultural and transhistorical volume of essays on the courtesan, defined her as a "social phenomenon whereby women engage in relatively exclusive exchanges of artistic graces, elevated conversation, and sexual exchanges with male patrons."[17] The sexual, intellectual, and artistic function of the courtesan must be understood, however, through the unique social and political circumstances in which she developed. As the lexical link between *cortegiano* and *cortegiana* (courtier and courtesan, respectively) attests, the prominence of the court (corte) in Renaissance Italy is inextricable from the figure of the courtesan.[18] Scholars have traced the origins of the Renaissance courtesan through a linguistic study of the use of *cortegiana, cortegiana onesta,* and other similar terms used to indicate the prostitutes frequented by elite men of the papal court in late fifteenth-century Rome.[19] The court, an entity that is at once a defined physical space and "a network of interpersonal relations," crucially provided a place "that witnessed new forms of identity negotiation and prestige, the definition of masculinity, and gender-specific roles, as well as the birth of modern politics and a modern ethics based on merit and individual self-interest," as Paola Ugolini aptly stated.[20] Therefore, the court situated the courtesan in close proximity to powerful political figures and furnished access to intellectual and artistic exchange, which in turn allowed for her to "slide in and out of agency, control, and influence."[21]

However, the imbalance in social class and gender difference between the courtesan and her male, socially elite patrons created a slippery "dynamic of privilege and constraint" from which her artistic practice of "self-promotion—indeed self-preservation" emerged.[22] In addition to the tangible services—sexual, aesthetic, and intellectual—she offered to her patrons, association with elite courtesans was also "closely meshed with constructions of elite manhood and male honour," as Tessa Storey argued.[23] Despite the role of courtesans in elite male self-fashioning, courtesans did not derive the same benefits from their relations with elite men. In fact, the courtesan's elite social status was fictional, dictated by the desires, demands, and whims of her clients and patrons. These circumstances constrained courtesans, like ambassadors, to be different things to different people, a condition amounting to existing in a perpetual performance space, both interstitial and alienating. The ambassador and courtesan alike served important social, civic, and political functions that afforded them privileges yet also restrained them.

In this comparative study of the ambassador and the courtesan in early modern Italian literature and culture, the two figures in question, at first blush, appear to be quite different. One imagines the early modern ambassador as traveling in open space from one center of power to another, gathering news and disseminating it in writing, as well as orally negotiating in person. The courtesan, in contrast, is imagined employing her body in the service of entertaining elite clients in the enclosed space of the urban *ridotto*, or salon. Although not inaccurate, these characterizations reinforce how these social actors ostensibly perform very different roles in society and culture, but their comparison allows for the emergence of salient points of convergence, particularly the position of their bodies natural in relation to the body politic.

Placing into dialogue the body natural with the body politic reveals the fracturing of the corporate metaphor, which becomes a less relevant representation of modernizing political structures, characterized by increasingly fragmented states in Europe at large and in Italy in particular.[24] An analysis of these commonalities shows the ambassador's and the courtesan's shared status as figures embodying a transition toward modernity at a time when the notion of the self coincided with the formation of the modern state. The examination of the ambassador and the courtesan through texts by and about them allows me to demonstrate both how these figures inhabited the tension, or friction, created by the two opposing forces of state and self, and in turn what they reveal about the negotiation between society and the individual in this transitional period.

The ambassador in the early Renaissance, as mentioned, was tasked with faithfully representing his government abroad with dignity, in addition to providing it with valuable observations and information about the countries to which he was sent.[25] An expectation derived from the humanist value held at the time that man had "no higher moral responsibility than duty his to country."[26] Although being elected as ambassador may well have been considered an honor, adherence to the collective morality that regarded the ambassador as "a tireless and selfless agent of state" was more aspirational than factual, however.[27] For instance, instead of embracing being elected as ambassadors, most members of the Venetian patriciate eagerly sought to avoid such diplomatic appointments, or committed immoral, irresponsible, or less than exemplary conduct while in embassy.[28] The increasing complexity of early modern politics and diplomacy dictated that the ambassador's charge went beyond mere message bearing; instead, the diplomat had to inhabit multiple selves at the same time. This conflict between collective ideals and individual practice is precisely the area this study probes.

The self, or one's identity, is an "elusive thing," as John Jeffries Martin stated in *Myths of Renaissance Individualism* (2004), making it difficult to understand precisely how the concept was formed or understood by the people of the Renaissance.[29] Martin urged that we at least understand the Renaissance self not merely as "a thing," but alternatively as a relation between the internal and external worlds of a given person, as something protean whose many forms changed depending on a particular individual's condition and circumstances. It is thus important to bear in mind that the notions of the self held by people of the Renaissance were "radically different from our own, but equally varied and dynamic."[30] Martin's relational conception of identity in the Renaissance offered a correction to Jacob Burckhardt's idea of individualism, articulated in *The Civilization of the Renaissance in Italy* (1860), that in the Renaissance "man became a spiritual individual and recognized himself as such," a development that he claimed distinguished the Renaissance individual from the men and women of the Middle Ages.[31] This study, while not seeking to define what may or may not have constituted the self, individualism, or identity in the Renaissance, aligns with Martin's relational conception of the Renaissance self in its examination of how the ambassador and the courtesan—figures tasked with representing different things to different people—negotiated the boundary, however porous, between their inner beliefs and their social and/or professional roles.

If the Renaissance self for Burckhardt comprised the ambitious ideals of the modern autonomous individual, postmodern critics saw instead that the early modern "human subject" was "remarkably unfree, the ideological product of the relations of power in a particular society," as Stephen Greenblatt claims in his influential New Historicist work *Renaissance Self-Fashioning from More to Shakespeare* (1980). The understanding of what constitutes the "self" in this view reduces the individual to a "cultural artifact" lacking independent agency and devoid of "identity freely chosen," and whose own subjectivity was so constrained by political, cultural, and social forces that willful self-fashioning, paradoxically, seemed quite improbable.[32] Yet, despite these issues, it is helpful to attenuate rather than discard these differing concepts of the Renaissance self. Virginia Cox redefined the concept of self-fashioning as how "Renaissance men and women consciously or unconsciously crafted their social personae" and proceeded to explain that self-fashioning is "a process profoundly influenced by cultural norms and power structures, but also allowing for some degree of individual agency."[33] In fact, though these notions are perhaps vulnerable to attacks of being ahistorical and even teleological, as Martin forcefully argued,[34] the friction between these two conceptions—a self-consciously autonomous self on the one hand, and a "cultural artifact" helplessly fashioned by society's powerful institutions and forces on the other—allows us to better understand the dynamic emergence of identity in the ambassador and the courtesan, social actors both privileged and disadvantaged, upon whom it was incumbent to represent different things, depending on the circumstances. Inhabiting social roles at the nexus of public/private and power/subject, the ambassador and the courtesan alike provide fertile ground to analyze the space between their internal worlds and their socially constructed selves.

I situate this study starting around the French invasion of Italy (1494)—which initiated the Italian Wars and the centuries-long destabilization of the peninsula—through the effects of the Counter-Reformation into the early seventeenth century. The initial invasion of Italy, via the hypothesis that this border breach allowed for the arrival and diffusion of syphilis, the "French disease," throughout Italy, establishes the link between military and sexual conquest, with the resultant consequences for bodies political and natural. Examining the tension between the body and its metaphor through the ambassador and courtesan is intriguing because their mediatory bodies represented a locus of negotiation, which attested to new demands of hybridity in response to societal transformation and crisis. The role of the body was thus central: The diplomatic body stood in for that of the sovereign state and was thus safeguarded theoretically by customary *ius gentium*, protections that originated in antiquity, guaranteeing the safe passage, immunity, and inviolability of diplomats. On the contrary, the body of the prostitute was the most public and "violable" body in Renaissance society, the incarnation of hospitality, whose body and voice were disciplined by moralistic legal statutes and maligned in male-authored literary texts. The freely circulating diplomat negotiated spaces as an official surrogate and rendered them in writing as solely personal experiences. Whereas the diplomat made the public private, the courtesan did the opposite: She transformed her closed-door encounters and personal correspondence into public texts.

The ambassador emerged as an important figure at this point in history, when meetings and conversations between princes became "useless, if not dangerous," leading to the dependence on diplomats to conduct international affairs.[35] The centralized nation-states of Europe, large and ambitious, required the establishment of an accordingly large diplomatic corps capable of conducting affairs simultaneously in disparate geographical spaces, both within and beyond Europe. In the early modern Italian context, given the numerous small political entities in the peninsula, a transition occurred from reliance on ad hoc diplomatic missions (straordinari) to the establishment of permanent embassies in an effort to maintain a "policy of balance of power" (politica dell'equilibrio). This equilibrium concept of international relations was an Italian invention that had already been in practice in the politically fragmented Italian Peninsula for many years, beginning with the Treaty of Lodi (1455), which created the Italian League, for which Lorenzo de' Medici, "Il Magnifico," is often credited.[36] In fact, at Westphalia in 1648, the chief mediators of the peace conference were Italian ambassadors: papal nuncio Cardinal Fabio Chigi (future Pope Alexander VII) and Venetian ambassador Alvise Contarini. The Peace of Westphalia was therefore a diplomatic rather than military triumph, due in large measure to this concept of the balance of powers, applied to Europe at large through the guidance of experienced Italian ambassadors.[37]

The establishment of the permanent embassy and resident ambassador required the increasingly autonomous role of diplomats, which in turn prompted negotiation of moral standards and special legal protections to codify the status of the ambassador. Seventeenth-century jurists and legal philosophers examined the complex legal and theoretical issues related to the movements of diplomats in space, and both the potential and limits posed by extraterritoriality, bringing about what Timothy Hampton calls "Baroque diplomacy," in which the ambassador assumes the role as his own ambassador.[38] This study is situated at the birth of modern diplomacy and the establishment of the embassy and resident ambassador.

For her part, the courtesan also acquired a new role in the Italian context as its fragmented political entities struggled to maintain tenuous relationships with the emerging nation-states in Europe and beyond. In fact, it was the Renaissance court, the institution at the center of political and cultural life, that "invented" the courtesan.[39] Celebrated humanist Lorenzo Valla (ca. 1406–1457) wrote a bold defense of pleasure, *De Voluptate* (*On Pleasure*, 1431), which he conceived as a young man while immersed in the homosocial and powerful world of the Curia in Rome.[40] In this text, Valla theorized that social problems, including infidelity and, importantly, the threat of cuckoldry, could be solved if "those charming women did not belong to particular private persons, or tyrants [. . .] but to the state itself, that is to all the people" (ille lepide mulieres non quorundam privatorum, prope dixerim tyrannorum, sed reipublice, id est ipsius *populi*).[41] Communal women, Valla suggested, reflect the assertions of both Plato and natural law that (sexual) pleasure must always be satisfied, and marriage is but an obstacle that unnecessarily fosters competition and division among men, and even civil strife.[42] Valla's formulation, therefore, can be considered an important justification of the courtesan and authorization of her practice as beyond purely personal pleasure seeking. The educated, glamorous, and refined courtesan was an "honorable alternative" to the common prostitute; she was only available to a small, elite group of humanist-educated men who, despite Valla's claim, were not representative of "all the people," but instead were precisely those men who wielded the power of the state.[43] As I discuss in more detail in later chapters, the unique Italian political situation demanded creative solutions, resulting in the concurrent authorization, exploitation, regulation, and containment of the "hospitality" of courtesans.

The ambassador and courtesan alike found themselves bound in a dynamic of freedom and repression, or privilege and restraint. As figures of mediation, both ambassadors and courtesans were motivated to narrate their own experiences. Emerging from the writings by the ambassador is a physical body fraught with the symbolism of the state's power but also rendered as the locus of suffering and sacrifice. While the ambassador was elected and reproached, the courtesan was praised and reviled, both the attraction of Venice and its scapegoat. The ambassador acted as the official representative of the sovereign yet was also the figure held culpable, and was subject to sacrifice should any disturbance occur. In the texts written by the ambassador and courtesan, therefore, it is possible to discern their negotiations between their internal and external experiences. Their individual subjectivities find expression within their own texts, where they are not confined to acting either as instruments of another's needs or desires, or as scapegoats.

Torquato Tasso (1544–1595), the great Italian poet of the late Renaissance, treated diplomacy in both *Gerusalemme Liberata* (1581) and *Il Messaggiero* (1582), his influential dialogue on the ambassador. Furthermore, in *Il Messaggiero* Tasso explicitly correlated diplomacy and prostitution by likening the messenger to a pimp. However, he quickly abandoned that suggestive line of inquiry, "leaving others to discuss the art of the pimp" (lasciando che dell'arte del ruffiano altri discorra).[44] Inspired by Tasso, Hampton titled his introductory chapter of *Fictions of Embassy* (2009) "Angels and Pimps: Toward a Diplomatic Poetics" and noted that "the connection between panderers and ambassadors is a cliché, which it would take a separate book to study."[45] In this book, I engage that line of inquiry, which has been deferred by influential male authors, by offering a sustained study of links between the ambassador and the sophisticated and aestheticized example of prostitution, the courtesan. Through a close study of *Gerusalemme Liberata*, in dialogue with *Il Messaggiero*, I contend that in the reconciliation of the ambassador and the courtesan, Tasso creates a space of freedom through a poetics of ambiguity and hybridity.

Both the ambassador and the courtesan are thus characterized by their liminal and ambiguous status, particularly in relation to, as well as within, the body politic. This requisite intermediary and conciliatory status, however, can easily or even necessarily result in alienation, estranging these figures from their own bodies, the very entity whose skin serves as a "privileged frontier," which facilitates the relation between "one's inner experience and one's experience in the world."[46] The root of this alienation from one's own body, the sacrifice of one's own corporeality, can be found in the modern imposition of being two (or more) things at once while also attempting to unite disparate sides. The physical body is a social and mobile entity that, unlike space, cannot be fully restricted, and therefore both the courtesan and the ambassador inhabit spaces of negotiation that are at times a privilege, and at others a danger.

My work hinges on the analysis of the embodied experience in texts by and featuring these figures. This attention allows us to discern how their bodies, their mobile material entities, negotiated geographical and discursive spaces, as well as spaces of identity, thus surfacing issues relating to extraterritoriality, hospitality, gender construction, and fictional practices. The practice of diplomacy was only possible because of a legal fiction (fictio iuris) that "takes the false for the true" by declaring the ambassador inviolable and guaranteeing him safe passage beyond the confines of his state.[47] Hampton established that the rise of a modern secular literary culture related to a new political practice incarnated by the early modern ambassador. The forgers of Italy's literary canon were often the same players who negotiated as diplomats both between Italian polities and with states beyond the peninsula.

Relations with courtesans offered elite men the possibility to fashion their identities and reputations, yet the courtesan's elite status was never consolidated in the same way, remaining instead imagined and conditional. As a subject of male-authored literary texts and works of visual art, as well as an author in her own right, the courtesan also populated the world of artistic fiction. Moreover, the courtesan embodies a fictional and interstitial space between morality and pragmatism. Publicly denounced as a moral and physical danger to the body politic, prostitution was, however, authorized, tolerated, and even exploited for its direct economic benefits as well as its indirect benefits to civil society and the maintenance of political order and social institutions, namely, marriage. The courtesan and the ambassador are thus figures of negotiation and keepers of peace. They alike depended on their eloquence and mastery of language and discourse for success, self-promotion, and even survival. They both arose from humanist-inspired circles, and these shared "fictional" humanist-invented origins of the ambassador and the courtesan reflected the fact that both human agents existed in a sort of "fiction" as well. The writings by and about these figures help us to understand how, in occupying fictional states, they negotiated between private and public personae, and navigated the resultant tension arising from shifting contingencies and loyalties; and to perceive how their selves as well as their bodies contended with such constantly changing demands.

Book Synopsis

Chapter 1, "From Mind to Body: Formation and Narration of the Early Modern Ambassador," places into dialogue humanist treatises on diplomacy with two early Renaissance travel narratives of Venetian ambassadors Ambrogio Contarini (1429–1499) and Giosafat Barbaro (1413–1494) in Persia during the late fifteenth century, in order to interrogate the distinction between diplomatic practice and theory. This juxtaposition reveals the privileged place of the ambassador as the so-called "mind" of the state in the *trattatistica*, or humanist treatise, and examines the tradition as well as the realities of the vulnerability and violability, and often futility, of the ambassadorial body in space and motion. For instance, Contarini narrated his embassy in a manner akin more to an account of a pilgrimage than of diplomacy. In these narratives, the arduousness and inefficacy of the diplomatic mission allowed for the emergence of the body natural, an aspect that I bring into dialogue with Zaccaria Pagani's *Viaggio di Domenico Trevisan: ambasciatore veneto al gran sultano del Cairo nell'anno 1512*, in which the ambassadorial body was rendered as semantically indistinguishable from a gift from one sovereign to another.

Chapter 2, "Ambassadors in 'Utopia,'" begins with a discussion of Hans Holbein's dual portrait *The Ambassadors* (1533), to destabilize public/private and foreigner/native binaries. I offer a reading of the painting as a work that illustrated the effacement of the Renaissance ambassador's personal identity. I then connect this reading with Steven Greenblatt's notion of "non-place" or "utopia" to frame the identity and existence of the office of the Renaissance ambassador as a "non-place"—a fiction or an interstitial irreality in which the ambassador was neither subject nor sovereign, neither foreigner nor native, and his actions neither private nor truly public.[48] The juxtapositions between these roles allow for a discussion of the growing influence of diplomacy on statecraft during the late fifteenth through seventeenth centuries. Two case studies in ambassadorial triumph and tragedy, the death and dismemberment of the contested ambassador Alberto Maraviglia (d. 1533), and the dangerous and virtuosic diplomacy of Henry Wotton (1568–1639), who also referred to himself as "Ottavio Baldi," provide for a discussion of these developments in diplomatic practice. No longer were messengers considered, nor did they act, as mere conduits, as implied by the terms *nuntius* (nuncio), *oratore* (orator), or *messaggero* (messenger). Yet the expansion of the diplomat's role, with its enhanced agency and responsibility, placed the ambassador in an even more vulnerable, even sacrificial position. As representatives of their state, their authority over its policies could be overestimated, and their culpability for its actions or aggressions exaggerated.

Chapter 3, "Tasso's Messengers: Ambassadors and Poets," establishes the correlation between diplomacy and poetry that Torquato Tasso created with his treatise on the diplomat, *Il Messaggiero*, and his chief work, *Gerusalemme Liberata*. Tasso's theoretical conception in his treatise on the ambassador is discussed to elucidate the centrality of the physical presence and aesthetics of the ambassador's body and how it relates to poetics. The rhetorical, physical, and aesthetic aspects of diplomacy in Tasso's theoretical formulation are then compared with the qualities of the ambassador characters in *Gerusalemme Liberata*. I closely read three episodes of diplomacy in the *Liberata* to show how the potential of diplomacy reached its height when the diplomatic and the poetic converged. The ambassador, liberated from reporting the demands of his sovereign, was granted the permission to deceive, the same license the poet grants himself. Deceptive practices, morally censured, were redeemed as essential tools of the negotiation of meaning and truth.

Chapter 4, "Armida's Mission: Reconciling Body and Language," contends that Armida, the beautiful, seductive, dispossessed Damascene princess through whom Tasso modernized the epic genre in *Gerusalemme Liberata*, is a hybrid of two composite figures—the courtesan and the ambassador—thus making her the figure of hybridization par excellence. Armida wielded her body and weaponized her sexuality, and through experience she came to understand that within *ragione di stato* (reason of state) politics, in which "all is permissible" (il tutto lice), morality was subjugated to pragmatic political interests, which entailed the disregard for agents and their bodies. This knowledge allowed Armida, in Tasso's fiction, to become the progenitress of the Este dynasty, thus surpassing the confines of the ambassador by establishing a state for herself: the Duchy of Ferrara. By situating herself within the body politic, of which Rinaldo occupied the "head," Armida transcended the traditionally generative role granted to the female body through political activation. Her triumph is authorial: She "rewrote" her own destiny, just as the poet authors the fates of characters. Armida took full advantage of the expectation of female vulnerability, performing it and utilizing the rhetoric of ambiguity to gain power and agency. This power to control discourse and manipulate people's responses is inherently diplomatic, representative of an ethos in which dissimulation becomes a necessary tool of power and freedom.

Chapter 5, "Controlling Her Corpus: The Courtesan as Political Writer," first contextualizes the courtesan in Venetian social, literary, artistic, legal, and medical history, to demonstrate the pervasive, though often futile, efforts to isolate, demean, and punish the body of the prostitute. The courtesan's fictional space of pleasure contrasts with the disciplinary restrictions placed on the body of the Renaissance prostitute, which ranged from the sartorial to the spatial and effectively excluded the prostitute from the body politic. In bringing the discussion once again to practice, I then situate Veronica Franco's (1546–1591) writing on prostitution, both explicit and implicit, in a political context by arguing that, in her *Lettere familiari a diversi* (1580), she reclaimed the body of the prostitute both for personal gain by relocating it within the body politic from which it was excluded, as well as to advocate for all prostitutes by aligning the health and integrity of the prostitute's body with that of the body politic.

This study, though not an exhaustive examination of either the ambassador or the courtesan, seeks nonetheless to demonstrate through these figures the conflict that arose between the state and the body in the changing political landscape of early modern Italy. The rise of *ragione di stato* political pragmatism coincided with the emergence of the modern subjectivity of the individual. This study contends that, through the analyses of writings by and about the ambassador and the courtesan, this convergence becomes particularly salient. The intersection of political and literary discourse created a space in which to appreciate both the vulnerabilities and privileges these figures embodied. As mediators, negotiators, and keepers of peace, as well as sacrificial entities, the ambassador and the courtesan employed diverse rhetorical strategies to situate and safeguard themselves in an alienating world in crisis and transition.

CHAPTER ONE

From Mind to Body

Formation and Narration of the Early Modern Ambassador

From "Oratore" to "Ambasciatore": The Formation of the Renaissance Ambassador

The role of the diplomat in early Renaissance Italy was still in formation throughout the 1400s, as the multitude of names used to refer to the office of the ambassador—*oratore, nunzio, messaggiero, legato,* and *ambasciatore*—attests. The Roman origins of early terms for the ambassador, such as *nuncius* and *orator,* convey the fact that these envoys reported orally. Indeed, *oratore,* a term used predominantly in the Florentine diplomatic context from the fourteenth to the sixteenth centuries, emphasizes the vocal and sonic aspects of an embodied diplomatic practice, yet does not account for the essential role of written communication in early modern diplomacy.

Early modern ambassadors wrote numerous and varied types of texts. Letters and dispatches were, of course, vital during the embassy. Since the Middle Ages, in Venice, ambassadors were required to draft reports—the famed *relazioni*—upon completion of a diplomatic mission and then deliver them orally to the Senate.[1] In the fifteenth century, it was mandated that the *relazioni* be recorded and registered in the Senate's archives. This decision to maintain these documents indicates an appreciation of their importance in a period in which the geopolitical landscape became more complex and threatening vis-à-vis Venice's political hegemony and economic stability. Though the clear intention was for the *relazioni* to be accessible only to Venetian governmental officials, these valuable and unique documents did not remain classified for long. Throughout the course of the sixteenth-century, the reports circulated widely in Europe, much to the indignation of the Venetian Senate. They were sold to both foreign governments and collectors alike, fetching high prices. Evidence of written *relazioni* does not appear until the late fifteenth century, and very few surviving *relazioni* date from before the sixteenth century. Venetian *relazioni* were valued even in the period for their unique qualities as "paint[ings] of political tableau," including observations of the "characters of princes and ministers, the attitudes and sentiments of peoples, and the strengths and weaknesses of states," as Donald Queller described.[2] Notwithstanding the remarkable interest in the *relazioni*, these reports related information of importance to the state, and the authors were considered mere vessels of this information; accordingly, they were expected to omit personal experiences, tribulations, or observations not relevant to the official mission. Consequently, the ambassadors who drafted these reports did not seem to have authorial intention or ambition.

Treatises on diplomacy appeared concurrently with the *relazioni*. These sought to define and dignify the office of the ambassador.[3] Treatises written by experienced diplomats, such as Étienne Dolet and Ermolao Barbaro, were concerned broadly with utilitarian discussions regarding the requisite qualities of an ambassador, as well as best practices. Others were more legal and abstract.[4] The growing number of these texts during the Renaissance indicates the need to codify the role of the diplomat, whose increasing importance coincided with the increasing demands and pressures on early modern states to respond to consequential matters beyond their borders. Riccardo Fubini stated that, particularly for Italian states of the fifteenth century, diplomacy became essential to their existence.[5] As the field of diplomacy grew in prominence in early modernity, it demanded the commensurate expansion of the authority of the ambassador. No longer was it sufficient for an envoy to practice the premodern sense of his function—a "'living letter' shorn of subjectivity, which spoke 'per se sed non de per se'—(through) himself, but not from (on behalf of) himself."[6] Instead, it was essential that the ambassador be considered a public official invested with authority, agency, and discretion. In *De officio legato* (ca. 1490), Ermolao Barbaro defined the objectives of the ambassador as far exceeding the conveyance of an unaltered message: "The purpose of the ambassador is [. . .] to do, say, discuss and devise everything he judges useful in order to maintain and increase the well-being ['ad optimum suae civitate status'] of their city."[7]

While understanding that diplomats were essential to the health ("well-being"/"optimum . . . status") and prosperity of their state, and granting greater authority to the ambassador, the state also implemented measures to control and restrict that same authority. Although this restriction and containment of an ambassador's agency may be interpreted as protecting the diplomat's person, the control of the messenger's message and intentions was a more probable reason. Venice, for example, forbade ambassadors from authoring their own instructions.[8] Measures such as the imposition of oaths were introduced to allay the states' anxiety that ambassadors might prioritize their own well-being or profit over that of the state or sovereign they represented.[9] The body of an ambassador therefore had to carry a message and represent the state, but it was not endowed with the state's powers; his voice had to speak the mind of the state, not his own. The navigation and negotiation of this boundary are examined in travelogues (viaggi) by and about Venetian ambassadors in the east during this period, in which the diplomat had to work with the increasing importance and scrutiny of diplomatic practice. The genre of ambassadorial travelogue represents a negotiation between public and private that allowed for the emergence of the voice of the diplomat, now relieved of the burden of recounting an official story.

Ius gentium in Theory and Diplomacy in Practice

Ius gentium, the Law of Nations, is a legal concept originating in Ancient Rome, which, in order to fulfill the demands of empire, established a universal, rather than territorial, law applicable to noncitizens.[10] In the early modern period, this concept began to be applied more specifically to relations between different nations, laying the groundwork for what would eventually become known as international law.[11] Discussions of *ius gentium* figured prominently in the literature on diplomacy and the ambassador in early modernity, attesting to the imperative of reinforcing and renegotiating customary conventions that guaranteed the safe conduct, immunity, and inviolability of diplomats.[12] Despite careful legal rhetoric, the body of the ambassador always inhabited a contradictory paradigm, crossing borders between individual and state, war and peace, violability and immunity, sacred and civilian, civilization and barbarism, dissimulation and authenticity, foreign and domestic, envoy and spy, diplomat and combatant—a few of the paradoxical categories in which the ambassador moved. The status of the ambassador's body thus proves to be a richly symbolic entity and a disputed territory. I examine the status and portrayal of the ambassadorial body as an entity fraught with contradiction and vulnerability, both uniquely protected as well as disputed. As the body of the ambassador is a surrogate for the state, its integrity and health is analogous to the integrity and health of the borders of the state itself, and the breach of the ambassador's body, as if it were a modern embassy, was—and still is—cause for fervent debate and conflict.

The body of the ambassador was, in theory, safe from harm. The *ius gentium* granted ambassadors immunity from prosecution, but most importantly, safeguarded their physical safety, at least rhetorically. Diplomacy, however, depended on contingencies, which meant that diplomatic theory and practice did not always coincide. The customary law, or legal philosophy, that should have protected the body of the ambassador may not always have prevailed. The ambassador could be used as a pawn in a conflict, possibly one that his presence was meant to avoid. In legal rhetoric, the ambassador was guaranteed safe passage and immunity, but in practice it was much more complicated to guarantee the integrity of that body, as the case of Alberto Maraviglia (discussed in chapter 2) demonstrates. The body of the ambassador was constantly displaced and dispossessed: The ambassador initially and theoretically stood in for the sovereign, and therefore the state; in practice, however, his body might have needed to be concealed or disguised, and his identity obscured, not only to assure his own physical security but also to fulfill his professional mission.

This chapter focuses on three *viaggi* by or about Renaissance Venetian ambassadors in the East. While Venice negotiated diplomatically with the important emerging European nation-states of the time, in addition to the papacy and other Italian states, perhaps its principal negotiating partner was the Ottoman Empire. The relationship was often unstable. In times of war with the Ottomans, Venice turned to Persia for allegiance and assistance. The Persian diplomatic mission was so critical that the Serenissima found it necessary to send two ambassadors to fulfill essentially the same embassy. Just twenty years after the fall of Constantinople, the Venetians were embroiled in the First Ottoman-Venetian War (1463–1479), which included the devastating loss in 1470 of Negroponte, the strategic trading territory in the Eastern Mediterranean of the Serenissima's *stato da mar* (maritime territories), in addition to Ottoman attempts to seize Cyprus, and other aggressions. The disastrous potential of further Ottoman encroachment to the west was the impetus behind dispatching two envoys, Ambrogio Contarini (1429–1499) and Giosafat Barbaro (1413–1494), to Persia in 1473.

Barbaro and Contarini were tasked with communicating a bold plan to defeat the Ottomans by waging a two-front battle, with Venice and her allies attacking from the west, and Persian allies—the Turkmen Aq Qoyunlu, led by Hasan Beg Bahador Khan, called Uzun Hasan (1453–1478)—from the east.[13] The first Venetian ambassador, Giosafat Barbaro, transported artillery, ammunition, and even soldiers to the Aq Qoyunlu. Barbaro took the sea route to the east, passing through the Adriatic, rounding Morea (the Peloponnese Peninsula, extending south of Greece into the Mediterranean), and continuing to Cyprus, where he scandalously remained for over a year, ignoring the Senate's demands for his immediate departure from Cyprus to fulfill his mission of delivering much-needed artillery to the troops of Uzun Hasan.

In his account Barbaro downplayed his official ambassadorial role. Unlike an official *relazione*, or even a text narrating the dutiful execution of his embassy, the adventurous story Barbaro offered portrays him as the protagonist, acting on his own command rather than on behalf and under the control of the state. Barbaro was sent to Uzun Hasan in early 1473 with the diplomatic order of enticing another attack on Mehmet II, this time with masses of artillery meant to facilitate the larger ongoing assault. We find out (not from Barbaro's text, I should add) that he never truly fulfilled this mission. Instead, Barbaro left Uzun Hasan's ambassador waiting for the better part of the year while he "ordered" ships about ("ordinai che le galee") and participated in strategic military planning during the Ottoman assault on Cyprus.[14] This quite clearly was not what he had been dispatched to do, but his active verbal forms (*ordinai, feci, andai*) and virile self-aggrandizement—"I, a man accustomed to a struggle and experienced with barbaric people" (io come uomo uso a stentare e pratico tra gente barbara)—spin his tale into one of bravery and exemplary diplomacy, and at the same time indicate his defiance of the Senate.[15] Barbaro's text essentially ignored his official mission in lieu of a revisionist account in which he reclaimed autonomy from his purported role as statesman.

In contrast, Contarini's account, which I discuss in more detail, is concerned with the physical struggles and the material negotiations of the body during the journey and offers a paucity of details regarding professional diplomatic protocol.[16] For this reason, much of the existing scholarly criticism has stressed that Contarini's propensity to narrate the physical difficulties he faced reduces the appeal of his travelogue to the reader, who hopes for marvel and adventure. The body of the ambassador, as described in the first person by Contarini, lacks any true sense of agency, independence, or uncertified identity. While he was the head of his cohort, his authority, and at times his dignity, ended there; the entire existence and survival of the group—their safety, their basic needs, their comfort, their route—were entirely dependent on the whims of the series of sovereigns (or their surrogates) under whose care they found themselves. Aspects of Contarini's narrative considered to be textual flaws by the criticism—its worries (affanni) and dangers (pericoli)—are, for the sake of my claims here, evidence of a valuable vantage point into the physical processes, difficulties, and realities of administering diplomacy in the early Renaissance. I look at the political implications of the movement of the diplomat's body extraterritorially and how the voice of the diplomat may or may not align with his own experience.

Contarini and Barbaro wrote and circulated individual accounts of their embassies upon return to the Serenissima. "Il viaggio di Ambrogio Contarini, ambasciatore veneziano"[17] and "Viaggio di Iosafa Barbaro alla Tana e nella Persia"[18] were eventually included in Giovanni Battista Ramusio's monumental three-volume *Delle navigazioni e viaggi* (1550–1559), one of the most significant compendia of travel narratives in the early modern period.[19] In the last section of this chapter, I examine a third account, *Viaggio di Domenico Trevisan: ambasciatore veneto al gran sultano del Cairo nell'anno 1512*, written by Zaccaria Pagani, a member of the ambassador's retinue, which narrates Domenico Trevisan's embassy to the grand sultan of Cairo, Qansuh al-Ghuri (1441–1516). Pagani offered an interesting point of view, both from within the diplomatic entourage as well as from the outside, as he was not the invested ambassador, but an informed and privileged observer.

In Contarini's text, originally published in 1487, the challenges and vicissitudes of the mission transform the narration of his embassy into an account that is stylistically related to pilgrimage narratives. Contarini expressed that he feared for his life numerous times, and members of his diplomatic entourage died of plague. Concluding his narrative, Contarini described the gravity of the dangers he encountered and reverently expressed gratitude for his "miraculous" survival:

> Ringraziando sempre il nostro Signor Dio e la sua Madre dolcissima, che mi aveva campato di tanti evidenti pericoli e affanni e condotto a salvamento [. . .] e benché corporalmente io fussi nel detto luogo [Venezia], *quasi l'animo mio dubitava, parendomi cosa impossibile, quand'io pensavo al tutto.* [. . .] Ma andandovi trovai nel canal della Zudecca mio fratello

> messer Agustin e due miei cognati, e abbracciati strettamente, parendo loro cosa miracolosa, perché tendevano per certo ch'io fussi morto (italics added).[20]

> (In eternal thanks to God Our Savior and His Sweetest Mother, who saved me from many clear dangers and sufferings and who led me to safety [. . .] even though I was in Venice, my soul almost doubted it, *seeming instead an impossible thing, when remembering it all* [. . .] However, returning home to Venice, along the Giudecca Canal, I found my brother, Mr. Agustin, and two of my brothers-in-law, and we embraced one another tightly, because to them my return seemed miraculous, so certain they were that I was dead.

In contrast, Barbaro, who almost certainly wrote his account in response to Contarini's, expounded on his active and indispensable role as a commander and military strategist, as well as his expert and seamless immersion with the eastern other.[21] Barbaro chose to begin his text with a separate narrative of his merchant past in the Tana, prioritizing from the outset his personal history rather than focusing on his role as ambassador.[22] In fact, as Daria Perocco noted, Barbaro's two distinct travels, one diplomatic and the other mercantile, seem to blend into one single account; this narrative confluence suggests that for Barbaro his personal experience as traveler was of greater importance than the public diplomatic role he was sent to fulfill.[23]

Reading the texts side by side offers the chance to compare their stylistic traits as well as their literary intent, topics that have not seen much other scholarly attention. Perhaps this lack of scholarship is because the texts were not written as literature, yet neither were they written as history, ethnography, geography, or political treatise. These ambassadorial travel narratives represent the emergence of a new genre, or subgenre, in which the practical and marvelous aspects, as well as the political utility, of the text itself fade into the context of the primary development: the emergence of a consciously first-person authorial voice that represents the material experience of the diplomat. This literary turn in the ambassador's writing, I argue, can be considered a rhetorical attempt at reclaiming the experience, and by extension the body, from the auspices of an official state mission.

There is evidence, even in current scholarship, of the difficult classification of the texts. Ugo Tucci referred to Giosafat Barbaro's text as a *relazione* because it was written upon return from, rather than during, the journey.[24] Daria Perocco distinguished between "travel report" (relazione di viaggio) and "travelogue" (diario di viaggio) on the grounds that the latter refers to a text written as the journey unfolds.[25] Donald Queller described the *relazioni* as "famed ambassadorial texts [that] are sui generis, not only among diplomatic documents, but among literary types."[26] The drafters of the *relazioni*, however, are rarely considered as proper authors in reference to their texts. Not known for stylistic virtuosity, the texts are often characterized as "businesslike," and drafted by authors of the "merchant oligarchy" who did not "claim" (or aim toward) "literary eminence."[27] That is to say, their texts were combed for pertinent and practical political information concerning matters of state as well as news coming from foreign lands.[28] Whereas in the *relazioni* the ambassadorial role overtakes that of the writer-narrator, in the *viaggi* the reverse occurs: The writer-narrator-traveler comes to the fore, and the official diplomatic role recedes to the background.

These texts are important to reevaluate as a literary type because they—like the Renaissance ambassador himself—are products of a transitional period toward modernity. Contarini and Barbaro's *viaggi* were contemporary to the first extant Venetian ambassadorial *relazioni*, the earliest of which dates to 1492.[29] The same year Columbus sailed to the Americas ushered in a new idea of the self, as individuals entered new geographies and challenged traditional literary and political structures. Unlike the official state-mandated *relazioni*, the *viaggi* served a distinct personal rather than official purpose. The physical, psychological, and professional sacrifice to the state, as well as a textual self-fashioning, became the focus of these texts, setting up a necessary conflict between the self and pure functionality. In these texts, we notice the ambassadors grappling with the gulf between the theoretical and philosophical *ius gentium* protections and the "sacred" nature of their missions. Through "innovative and fertile narratives," which privilege the physical trials of the body natural, these accounts of ambassadorial "bodies moving through space" reclaim the narrative by framing it within their own experience.[30] Contarini's account aligned with that of a pilgrim; Barbaro's became a tale of marvelous adventure and personal bravery; Pagani's represented the awe of the observer, lucky to be one step removed from harm's way. The legal fiction of inviolability or immunity made way for the narrative fiction of the travel writer as the personal experience bled into the official account.

The audience for which the texts were originally written was most certainly Venetian, as none were inflected or infused with Tuscanized touches: They were written in *veneziano*. The *viaggi* likely emerged from the practical, and particularly Venetian, genre of the merchant text.[31] Contarini's text alone had, in addition to its 1487 *princeps*, six additional editions in the sixteenth century before it was modified in adherence to linguistic and rhetorical reform championed by Pietro Bembo and reframed under a geographical rubric in Ramusio's *Navigazioni e Viaggi* (1559).[32] Merchant texts were informal in nature and often written anonymously, not out of discretion, but instead because of the utter unimportance of the writer, whose utilitarian purpose was simply to disseminate essential information to the numerous other nameless and faceless men of commerce.[33]

Like Marco Polo before them, neither Contarini nor Barbaro were writers or poets, or even humanist scholars. What distinguishes them from a figure like Polo, who went East along with his merchant father and uncle, however, is that they were not exclusively merchants, and their voyages were not commercial in nature. By the late fifteenth century, most members of the Venetian patrician class had mercantile roots, but Contarini and Barbaro were traveling principally, even if begrudgingly, as statesmen. Another aspect that distinguishes them from Polo, their literary predecessor, is that their narratives were written by the travelers themselves, and importantly in their own voice, as well as in their Venetian language.

While the texts of Marco Polo and John de Mandeville before him were considered "extravagancies," the travel writers *avant la lettre* of early modernity seem obsessed with convincing the reader of the authenticity of their written testimony and personal experiences.[34] Contarini ended his account by apologizing for his inelegant style, which was the result of his overriding desire to "expose the truth like this, rather than adorn a lie with beautiful and elegant words" (esporre la verità a questo modo che ornar la bugia con belle ed eleganti parole).[35] Similarly, Barbaro stated in his exordium that he hesitated in writing and speaking of his travels because the things he would recount might appear to be lies ("forse parranno bugie") to those who had never been out of Venice.[36] My aim is not to draw distinctions between truth and falsehood, but instead to call attention to moments within the narration that suggest an authorial selfhood.[37] While the writers both try to erase their narrative presence by insisting upon the "truth" of what they saw, heard, smelled, touched, or tasted—akin more to an act of recording or reportage than narrative writing—there are moments within both texts that suggest not only the author's presence, but his literary self-portraiture.

Contarini recounted his three-year journey—from Ash Wednesday, January 1474, to Easter Sunday, April 10, 1477—over land from Venice to Tabriz, the capital city of the East Azerbaijan province in the northwestern part of present-day Iran. This account was written almost immediately upon his return from Persia and published for the first time in 1487, while the author was still living.[38] Yet, despite its fortunes at the press, Contarini's text has its detractors. Contarini has received cursory mention in a few studies, and his inclusion has little to do with the text as a whole, which is instead culled for historical or "documentary" or "diaristic" information, rather than considered as a literary text in the wider sense.[39] Marica Milanesi, the editor of the only modern edition still in print in Italy of Ramusio, credited Contarini's observational skills, yet faulted him for granting too much space to the "persona of the protagonist" (la persona del protagonista).[40] The reasons for this censure represent precisely the nascent literary merit and fictional impulse I wish to highlight. The text poses intriguing questions related to the portrayal (or self-portrayal) of the "persona" who wears the ambassadorial guise, which revealed itself to be of central importance to Contarini throughout his office as Venetian ambassador.

"Tutti cinque vestiti di grossi panni alla todesca": Concealing and Clothing the Ambassador

Garbed in "heavy German-style garments" (grossi panni alla todesca), Ambrogio Contarini, the elected ambassador to the "most illustrious Lord of Persia," departed Venice in January 1474, with the Venetian Senate's order to seek to convince Uzun Hasan to take up arms once again against the Ottomans, who had just handily defeated his troops the previous August.[41] In the company of only four others—a priest, an interpreter (turciman) and two servants—Contarini, the ambassadorial surrogate for the government of Venice, was sent on a diplomatic mission that required over six thousand miles of travel by foot and on horseback and ended up lasting over three years. The priest, while also doubling as secretary (cancelliere), saw to the spiritual well-being of the group and the administrative needs of the ambassador; the interpreter ensured verbal understanding between Venice and her allies and foes; and the two servants, one imagines, were left in charge of the essential tasks: food preparation, laundry, tending to the horses, and the preparation of camp, among other responsibilities. It is easy to see the logic of including each of these members in the group traveling with the Serenissima's elected ambassador. Notably absent from the entourage, however, was a person whose responsibility it was to ensure the physical safety of the ambassador and the group traveling with him. No member of Contarini's group had had prior experience with this route. The ambassador should have been guaranteed safe passage, but the uncommon practice of sending ambassadors with guards signaled that the sacred status of the ambassador was, in reality, only theoretical. The omission of a guard or security expert in this particular case seems odd given that the Senate must have considered the perils of the undertaking.

Unlike most other Venetian diplomatic travel, this *viaggio* was intentionally sent over land rather than by sea. The steady westward advancement of the Ottomans foiled any plans of reaching Persia from the West, thereby threatening the sea routes at the time. Contarini and company traveled north from Venice into German lands, passing through Poland and other territories of what is now considered Eastern Europe, through present-day Ukraine, toward Russia, southward through Georgia and Azerbaijan, and then finally into Tabriz and what is now Iran. After initial difficulty in securing a guide to lead them out of Venice and into Germany, Contarini, without mentioning how, noted that he finally "found one Sebastian, a German" (trovai un Sebastian todesco), perhaps a merchant. His seemed to Contarini to be "an emissary sent from God" (mi parve un messo da Dio), who graciously led them from Conegliano to Nuremburg via the Brenner Pass.[42] Contarini did not indicate any type of compensation given to Sebastian, instead focusing on the bond forged between them. Before parting ways, Contarini conveyed his genuine gratitude to and affection for Sebastian the German by noting that the two embraced "tightly" (strettamente) before bidding each other farewell.[43] This detail, ostensibly devoid of any further significance, could be read as another sign of the vulnerability of the ambassador. Contarini entrusted his fate and that of his cohort to this anonymous man, whose only biographical information decipherable to Contarini was his Germanness. Contarini depended on Sebastian's local knowledge to lead the group through a treacherous stretch of the Alps in the middle of winter. Upon safe arrival, one imagines that the "tight embrace," which Contarini took the time to remember and record, could signal the tenuous relationship between the ambassador and safety. Even while protected by an ancient customary law, the ambassador was left to fulfill his mission independently and ensure his own safety, continually relying on the mercy of strangers.

This was Contarini's first diplomatic mission, yet his palpable sense of defenselessness was not due to inexperience. By the time he was elected ambassador, Contarini had already been a seasoned traveler, merchant, and naval commander, having lived for long stretches in Constantinople, on the Barbary Coast, and in Southern France, in addition to having commanded a galley for Venice during the First Ottoman-Venetian War.[44] Notwithstanding his previous experiences abroad, however, Contarini's text reveals a sense of the body of the ambassador as one that is quite vulnerable, regardless of the *ius gentium* protection.

Returning to the physical appearance of the ambassador as he embarked on his diplomatic travels, Contarini made special note of the style of dress he and those accompanying him wore: "Tutti cinque vestiti di grossi panni alla todesca. Li danari li quali portai con me erano cusciti nei giupponi del detto prete Stefano e mio, il che non era senza affanno" (All five of us were dressed in heavy German-style garments. The money we carried had been sewn into my coat and that of the aforementioned priest, which was not [done] without some trouble).[45] Besides a brief mention of the names and basic roles of each member of his group, Contarini makes no other mention of any of their other defining physical characteristics, nor does he emphasize the importance of their clothing. The German-style dress, of course, could be because their mid-winter departure and northerly route demanded heavy clothing to survive the elements. If this were the case, however, it would remain an isolated reference in Contarini's account of the relations between the dress of the group and the dictates of the climate. Although the physical state of the group was a fundamental concern of the narrator from the diary's outset, there were, however, many more occasions in which dress was underscored to indicate the need to conceal identity or to conform to the norms of the host culture. On all occasions, it warrants emphasis, revealing how the ambassadorial body had to adapt to a given setting.

In the description above of the group's heavy German-style garb, Contarini also mentioned an essential concealment: The money that they carry was sewn into the inside of both his garment and that of his chaplain-secretary, prete Stefano Testa. This detail provides an interpretative key to the way in which the reader is to consider Contarini's mention of their heavy, un-Venetian garments: That which was essential, of fundamental importance to their success, was concealed in their interior, not communicated on their exterior. This act of disguise was not without its downside: The two members of the entourage that carried the concealed cash were also psychologically burdened by the anxiety that accompanied the risks associated with carrying valuable items, in particular money.

One wonders if this distress might have been in some part associated with the displacement of identity. The body of the ambassador, after all, was supposed to be universally sacred (*ius gentium*) and protected by those encountered outside of his own state. Yet, along with the ambassador himself, the identity of each member of his entourage was obscured by the "grossi panni alla todesca," as any association with the body of the ambassador brought along with it a degree of risk to all those who encircled him. This paradoxical role of the body of the ambassador—supposedly granted universal safe passage yet whose identity had to be suppressed to reduce the risk associated not only with his mission but also in terms of his identity—was one that the author evoked repeatedly in his account of his diplomatic mission and travels.

After bidding farewell to his previous guide, our narrator once again underscored his vulnerability and lack of support by mentioning that he was unable to proceed without procuring a replacement guide, a duty that was solely his responsibility:

> Adí X marzo 1474 con una guida giungesimo in Norimbergo, terra bellissima, la quale ha il suo castello e li passa un fiume per mezo. E cercando io guida per voler seguire il mio viaggio, *l'oste mi disse che quivi si trovavano due ambasciadori della maestà del re di Polonia, e confortommi ad accompagnarmi con essi*: la qual cosa intesa mi fu di grandissimo contento, e *per prete Stefano feci saper alle magnificenze loro chi io era, e che volentieri parleria con esso loro*. Intesa che ebbero l'ambasciata, mi mandorno [*sic*] a dire che l'andare era ad ogni mio piacere (italics added).[46]

> (On the tenth of March 1474, with a guide we reached Nuremburg, a beautiful land, which has its castle and is traversed by a river. Desirous to continue my journey and in need of finding a guide for myself in order to do so, the host informed me that here in *Nuremberg were two ambassadors of His Highness King of Poland, and he persuaded me to meet with them: Learning this made me exceedingly happy, and through prete Stefano I informed their Magnificences who I was and let them know that I would gladly converse with them*. Having learned that they had an embassy, they sent [a message] informing me that I was more than welcome to visit any time I wished to come.)

Luckily, the host knows that two ambassadors of the king of Poland are currently in Nuremburg, and persuades Contarini to make their acquaintance. One would think that the ambassador would either already have possessed this information or at least would have had access to it by more official channels and would not have needed to be "persuaded" by "the host" to meet his fellow diplomats. Despite the roundabout way by which Contarini learned of the ambassadors' presence in Nuremberg, he proceeded to act in accordance with expected diplomatic protocol by sending his own designated surrogate, prete Stefano, to meet the ambassadors, who most probably greeted Contarini's envoy with their own surrogates, demonstrating the irony of his position.

The body of the ambassador itself was not considered official without its presence being first announced by another emissary. This procedural diplomatic language was understood and reciprocated, and Contarini was then invited to their embassy. Despite his previous, professionally questionable, diplomatic negotiations with "the host" rather than local dignitaries, Contarini protected himself from possible allegations of inexperience by exhibiting courtly competence in his greeting of the Polish ambassadors:

> Cosí me n'andai, e trovai esser due de' primi di sua maestà, uno arcivescovo, l'altro messer Paolo cavalliero; e fatte le debite salutazioni, *li certificai come io andavo alla maestà del loro re con lettere di credenza, i quali, non ostante il mio abito,* certamente assai mi onorarono, accettandomi di buona voglia in loro compagnia, con larghissime offerte (italics added).[47]

> (Thus I went off and learned that the two ambassadors were two of the king's highest ranking men, one being an archbishop and the other, Sir Paolo, a knight; And, after having performed the necessary greetings, *I confirmed my presence before their king with a letter of credentials, and, despite my clothing,* they most certainly honored me greatly, accepting me quite willingly into their company, with very generous offerings.)

In stating that he presented himself to their king, Contarini in truth presented himself directly to the ambassadors, and only indirectly to the king. The king of Poland, in this instance, was represented in his absence by the ambassadors, who verified Contarini's identity as an official ambassador of Venice. Their acceptance of his credentials allowed him to eventually make the direct acquaintance of the sovereign himself.

Despite the diplomatic finesse Contarini exhibited in his salutation of the Polish ambassadors, he was conscious of some discord between the mastery of verbal and procedural diplomatic protocol and his physical appearance, cloaked in "heavy German garments." Contarini himself underscored this sartorial incongruity by noting that, upon arriving to make the acquaintance of the Polish ambassadors, undignified garments were cloaking his ambassadorial body: "despite my clothing" (no ostante il mio abito).[48] Confirming that the seemingly casual mention of "grossi panni alla todesca" at the beginning of the text is significant, the garments were once again mentioned at a key moment. In the first mention of the clothing, "tutti cinque vestiti di grossi panni alla todesca" (all five of us dressed in heavy German garments), Contarini offered a description of his clothing but also pointed out that he was dressed identically to that of his entire group. This assimilation acquires significance only after considering the second mention of his garments, at the moment in which he makes the acquaintance of the Polish ambassadors. This was the first encounter with other diplomats on the trip, as well as the first meeting with other individuals of an equivalent patrician status. Given that there is no textual evidence that Contarini's discomfort regarding his attire was provoked by any reaction on the part of the Polish ambassadors, one is left to wonder whether his unease was because his clothing contradicted his diplomatic and noble identity. While wearing rustic German clothes, prete Stefano announced Contarini to the ambassadors. Contarini, the invested ambassador, then arrived wearing garments identical to his subordinate. The lack of visual distinction between the official ambassador and his subordinate could be a reason Contarini directed the reader's attention back to his own physical presence and appearance as ambassador.

These two moments in the text allow the clothing to reveal itself as triply inappropriate, or misleading: Contarini's patrician identity was rendered indistinct from that of his lower ranking companions, all being equally rustic and unrefined; his official status as diplomat of the Serenissima was not apparent by his appearance, which had to be "certified" by a "letter of credentials" (lettera di credenza); and his Venetian origins were betrayed by the "Germanness" of his clothing.[49] Perhaps Contarini's intended reader would have also been concerned about the impression provoked by a Venetian patrician presenting himself in "heavy German-style clothing"; regardless, it is understandable, even to contemporary readers, that a degree of anxiety would be provoked if one's appearance seemed indecorous or less formal than it should be. What is surprising, however, is that the ambassador finds himself exposed to such a potential embarrassment: Was this not precisely the type of encounter for which a diplomat traveling on official state business should have been prepared? And perhaps it is even more significant as this is the *only* anxiety mentioned by Contarini, who did not reveal any other concerns about the meeting or its outcome. The state of his body and the impression it made upon other diplomats was his most pressing worry. This small detail points to an intriguing inconsistency between the physical appearance of the ambassador and the formality of his handling of other diplomatic protocol: He immediately dispatched prete Stefano to arrange a meeting and present him, bearing the official and expected "letter of credentials." In this case the body of the ambassador was not vulnerable to physical harm, but was instead subjected to judgment due to the established diplomatic norms and expectations imposed upon his body. The anxiety is perhaps attributable to Contarini's paradoxical identity; in other words, the knowledge that his body coincided only metaphorically and rhetorically with the body politic was what provoked discomfort.

The concerns about breaching sartorial protocol are revisited just a few short pages later, but under quite different circumstances and with quite different results:

> Adí 11 da mattina mandò ["re Casimir, re di Polonia"] a presentarmi una *veste di damaschin negro,* chiamandomi da sua maestà, e *per esser così loro costume, con la detta veste indosso me n'andai,* accompagnato da molti uomini da conto, e fatte le debite riverenze e salutazioni gli presendai [*sic*] il presente mandatogli dalla nostra illustrissima Signoria, e dissi quanto m'accadeva. Volse che io desinassi con sua maestà. Usano mangiar quasi a nostro modo, benissimo apparecchiando e abbondantemente. Finito il desinare, tolsi commiato da sua maestà e tornai al mio alloggiamento (italics added).[50]

> (The morning of the 11th, King Casimir [IV] of Poland sent me a gift consisting of a garment made of black damask. His Majesty summoned me, and *as was their custom, I went to him dressed in the said garment* and accompanied by many men of noteworthy stature. After having made the requisite bow and greetings, I presented him with the gift sent by our illustrious Signoria, and I recounted what I had encountered. He insisted that I dine with His Majesty. They dine almost as we do, abundantly and in a most well-appointed manner. Once the meal had ended, I took my leave from His Majesty and returned to my residence.)

The most obvious difference between Contarini's previous encounter with the Polish ambassadors is that in this case the Venetian ambassador was summoned by the sovereign himself, Casimir IV, king of Poland. Just as in his previous diplomatic encounter, however, Contarini once again made special note of the sartorial details. This time there was no chance of transgressing the dress code; the king had provided his costume. Contarini was not satisfied in offering a vague description of his attire; instead, he presented details that allowed for an appraisal of the material of the clothing and situated the garments in specific social, geographical, and economic contexts. The "heavy German-style clothing" alluded clearly to unrefined, utilitarian clothing, much more suited to disguising than adorning the ambassadorial body. Germany, not known for its refined textile tradition, was evoked instead as a guise to conceal the ambassador's true origins and status; the provenance of the "heavy clothing" is never offered, and the reader is in no way encouraged to take the non-luxurious garments as having been received as diplomatic gifts.

Alternatively, in this instance, the reader is made aware not only of the origins of the garment but also its color and quality. The term *veste* (robe) is used instead of the more familiar and general term *panni* (clothes), to more suitably designate the luxurious and exotic nature of the "black damask" (damaschin negro) with which Contarini was presented by "His Majesty" (sua maestà). The type of cloth, damask, connotes ceremony and prestige, and was reserved for the most formal of occasions. While these details most certainly serve to elevate the perceived status and importance of the ambassador, in conjunction with his other references to garments and their diplomatic importance, Contarini offered us an insight into the purposes, roles, and significance of the cloaked ambassadorial body. As with the "heavy German-style clothes," Contarini's body was once again enveloped by foreign cloth. By donning the black damask, it is clear that the ambassador must not only present his body in a suitable fashion but also conform to "their custom" (lor costume), which in this case required a visiting diplomat to render himself sartorially indistinguishable from the others belonging to the court. This lack of distinction is a theme that harkens back to the outset of the mission, when Contarini's body shared the same clothing as those who surrounded him; the principal difference is that here, instead of appearing similar to the servants in his retinue, he blended in with "many men of noteworthy stature" (molti uomini da conto).[51]

"Questi è come la persona del nostro re": Safe Conduct of the Ambassadorial Body

> Stemmo nel detto luogo fino a dieci dí, dove giunse il detto ambasciadore; e la mattina che fummo per partire volse che udissimo la messa, e benché per avanti gli avevo parlato del mio essere lí, nondimeno, udita la messa e *abbracciati insieme, l'antidetto Pammartin mi fece pigliar la mano del detto ambasciadore, e dissegli: "Questi è come la persona del nostro re, e però fa che tu lo conduca a salvamento in Capha"*; e ciò fece con parole tanto calde quanto dir si potesse. *L'ambasciadore rispose che 'l comandamento della maestà del re era sopra la sua testa, e quel che sarebbe di lui saria eziandio di me.* E con questo tolsi commiato da sua signoria, ringraziandola quanto seppi e potei e come egli meritava di tanto onore che mi fece. In quei giorni che stetti lí spesse volte mi visitava di vittuaglia (vettovaglie) (italics added).[52]

> (When the ambassador arrived, we had already been there for ten days, and the morning that we were to depart, he (His Majesty) wanted us to attend mass, and even though I had previously told him (the Polish ambassador) about my being there, nonetheless, after having heard mass, *we embraced, and the aforementioned Pammartin had me take the hand of the ambassador, and he told him: "He is like the person of our king, and thus ensure that you conduct him safely to Capha"; and he did so with words as warm as one is able to muster. The ambassador responded that the commandment of His Majesty the King was on his head, and whatever happened to him, would also happen to me.* And with this we took leave from His Majesty, thanking him as much and as well as I could, for he was deserving of as much honor as he showed me. During the days in which I was there, he visited many times and brought provisions.)

This passage discusses the arrangement of Contarini's safe passage in the journey from Kiev to Caffa (modern-day Feodosia) on the Crimean Peninsula, which was a Genoese colony under the protection of King Casimir IV of Poland at the time of Contarini's arrival but would fall to the Ottomans in 1475. There are numerous references to the physical body and its roles, both metaphorical and ritualistic, in diplomatic communication and conduct. Contarini communicated in a corporeal fashion—"we embraced" (abbracciati insieme)—his positive rapport, and thus successful diplomatic mission, with Pammartin, the governor and most senior exponent of the Polish crown. This contrasts with the way in which he expressed his relationship with his equal, the unnamed Polish ambassador, which was described in decorous rather than bodily fashion: "The guides of His Majesty the king provided me with good and excellent company, with whom I employed courtesy" (Dalle guide della maestà del re ebbi buona e ottima compagnia, alle quali usai cortesia).[53] The name of the Polish ambassador is not mentioned because it would have been unnecessary to do so, since his personal identity, like Contarini's, is subsumed by his ambassadorial identity.

After the pregnant embrace between Contarini and Pammartin, the governor/lord of Kyiv, another symbolic and gestural moment occurs in which the Venetian offers important details of the exchange.[54] Pammartin, the officiating party, "ha[d] him [Contarini] take the hand of the ambassador" while he uttered a significant and performative phrase by which he conferred upon Contarini a new, albeit transient, status and citizenship for the travel to Caffa. The exact rank of this new status or identity, however, is somewhat open to interpretation. One possibility is juridical in nature. When Pammartin referred to Contarini as "[he] is like the person of our king," he was exercising the legal authority of his position to invest Contarini with the legal status equal to one of his king's "people," courtiers, or subjects more broadly. This protective gesture embraced Contarini by extending to him the same rights enjoyed by his people. In legal terms, however, such a privilege also subordinated Contarini. In exchange for legal and physical protection, Contarini now also bore the responsibility and expectation that he adhere to the laws and the standards of conduct of Pammartin's subjects or face the same consequences.

On the other hand, the presence of the definite article, as opposed to the indefinite, opens the possibility for a different, and perhaps less probable, but quite intriguing interpretation. The text reads "[he] is like *the* person of our king," not "a person," and thus may therefore be read as Pammartin conferring unto Contarini the status of his sovereign, the king of Poland: "He [Contarini] is to be considered as the persona of our king [the embodiment of our king; that is, treat him as you would our king], and therefore be sure to [you must] conduct safely him to Capha."[55] The translation here was done as literally as possible to highlight Contarini's exact lexical choices, particularly the word "persona." This semantic choice is noteworthy because the body of a king was a sacred entity, and conferring it, even rhetorically, unto another statesman of considerably inferior rank was a significant gesture that once again obscured the ambassador.

The Hakluyt Society translation of Contarini's text renders the phrase as follows: "When Mass was over, we embraced each other, and Pammartin made me shake hands with the ambassador, whom he requested, with much warmth, to consider me as the person of his king, and conduct me in safety to Capha."[56] The first difference is that the translators converted the text from direct to indirect discourse, thereby negating the performative and ritualistic aspects of Pammartin's phrase. Also, instead of *pigliar mano,* which could be translated as "hold the hand," suggesting a lingering gesture, the translators render it as a momentary "shak[ing of] hands," which if done before an agreement suggests a mere greeting, whereas if done at the end of a discussion indicates a pact.[57] This "holding of hands" rather than the hasty "shak[ing] of hands" suggests a more solemn ritual, more akin to a wedding ceremony during which the bride and groom grasp hands while reciting their binding vows. The anglicized translation, "shake hands," results in a descriptive rather than interpretative rendering, an expedient choice that certainly accounts for the physical interaction that took place; however, it demonstrates little attention paid to the meaning of such an encounter.

Either accepting the status as "the person of the king [of Poland]," or that of one of the subordinates, the "people," of the king, what both meanings share is that they represent a double displacement of identity for Contarini. In accepting the role and order of Venice's Senate as ambassador to Uzun Hasan, Contarini effectively set aside his own identity in lieu of his assumption as that of the surrogate for the Republic of Venice. The second displacement of identity—the rhetorical assumption of the "person of the king [of Poland]," or one of his "people"—was done not out of duty to or by order of his country, but instead as a courtesy and gesture of solidarity between Venice and the host country of Poland. Just as he was asked previously by Casimir IV to don the black damask robe, here Contarini as ambassador underwent another concealment, this time rhetorical rather than sartorial. While Pammartin's pronouncement was clearly made to protect Contarini, it nonetheless underscores the ambassador's lack of agency over his own body and identity. The survival of the ambassador often depended not only on the goodwill of others but also on the double concealment of his identity, both of his private personhood and his official status as ambassador.

The Polish ambassador's response in Contarini's original, "L'ambasciadore rispose che 'l comandamento della maestà del re era *sopra la sua testa*, e quel che sarebbe di *lui* saria eziandio di me" (The ambassador responded that the commandment of the King's Majesty was *above his head*, and whatever happens to him would also happen to me; italics added), contains an interesting, perhaps menacing, and certainly cryptic bodily metaphor: "above his head."[58] The Italian phrase, "sopra la sua testa," is also ambiguous as it could mean that the task is superior to one's capabilities or, conversely, that one understands and accepts the duties and the inherent responsibility, which in English would be synonymous to "[it is] on his head," meaning that the responsibility for the successful completion of the task falls to him.[59] In a literal English translation, "sopra la sua testa" would be rendered as "above his head," which would express an overwhelming sensation on behalf of the ambassador, an awareness that it is beyond his capabilities to truly guarantee the safety of Contarini. Yet he proceeded to assure both Contarini and Pammartin that he would do all that he could to assure Contarini's safe conduct, "and whatever happens to him would also happen to me."

The way in which Contarini paraphrases this last portion of the Polish ambassador's words is also unclear: To whom does "lui" (he/him) refer, the ambassador himself or the king of Poland, whose privileges Pammartin's pledge may confer upon Contarini? The 1863 Hakluyt Society edition erased any possible ambiguity by translating the phrase as follows: "The ambassador replied that the command of His Majesty the King *should be observed*, and that I should be treated in the same manner as if I were the king himself."[60] The bodily metaphor was omitted, whereas the second part of the ambassador's response was spelled out more clearly. The Hakluyt translators read "lui" as "king," and rather than attempting to interpret, they repeat, in Pammartin's words, the more subtle meaning concealed in the ambassador's ambiguous response. It is impossible to know if Contarini chose his wording to include purposefully the ambiguous bodily metaphor "sopra la sua testa" or whether this phrase is simply a colloquial phrase that was included without any other meaning. What is significant, however, is that the ambiguity, purposeful or not, aligns with Contarini's understanding of the very real and unpredictable insecurity inherent in his office as foreign ambassador, no matter how vehemently a sovereign promised to ensure his safety.

Contarini then describes his gift exchange with Pammartin: "In quei giorni che stetti lí spesse volte mi visitava di vittuaglia. Io gli presentai un cavallo portante tedesco, il qual fu uno di quelli con li quali mi parti' da Mestre, e gli altri, perché integri, volsero che gli lasciassi tutti lì e pigliassi cavalli del paese"[61] (During the days I was there, he came many times with provisions. I presented him with a German pacing horse, which was one of those with which I traveled from Mestre; because the other horses were ungelded, they wanted me to leave them behind and take instead the local horses.) Gift exchange between a traveling emissary and a foreign sovereign has been a cornerstone feature of diplomacy since antiquity, but here it went beyond an expected account of gifts received and offered. First, Contarini seems to justify the reason for which he presented Pammartin with a gift: "During the days I was there, he came many times and brought provisions." This detail suggests that his choice to gift a German pacing horse was personal and in direct correspondence to the kindness and generosity with which Pammartin treated him.

This moment of agency and independent decision-making by Contarini suggests that this saddle horse was not presented to Contarini with the express purpose of being an official gift from the Venetian Senate, but instead to be used as his own precious mode of transportation.[62] He also went on to note that this was a horse that had accompanied him throughout his long diplomatic journey since his departure from Venice—"which was one of those with which I traveled from Mestre"—and thus possibly a horse of which Contarini is particularly fond, and valuable also because the animal had successfully and reliably transported him thus far. The horse was therefore a personal gift, offered by Contarini himself as thanks for the special courtesies and provisions (vittuaglia) from Pammartin, rather than one given on behalf of the Senate for diplomatic and political purposes.

The horse also represents another moment in which Contarini noted the symbolic importance of his appearance: "Because the other horses were ungelded, they wanted me to leave them behind and instead take the local horses." The fact that Contarini and his entourage were traveling to Caffa on ungelded horses (integri) perhaps prompted concern on the part of the Poles, who "wanted" him to abandon his own horses and take horses that conformed to the place in which he now found himself, "del paese." The note of Ramusio's modern editor mentions that "the Tatars only used neutered horses" (I Tartari usavano solo cavalli castrati), the reason for which Contarini was advised to abandon his Western horses for those that would follow Tatar standards.[63]

Despite the statement of the Tatars' horse preferences, there are at least two possibilities that account for why the reproductive potential of Contarini's horses was of issue. The first reason returns to the importance Contarini has given to his own appearance and its symbolic importance. The appearance of his horses (in this case, the fact that they are ungelded) also reflected upon his persona. Horses were often of significant symbolic value for ceremonial use and, as we have seen, valuable gifts. In addition to their ceremonial value, horses were also essential in war. Their bellicose potential, perhaps underscored by their ungelded state and thus more virile appearance, could perhaps have been interpreted as an affront, thus risking the provocation of a belligerent reaction from the Tatars. Or more simply, their appearance could have undermined Contarini's diplomatic intentions since he did not educate himself as to the Tatar customs. While the reason for this it is not elaborated on by Contarini or the editors, it is plausible to infer that whatever the Tatars' interpretation of the ungelded horses might have been, all aspects of the visual appearance of the ambassador—from his garments to the presence or absence of his horses' testicles—were symbolic carriers of meaning, particularly in the absence of direct verbal communication due to the reliance on interpreters.

The first encounter in this mission between Contarini and non-Europeans, the Tatars, was brokered by Pammartin's unnamed Polish ambassador. The discomfort and insecurity Contarini felt were mirrored in the geographical and environmental difficulties of the journey, in addition to his own physical limitations. A leg ailment rendered Contarini unable to ride horseback, and he had to travel instead on a small cart.[64] Contarini was thus at the mercy of his traveling companions. His reliance upon others for survival and completion of his ambassadorial mission is reiterated in the next episode he narrated, entering into a "deserted countryside" (campagna deserta) and crossing the Dnieper, which separated Russia from Tartary (parte la Tartaria dalla Rossia verso Capha). Traversing such a vast and forceful body of water, "more than one mile wide and very deep" (larga piú di 1 miglio e molto profonda), was a risk or "danger" (pericolo) for which Contarini and his entourage were not prepared.[65] Their safe crossing was facilitated by the ingenuity of the Tatars, who fashioned makeshift rafts out of gathered wood (legnami), on top of which rode Contarini along with his entourage and all their belongings. The Tatars and their horses entered the water and towed the rafts across the river, yet Contarini instead thanked God for their safe arrival on the opposite riverbank.

At this point in the narration, Contarini made explicit his distrust of the Tatars: "Passati dall'altra banda e dismontati in terra [. . .] stemmo tutto quel giorno co' Tartari; e *alcuni lor capi molto mi guardavano, e fra loro fecero di molti pensieri*" (Once we crossed to the other side and made our way on land [. . .] we spent the whole day with the Tatars; and *a few of their leaders were looking at me and among themselves communicated many thoughts*; italics added).[66] Contarini does not clarify how he became aware of the Tatars' "many thoughts," but he later determines that these suspicions were warranted, given that shortly thereafter the accompanying Polish ambassador's interpreter arrives to inform Contarini that the Tatars "had decided to deliver [him] to their emperor" (li detti Tartari avevano deliberato di menar[lo] al loro imperadore).[67]

The Tatars had plainly realized ("ben lo avevano inteso") that Contarini was a man of a certain stature, and it was therefore incumbent on them to present him to their leader. The interpreter's news provoked great anxiety in Contarini, yet he did not mention the reason for this fright nor what he imagined or knew would become of him if he were indeed to be brought to the Tatar leader. Contarini thus resorted to entreating the interpreter (*turcimano*) to "beg [the ambassador] to remember the promise he made to Pammartin on behalf of His Majesty the King of Poland" (mi racconmandai al detto turcimano, pregandolo si ricordasse della promessa che fece a Pammartin per la maestà del re di Polonia).[68] To ensure that the interpreter fulfilled this desperate request, Contarini mentioned that he even "promised him a sword" (gli promisi una spada), at which point the interpreter responded that he wants to serve Contarini, comforted him, and then returned to his ambassador. The interpreter proved to be a trustworthy go-between, given that the ambassador succeeded in dissuading the Tatars from taking Contarini captive by assuring them that he was Genoese. The shift in identity, from Venetian to Genoese, assured the release of the ambassador because of the Genoese colonial presence in this part of Eurasia, which afforded them certain privileges with the Tatars.

This clever move on behalf of the Polish ambassador amounted to yet another displacement of Contarini's identity. This time, instead of donning foreign garments, he was verbally clothed with Genoese citizenship: "[The ambassador] sat down and drank with the Tatars, and with many words was able to assure them that I was Genoese, and resolved the matter with fifteen ducats" (Si mise [l'ambasciatore] a sedere e bere con li detti Tartari, e con molte parole accertandoli ch'io era genovese, l'acconciò in ducati 15).[69] The mention of the exchange of fifteen ducats from the ambassador to the Tatars lends doubt as to whether the Tatars believed that Contarini was Genoese, but what is certain is that such an identity was considered to be plausible enough to allow them to accept that as fact. The remainder of Contarini's journey contained similar moments of dangerous diplomatic situations, cryptic symbolic corporeal language—both via dissimulation and simulation—and the resultant physical hardships suffered by his body as it negotiated space, politics, and geography on behalf of Venice. Contarini's text was constructed by a corporeal language by which he revealed the violability of his, and thus the ambassador's, body more generally while also exerting rhetorical control over the body of his text by way of writing it. By likening himself to a pilgrim, a figure who elects to undergo physical hardship and geographical displacement for a cause greater than himself, Contarini regained ownership over his own experience, and in doing so, purified, or exorcized, the corporeal suffering he undertook on behalf of the state.

In Contarini's text there is a problem of correspondence between the spiritual, self-effacing mission of the pilgrim who claimed to have undertaken great sacrifices for "the universal good of all Christianity" and the patrician statesman appointed to fulfill a diplomatic mission that had less to do with the survival of Christendom and more with that of the Venetian mercantile economy. The text itself was based on a dual mission of the author's own devices: one sacred and the other profane. This binary is established from the journey's outset in the author's preface ("il proemio dell'autore").

Contarini established that he was chosen (eletto) for this mission by the Serenissima's government. He did not minimize the importance of the diplomatic assignment, noting the illustriousness of the sovereign to whom he is was sent to persuade. He also highlighted the physical dangers and general difficulty of such a lengthy and grueling trip. He, however, cloaked himself rhetorically as the humble servant who was called upon to fulfill a duty too important to refuse: "considering the great desire of my illustrious Signoria and the universal good of all of Christianity" (considerando il gran desiderio della mia illustrissima Signoria e il bene universal di tutta la cristianità).[70] The editorial note regarding the dates claimed above by Contarini states that he was observing the *more veneto* calendar, which indeed in the year 1473 had its Ash Wednesday fall on the 23rd of February. The reader is thus encouraged to take his return date, April 10, 1477, as reliable as well. It is not revealed until the end of the text that his return home falls on Easter Sunday. The narration is thus situated literally between two liturgical dates. The emergence of a traveler from a long, arduous journey on Easter Sunday has biblical origins; it is no coincidence that Contarini's *viaggio* and Jesus's sojourn in the desert both lasted precisely forty days. However, it also has literary precedents in the Italian context, most importantly that of Dante Alighieri, a model to which Contarini seems to adhere.

Although his journey actually lasted three years, the dates that the author would like the reader to focus on are not those that pertain to the calendar years, but instead those of the Christian liturgical one: Ash Wednesday to Easter Sunday, the period of Lent, the holiest part of the year. This framing premise, in which the civil calendar is secondary, has the effect of essentially collapsing the time of the narrative from three years to forty days; the writer would have the reader imagine his travels—or, better, pilgrimage—as also having lasted only forty days. Contarini assimilated his story with that of Jesus's as well. The forty days that Jesus spent fasting in the desert are symbolically recreated by the Catholic ritual of Lent; Contarini undertook the symbolic period of Lent while also geographically undergoing Jesus's desert *viaggio* by spending the same amount of time (he would have us believe) in the Orient, supposedly for "the universal good of all of Christianity."[71]

The text thus reveals itself to be infused in a matrix of travel, and therefore links travel writing with religious pilgrimage. Dante was not the only narrative antecedent for Contarini. Numerous Franciscan missionaries of the prior centuries certainly provided a model, particularly the widely diffused text of Friar Odorico da Pordenone (written/dictated in 1330) and Petrarch's fictional pilgrimage guidebook, *Itinerarium ad sepulchrum domini nostri* (Itinerary to the Sepulcher of Our Lord, written in 1358), which associate a journey to the East as one undertaken for religious purposes. This, however, is not a crusader text. The duty assigned to Contarini was that of enticing Uzun Hasan to take up arms against Mehmet II, a fellow Muslim.

Contarini did not reduce his entire ambassadorial mission to a spiritual pilgrimage, but proceeded with this dual-track narrative, intertwining competing narrative strategies and genres within the same text. Two concurrent calendars date the journey; the text is ostensibly a nonfiction account of a real diplomatic mission, but it is framed in a fictitious manner that calls into question that very nonfiction nature. These conscious narrative strategies, similar to Barbaro's omissions, mark the evolution from the utilitarian and fiscal merchant handbook to a literary work in which the writer is not merely a merchant communicating practical information, but an author engaging in self-fashioning. Contarini appears as the reluctant, dutiful, and self-sacrificial pilgrim; and Barbaro, the freelance admiral, exemplary diplomat, and burgeoning ethnographer.

Reading Contarini and Barbaro's *viaggi* closely, what emerges is the distinction between practice and theory in diplomacy. Juxtaposing these two narratives with contemporary diplomatic treatises, Ermolao Barbaro's *De Officio legati* in particular, one can appreciate the freedom these writers created for themselves. The privileged place of the ambassador as the humanist "mind" of the state in the *trattatistica* tradition contrasts with the conflicting realities of the vulnerability and violability, and often futility, of the ambassadorial body moving in space. In recounting their own embassies, each ambassador dealt with the realities of the burden of representing the entire body politic, when ironically their own bodies were so vulnerable despite the sacred title of "ambassador."

In Silk and Chains: Pageantry and Prosecution of the Ambassadorial Body

I now look at the political implications of the clothed ambassadorial body in Zaccaria Pagani's *Viaggio di Domenico Trevisan: ambasciatore veneto al gran sultano del Cairo nell'anno 1512*. The text of this fascinating encounter, recently published in its first critical edition by Laura Benedetti and Enrico Musacchio, merits a more exhaustive treatment than I can offer here.[72] However limited, it is my hope that my reading is nonetheless successful in demonstrating, through Pagani's *viaggio*, how the body of the Renaissance ambassador was an entity both protected and vulnerable, and how his dress was tantamount to a political act.[73] The ambassador's clothing, often lavish and always highly symbolic, was the site of a double encounter: of his person and office, as well as of his land and that of the foreign sovereign. The ritualized encounters between ambassador and foreign sovereign are central to Renaissance diplomatic *viaggi*, or travelogues, whose most intricate passages detail sumptuously the clothing of the Venetian dignitaries and their hosts, including weave, weight, and material of the fabrics. The clothed ambassador is rendered in a manner indistinguishable from the extravagant gifts, overwhelmingly garments and fabrics, brought with the diplomatic entourage. Ambassador and diplomacy are reduced to the visual impression made by their impeccable and sumptuous Venetian apparel and gifts.

Zaccaria Pagani's narration of Domenico Trevisan's 1512 voyage to the Mamluk grand sultan of Cairo, Qansuh al-Ghuri (1441–1516),[74] offers a glimpse into the most extravagant diplomatic pageantry against the backdrop of complex geopolitics. Since the fall of Constantinople in 1453, the steady advance of the Ottoman Turks into Venice's Eastern *stato da mar* had relentlessly threatened the Serenissima's control of commerce in the region; additionally, the Portuguese discovery of a sea route to India effectively ended Venetian domination of the spice trade and diminished it commercially.[75] The *viaggio* offers only scant contextualization of the purpose of the mission, directing the reader's attention instead to the surface of the diplomatic encounter—its rituals, its gift exchanges, its pomp, its exotic locales—which is a striking contrast to the silence regarding the depth of the serious matters that demanded Venice undertake the expense and effort of sending a special envoy all the way to Cairo.

The reasons for and objectives of the embassy were multiple and varied. Trevisan was sent as a special envoy for three reasons, two of which were significant to the Venetian economy: a dispute over the price of black pepper, as well as access to pilgrimage sites in the Holy Land—in addition to a most pressing political issue and international controversy, the "Zen affair." Pietro Zen (1458–1539), Venetian consul at Damascus, was imprisoned in Cairo under suspicion by the Mamluks for his dealings with the Safavid rulers of Persia.[76] The delicate nature of this mission is apparent, since Trevisan—a Venetian ambassador—was sent to remedy the alleged improprieties of Zen, a fellow diplomat. Regardless of Zen's guilt, his imprisonment by the Sultan seems to have been designed, at least in part, to constrain Venice into finally sending an ambassador to negotiate directly with the Sultan, to resolve issues beyond those involving Zen. The two diplomats, Zen and Trevisan, are thus revealed to have been pawns in a proxy war between the Mamluk Sultanate and the Venetian Signoria, which was situated in a broader geopolitical context that included the Ottomans, Persians, French, and the members of the Holy League, whose shifting alliances contributed to the region's destabilization.

Little is known about Zaccaria Pagani, the author of this *viaggio*, other than that he was a member of the ambassador's retinue, of Bellunese origins, and affiliated with Andrea de Franceschi, Venice's ducal secretary.[77] Pagani thus offers an interesting point of view, both from within the diplomatic entourage, as well as from the outside, as he is not the invested ambassador, but instead an informed and privileged observer. Pagani's manuscript of the *viaggio* was housed in the Biblioteca Piloni near Belluno,[78] where it languished in obscurity until the late nineteenth century, when the Piloni family sold its library collection. At that point the book came to the attention of Niccolò Barozzi (1826–1906), a Venetian scholar, editor of some of Marino Sanudo's diaries, and the director of Museo Correr. Barozzi published an edited version of the manuscript in 1875, in which he translated the text's original Venetian into Italian.[79]

The text documents the efforts of the Venetian government to send one of its most trusted and seasoned diplomats, Domenico Trevisan (1446–1535), to lead the embassy to the Sultan. Since his first diplomatic mission, accompanying Ermolao Barbaro (1454–1493) to congratulate Maximilian I on his election as king of the Romans in 1486, Trevisan had participated in many of Venice's most important and complicated embassies. He was involved in the negotiation of peace between Ferdinand I of Spain and Charles VIII of France, lobbied successfully for an end to Julius II's excommunication of Venice, and brokered the inclusion of the Serenissima in the Holy League, in addition to making numerous other prestigious and delicate missions to places such as Rome, Milan, and Constantinople. Trevisan had accumulated wide-ranging expertise, and his election to lead this particular mission to the last of the Mamluk rulers signaled its critical importance to Venice.[80] This embassy was an opportunity for Venice to demonstrate to the Sultan its undiminished splendor and economic power despite its vulnerability.[81]

Venice's economy was damaged by the diversion of the spice trade from land to sea at a time when French agents (commercial rivals of the Serenissima and enemies of the Holy League) were attempting to tarnish Venice's reputation in Egypt in order to usurp its privileged commercial agreements with the Mamluks.[82] As a response, the Venetian senate instructed that Trevisan's embassy would transport copious amounts of precious objects, including silver and clothing (*arçenti* and *veste*), in proportion with their "need and desire" (bisogno et desiderio) to make a positive impression.[83] The Sultan also anticipated the arrival of a Venetian ambassador quite anxiously. In fact, in one of his meetings with Zen after his imprisonment in Cairo, the Sultan expressed resentment that Venice had neglected to reciprocate his diplomatic overtures despite having received, a few years earlier, the Mamluk ambassador and interpreter Taghri Berdi ("Tagavardi" in Zen's correspondence).[84] This affront was exacerbated by the fact that the Sultan knew Venice had recently received Persian ambassadors. Venice clearly understood that the Sultan would not release the imprisoned consuls and merchants, resolve the problems that led to their arrest, or allow Venetian galleys to resume commerce without dispatching an ambassador of great dignity (*solenne*) to Cairo.[85] Zen himself echoed the desperate need for a particularly "distinguished" ambassador (l'orator, e honorato) to avoid a potential military conflict, "se non verà ambasador, le cosse non anderà bene [. . .] la guerra fa mal d'ogni canto" (if an ambassador does not come, things will not go well [. . .] war is harmful no matter the reason).[86]

The mission phase of the distinguished and anticipated ambassador's *viaggio* began after three months at sea as the ambassadorial galleys approached Alexandria. Trevisan entrusted his own messenger (that is, a messenger's messenger) with his letters so that they could be sent by land directly to the vice consul of Alexandria, who would in turn dispatch the news of the ambassador's imminent arrival in Cairo. It is this action that set in motion the characteristic pomp of the encounter between the Signoria of Venice and the grand sultan's court. The first act was played by the admiral of Alexandria, who met the ambassador's entourage with "a most ample safe conduct" (un salvacondotto amplissimo), the nature of which, Pagani informed us, "made it clear that his Magnificence was expected with great desire" (il tenore del quale è copiato in questo scritto, facendo intendere che aspettava sua Magnificienza con desiderio).[87] This rare interpretative comment by Pagani intriguingly exposes the political significance of each sign, each object, each gesture, and how each individual detail must be interpreted and understood in the context of the diplomatic encounter, whose language was more visual and material than it was verbal.

Throughout the *viaggio* of Trevisan, each surface the ambassador encounters, physically or metaphorically, is covered in cloth. I find this layering significant as it is representative of the diplomatic meeting itself, which is always one or more layers removed from a true, direct encounter, symbolic of the many layers of contact separating parties, such as the communication messenger's messengers, as we saw in Contarini's *viaggio*, in the previous section. The first Mamluk official the ambassador encountered was the admiral of Alessandria, who was also accompanied by the royal secretary, the *dawâdâr* (*diodar* in Venetian), a term whose literal meaning, "the bearer of the royal inkwell," belies the fact that he became one of the most prominent ministers in the sultanate's power structure during this period.[88] Besides these two high-ranking dignitaries, the entourage comprised "an infinite multitude of people on horseback and on foot" (infinita moltitudine di persone a cavallo e a piedi), in addition to seven other horses for the sole purpose of transporting the ambassador and his company.[89] The horses and camels before them were also clothed in fine silks. As the Venetian ambassador rode into town, the roads were lined with spectators and also covered with "scarlet cloth" (panni di scarlatto). The gates of the *fondaco* (fontego) were cloaked as well with crimson velvet and "other silks" (altre sete").[90]

Once in Cairo, the ambassador proceeded to the palace and entered the courtyard, where the reader is finally offered a glimpse of the sultan, seated upon a high "pulpit," or platform (*mastabe*), which was, Pagani noted, covered in green velvet. The sultan was fully clad in a white robe, on top of which was layered a green goat-hair cloak. On his head was a large, elaborate two-horned headdress that Pagani claimed defied his descriptive powers: "I wouldn't know how to describe [it]" (non saprei descrivere) he said after describing it. In fact, his description of clothing, as well as gestural and bodily language, was so vivid and colorful that it inspired Cesare Vecellio to use it as a source for his influential illustrated costume book, *De gli habiti antichi et moderni di diversi parti del mondo* (1590),[91] in which appeared a nearly identical image to the watercolor of the Sultan that accompanied Pagani's *viaggio* (Figure 1.1).[92] Flanking the Sultan were at least twenty young men to his right, similarly dressed in white and donning the same headwear, along with an "infinite number" (infinito numero) of others standing at attention.[93] Then, like a bride accompanied by her attendants, the Venetian ambassador entered in a brocaded attire with tight sleeves, on top of which was worn a golden mantle lined with ermine fur ("vestito di broccato a maniche strette, con un manto di ristagno d'oro, di sopra foderata di armellini").[94] The "ristagno" fabric of this garment was particularly prized for its luxurious composition of heavy silk interwoven with gold.[95] Its lengthy train required four dedicated members of the diplomatic entourage to carry it as the ambassador approached the sultan, and then to lift and carry the train again as the ambassador backed away, to ensure that Trevisan did not tread on the garment and then trip over it.[96]

The apparel of the other members of the Venetian entourage was also described in splendid detail meant to underscore the fine nature of the fabrics: scarlet- or crimson-colored damask, all floor length. Once the ambassador saw the Sultan, he immediately removed his velvet cap, bowed, placed one hand on the ground, then brought both hands to his mouth, and finally raised both arms above his head. The procession of the ambassador halted about twenty paces before the Sultan, a space covered in fine carpets, on which it was prohibited to tread. At this point, after a similar display of reverence, the ambassador placed his hand at his breast and displayed a ducal letter, the appearance of which was also richly described by Pagani. The letter, like its carrier, was finely dressed

Figure 1.1. Cesare Vecellio (attributed). *The Grand Sultan of Cairo, Qansuh al-Ghuri.* MS Paris, Bibliothèque Nationale de France, Archives et Manuscripts, Italien 2111. Photo courtesy of Bibliothèque Nationale de France.

and composed of paper tinged in the prized purple color known as *pavonazzo*. The embellished envelope featured a gold pendant seal and was further decorated with golden cords and bows. Its message, indicating the task of the ambassador, was also written in bright gold ink on the strikingly hued paper. Once the letter was displayed, the ambassador then kissed it, lifted it above his head before passing it on to the head *memendar* (the official escort of the ambassador), who transferred the letter to the sultan, opened it, and read aloud the contents.[97] The precise description of the document and the ritualized treatment of it reveals Pagani's disinterest in its substance, which he neither transcribed nor summarized.[98] What was shown to be of high importance was instead the gestural, visual, and corporeal language accompanying the presentation of the letter. The medium here really is the message.

The same attention to detail was also dedicated to the presentation of the gifts to the sultan. The presentation of the gifts preceded the arrival of the ambassador and thus set the stage for the reception of the ambassador, the most lavish gift of all. In discussing the gifts, the detail took such precedence that Pagani abandoned narration and instead composed a list so that every aspect could be clerically detailed, from the gift's value in *ducati* to the number of each item gifted, and so forth. To convey the extraordinary detail, I offer a brief transcription of one of the numerous lists included in the *viaggio*:

> The Signoria of Venice presents to the Gran Sultan by way of the Magnificent Venetian Ambassador.
>
> Gold Soprarizzo cloth with a pavonazzo background, value: 30 ducati per braccio . . . . 1 garment
>
> Gold Soprarizzo cloth with a crimson background . . . . 1 garment
>
> Gold Ristagno cloth 2 garments
>
> For a total of 8 gold-threaded garments
>
> Multiple-pile crimson-colored Velvet . . . . 2 garments
>
> Low pile crimson velvet. . . . . 3 garments
>
> Green flat velvet . . . . 3 garments
>
> Lionato low pile velvet . . . . 3 garments
>
> Pavonazzo flat velvet . . . . 3 garments
>
> For a total of 14 velvet garments

Lista del presente mandato al Serenissimo Soldano a mezzo del Magnifico Ambasciatore Veneziano.

Panno d'oro soprarizzo in campo pavonazzo da 30 ducati al braccio		vesta 1
Panno d'oro soprarizzo cremesin		vesta 1
Ristagno d'oro		veste 2
	Ori	veste 8
Velluto alto basso cremesin		veste 2
Velluto pian cremesin		veste 3
Velluto verde pian		veste 3
Velluto lionado pian		veste 3
Velluto pavonazzo pan		veste 3
	Velluti	veste 14

And so on with the satin garments, which totaled twenty-six and ranged in color from turquoise to a rich blue (alessandrino), to green, to crimson, to straw hued. Then come the damasks, followed by the pelts, then the sable and ermine furs, which totaled over five thousand pieces. Also gifted were fifty large pieces of Piacentino cheese, one of the most coveted diplomatic gifts. This list is followed by similarly detailed and exhaustive catalogs of gifts intended for the sultaness and other distinguished members of the Mamluk court: the royal secretary (the *dawâdâr; diodar* in Venetian), the grand admiral, the official escort (the *memendar*), and the Sultan's secretary (*chatibiser*).[99]

What I want to impress here is that the lists of objects gifted to the sultan, the sultaness, and other dignitaries—the majority of which were textiles—in the end become indistinct from the list of individuals, esteemed ambassador included, which Pagani described, all of whom are referred to in a similar, systematic, and detailed manner—rank, clothing style, color, and fabric type—rendering all agents effectively indistinguishable from the objects they bore. The visual was privileged over the verbal, and although Trevisan is referred to often by the title that indicated his role as oral message bearer, "Clarissimo Oratore" (Most Distinguished Orator), there is no description, transcription, or other representation of his verbal exchanges. Instead, Trevisan's language is a visual idiom of grandeur, luxury, and pageantry.

Following the exhaustive detail of the gifts, Pagani offered cursory, matter-of-fact description of the reasons behind the international scandal that necessitated the embassy:

> In detto luogo per lo spazio di due ore, e fu fatta grande disputazione tra esso Magnifico Oratore e detti mori di cose assai, tra le quali di un Ambasciatore del Sofì, il quale fu a Venezia già tre anni, che loro dicevano che era andato a domandar artiglierie e gente alla Illustrissima Signoria per andare contra il Soldano.
>
> (In this place, for two hours, a great discussion occurred between the Magnificent Orator and the aforementioned Moors about many topics, among which was pertained to an ambassador of the Sofì [Ismail I], who has already been in Venice for three years, and whom they [the Mamluks] claim had gone there to request artillery and troops from the Most Illustrious Signoria in order to wage war against the Sultan).[100]

This discussion is then followed by several pages of detailed description of the food and drink consumed, as well as a tour of the sultan's African menagerie, comprised of animals Pagani had never encountered, including a giraffe, elephant, and lions, which so impressed the author that he included minute details reminiscent of those of a comparative zoologist.

The pageantry then took a serious yet theatrical turn when an encounter was staged with Pietro Zen at an audience with the sultan. The yearlong imprisonment of the embattled Venetian consul of Damascus was one of the main reasons for Trevisan's embassy. Zen was paraded out in public during a formal meeting between the Venetian ambassador and the sultan. Pagani identified him as the "Magnificent Sir Zen, most worthy Consul of Damascus" (il Magnifico messer Pietro Zen degnissimo Console di Damasco) and then offered a remarkably detailed description of his clothing—"wearing a scarlet [robe] with ducal sleeves" (vestito di scarlatto con maniche alla ducale).[101] Pagani then preemptively declared Zen's innocence before skewing the issue by stating that the sultan believed Zen "made a mistake" (abbia fallato).[102] Ambassador Trevisan, in this moment, was expected to deny aloud the Serenissima's involvement in Zen's affairs, and after a discussion that was neither transcribed nor summarized, in which "many other words were said" (fatte altre molte parole), then Trevisan himself, in the presence of the sultan, recreated Zen's imprisonment. He placed chains around the imperiled consul's finely clothed neck: "In the presence of the Lord Sultan, the Magnificent Ambassador, by his own hand, placed the chains around the neck of the aforesaid Magnificent Consul of Damascus" (In presenza del Signore Soldano, il Magnifico Ambasciatore di sua mano pose le catene al collo al prefato Magnifico Console di Damasco).[103]

This was a remarkable moment when Trevisan encountered a fellow member of the Venetian diplomatic corps and was expected to (re)enact Zen's imprisonment and symbolic punishment in front of, and on behalf of, both the Mamluk sultan and Venice itself. I view this as a moment in which the two realities of the ambassador came into conflict. On one side was Trevisan, enjoying privileged status as a lavishly welcomed and highly anticipated guest, while on the other was Zen, a condemned prisoner whose life depended on the dictates of a foreign sovereign and the negotiation skills of his fellow ambassador. Zen's ritualized humiliation, or ceremonial punishment, was as much a message to Trevisan as it was an appeasement to the sultan, for it demonstrated the risk that accompanied the privileged diplomatic body, which could quickly become a vulnerable, imprisoned one.

In essentially opposite ways, both Contarini and Pagani's texts demonstrate the vacillation between distinction and likeness that defined the ambassador's privilege and predicament. The ambassador inhabited a world in which the need for disguise and ceremony shifted rapidly and, in both cases, the ambassador was a foreigner to his own self. As an insider to his state, he had to sacrifice his own identity and don that of his sovereign, submitting every action to political interpretation. As a surrogate of the state to a foreign sovereign, the ambassador could theoretically be considered an insider or sometimes, as we have seen, a prisoner. The cloth that adorned the ambassador, while often luxurious, also distanced him from his personal identity, imprisoning his body natural within the body politic. Many overt demonstrations of authenticity were undertaken, but those same rituals covered, layered, and complicated the surface, obscuring it and thus widening the gap between the surface and the truth.

CHAPTER TWO

Ambassadors in "Utopia"

In this chapter, I discuss how the political imperatives fulfilled by the early modern ambassador often required, to meet those collective needs, that the individual sacrifice aspects of his personhood. I first focus on the body of the ambassador. Although his body is indeed of flesh, the role of the ambassador is a work of fiction: He inhabits an existential nonidentity, a fiction, neither his own nor truly that of his sovereign; he is also physically in limbo, for he is legally inviolable (a truly impossible thing but a useful fiction) yet still vulnerable. The ambassador also exists in geographical "utopias," or non-places, evoked by Stephen Greenblatt in his important discussion of Hans Holbein's iconic painting *The Ambassadors*: "They who seem to be present before us exist nowhere, exist then in utopia."[1] Setting aside for now the aesthetic implications of Greenblatt's insight, for the purposes of the present argument, it can also illuminate the spatial predicament of the ambassador. While traveling, the ambassador's identity and safety were contingent upon outside forces, and the establishment of the embassy also represented an indistinct, and in a sense a fictitious, space, belonging neither to the country that surrounded it nor to the one that sponsored it. The appearance of the ambassador was a highly symbolic entity, and each of its elements was open to scrutiny and interpretation, at times with devastating consequences.

In addition to a discussion of *The Ambassadors,* I examine the figure of the early modern ambassador and orient the spaces in which he worked and moved by way of two case studies in early modern diplomacy. Each of these is extraordinary, but together they bring into relief general concerns and potential privileges of these emissaries. Early modern Europe was evermore interconnected by commerce and imperial designs on "new" geographies encountered, as well as the threat of known but feared peoples and states to its east. Swiftly shifting alliances, religious strife and schism, the centralization of power in the nation-states, and unstable alliances in the Italian peninsula all warranted the development, codification, and professionalization of diplomacy.[2] Both cases that I discuss left behind a paper trail attesting to their contemporary importance. The case of Alberto Maraviglia (ca. 1485–1533) became, as Timothy Hampton states, a "cause célèbre, almost a kind of Rorschach test, for Renaissance diplomatic writers."[3] Maraviglia's case was a prism through which contemporary thinkers refracted Renaissance diplomacy into its elemental parts. Each thinker who discussed the case, from French philosopher Michel de Montaigne (1533–1592) to the expatriate Italian jurist Alberico Gentili (1552–1608), constructed an idiosyncratic interpretation, indicating the richness of the case, particularly in terms of the dangers and uncertainties, both legal and practical, that the early modern ambassador faced. The fragility of the diplomatic profession, as well as the inconsistent way it was applied and manipulated in foreign relations, is also elicited.

The subject of the second case study, Sir Henry Wotton (1568–1639), however, left behind numerous letters as well as scholarly and literary texts through which he narrated his story personally.[4] Wotton served as English ambassador to Venice on three different extended embassies over a nearly twenty-year period (1604–1623), an experience that indelibly modified Wotton's own personal identity.[5] The case of Wotton demonstrates how fictionality is reclaimed by the ambassador. For Wotton, the ambassador was no longer only subject to the legal fiction of diplomatic immunity (*ius gentium*), but importantly he instead created a fiction of himself—and/or recreated himself as a work of fiction.

Ambassadors to Nowhere: Holbein's The Ambassadors

Perhaps no work, visual or textual, better illustrates this phenomenon than Hans Holbein's *The Ambassadors* (Figure 2.1). Although the scholarship on this painting is extensive, I offer an approach that interprets the work as a testament to the instrumentalization of the ambassador: a figure who is dispossessed of his own body and sent to inhabit a non-place, neither fiction nor reality, as an

Figure 2.1. Hans Holbein the Younger. *Jean de Dinteville and Georges de Selve (The Ambassadors)* (1533). Oil on wood, 207×209.5 cm. Image Number NG1314. National Gallery, London. Photo courtesy of National Gallery, London.

instrument of the state. The notion of ambassadorial instrumentalization I employ here is inspired by Francesco Guiccardini's *Ricordo* number 171 in which the metaphor of a crossbow (balestra) and its arrows (freccie) are used to describe the relation between a prince and his ambassador:

> Diceva el duca Lodovico Sforza che una medesima regola serve a fare conoscere e principi e le balestre. *Se la balestra è buona o no, si conosce dalle freccie che tira; così el valore de' principi si conosce dalla qualità degli uomini mandano fuora.* Dunche si può arguire che governo fussi quello di

> Firenze, quando in uno tempo medesimo adoperò per imbasciadori el Carduccio in Francia, el Gualterotto a Vinegia, messer Bardo a Siena e messer Galeotto Giugni a Ferrara (italics added).[6]

> (Duke Ludovico Sforza used to say that princes and crossbows could be tried by the same rule. *Whether the crossbow is good is judged by the arrows it shoots. So too, the value of princes is judged by the quality of the men they send forth.* We can guess, therefore, what sort of government there was in Florence when it employed as ambassadors simultaneously Carducci in France, Gualterotti in Venice, Bardi in Siena, and Galeotto Giugni in Ferrara.)

This maxim is interesting and worth discussing here because it sheds light on the complexity of the figure of the early modern ambassador.

Elected ambassador of Florence to King Ferdinand of Aragon in 1511, Guicciardini was resident at the Spanish court during the period in which, under strong Spanish influence, Florence restored the Medici to power. In his maxim, Guicciardini, an experienced ambassador, reproduced a metaphor from the point of view of a prince, Duke Ludovico Sforza: the ambassador, likened to a weapon or, better, to the missiles (arrows) it launched. The arrows, essential to the functioning of the weapon, were nevertheless intrinsically impotent. Without the power of the princely weapons that "sent them forth," ambassadors, like idle arrows, lacked any power to impact. The prince, fixed in the place of launch and thus distant from the place of impact, however, was judged by the qualities of the ambassador he "sent forth." The ambassador, impotent yet essential, was distinct and different from the prince, yet paradoxically also a reflection of him, his qualities, and the state he incarnated. The ambassador was an instrument, a tool whose usefulness was determined by whether he fulfilled the mission for which he was "launched." His agency was thus circumscribed and dependent on the desires of the prince who "sent him forth." And taking the metaphor to its extreme, we can conclude that the ambassador, once launched, was also incapable of propelling himself back home; he had to passively depend on the actions and the will of the prince to return him to his place of origin.

Let us now look closer at Holbein's *The Ambassadors* (1533) to further illustrate the types of questions confronted by the study of the figure of the early modern emissary. This contemporary work of visual art is as archetypal as it is enigmatic. This portrait, featuring two Renaissance diplomats, depicts myriad objects that define and illustrate the achievements, culture, and conflicts of its time: a printed Lutheran hymnbook alongside a book of merchant profit calculations, which happens to be cracked open just enough to make its contents legible; globes both terrestrial and celestial; a lute with a broken string; flutes; astronomical (toquetum) and navigational tools; and tapestries, curtains, and elaborately colored mosaic flooring all indicate a learned and courtly setting. The symbols of the seven liberal arts—the trivium and quadrivium—of a proper humanist education are carefully depicted. The attention paid by Holbein to the details of the objects extends to the clothing of the ambassadors, which richly reproduces and even enhances the laborious work the tailors, embroiderers, and furriers undertook in the production of the garments, heightening the observer's awareness of the elaborate workmanship of these manufactured garments and objects, which, Holbein suggests, includes the painting itself, as John Berger argued.[7] The clothing of the anonymous ambassadors is thus "professional," appropriate to their post, and points to use in ceremonial and the most formal of courtly occasions. The sumptuous rendering of the garments holds the eye of the beholder on the surface of the image purposefully, thus resisting the interpretation of what lies under the garments. For my reading, what is most striking is that the use value of the human figures lies in their courtly appearance, their exterior—not in what they accomplished as individuals. Their lack of individuality embodies, in a sense, the ambassadorial role they represent. The ambassador thus becomes an object, a symbolic gift from one sovereign (state) to another, an instrument of negotiation and diplomacy, just as the globes are instruments of navigation; the sundial, of timekeeping; and the merchant handbook, a tool of commerce.

The objects are clearly identifiable to the intended viewer.[8] As has been well noted, the details of Holbein's composition include several examples that reveal the imprecision and imperfection of the instruments displayed: The lute has a broken string; one side of the tetrahedral sundial shows a time of 9:30 and another, 10:30; the celestial globe is shown from the latitude of Spain or Italy rather than the portrait's location of London. Consistent with this undermining of the advancements and achievements represented in the painting is the most emblematic aspect of its composition: the large, anamorphic skull in the foreground. This figure underscores mortality, the ultimate human flaw. This imperfection, when compared to the immortality and perfection of the Christian deity, is figured by the anamorphic memento mori, which from the correct vantage point successfully eclipses and nullifies all forms of material culture as well as those of earthly status and achievement, present or alluded to in the composition. What was in one moment a space is suddenly erased. Holbein's skillful anamorphosis manipulates space, time, and perceptions of reality, and reflects the instability of the non-place, the liminality, inhabited by the ambassador.

The Ambassadors continues to provoke scholarly interpretations of the double portrait's "unusual character," its "secret."[9] The enigmatic quality of the painting does much to attract such attention and attempts to decode its meanings. One recent article dedicated to the painting applies phenomenological interpretative tools to suggest that the artwork tries to speak through what it conceals: "They [the anamorphic skull and the concealing draperies in the background] tell us that the modus operandi of *The Ambassadors* is regulated by a principle of concealment. *The Ambassadors* is a painting that hides by showing."[10] The most important and telling question to pose about the painting, according to Kenaan, is why Holbein portrayed two men in a stylistic and figurative language usually reserved for the portraiture of a married couple.[11] Because neither of the subjects ever married, the "main concern" of the painting may be that the two shared an "intimate" friendship and possibly this "secret" or "forbidden" relationship.[12] I mention this study not to agree or to disagree with its assumptions or conclusions, but instead to cast it as an example of how often in *The Ambassadors* scholarship there is a singular focus on the biographical and historical details of the dual portrait's subjects. The painting itself—from its general title to its lack of biographically identifying details—precisely resists such attempts at circumscription and limitation of meaning, however. It was not until 1900, nearly four hundred years after its creation, when Mary Hervey undertook the painstaking archival research, that the sitters' identities were established; until that point the subjects were known only as "ambassadors."[13] The debate that raged about the identities of the subjects of the double portrait attests to the curious lack of detail attributed to the identities of the portrait's subjects, and even its subject-patron, Jean de Dinteville.

Dinteville (1504–1555), on the viewer's left, was Francis I's ambassador to Henry VIII of England, and on the viewer's right is Georges de Selve (1508–1541), bishop of Lavaur, Francis's ambassador to Venice. The two ambassadors, uncentered in their portrait, are positioned at the edges of the composition, and the painting's center is occupied by a double-tiered table on which the two men casually rest their arms. The table is crowded with the abovementioned items, and Holbein is careful to make each individual item easily identifiable, not blocked or obscured by the bodies of the titular figures. Besides a medallion of the Order of St. Michael around Dinteville's neck, and Selve's black clerical robe, however, the personal identities of the ambassadors are not apparent by symbols on their persons. Anonymity is not atypical in Renaissance portraiture, yet the artist often explicitly renders the identities and likenesses of the individual sitters, as did Raphael in his portrait of Julius II, and Holbein in his unmistakable portrait of Henry VIII.[14]

In the case of *The Ambassadors*, however, the painting's iconic nature is perhaps owing to its enigmatic qualities. Art historians and scholars intervened through intensive archival research to identify the figures represented. The symbols associated with the figures are mostly generic representations of nobility: Dinteville's dagger and sword, along with his medal, indicate his noble status and place at court. These objects are symbols that speak to the general characteristics of an ambassador's education and class, rather than the historical identities of the depicted ambassadors. Nonetheless, the robed Selve, clearly a clergy member, is depicted leaning his elbow on an unidentified book, the edge of whose pages reads "ÆTATIS SVÆ 25," which happens to indicate Selve's age of twenty-five in 1533, the year of the portrait's execution. This reference to Selve's age is repeated by an even less visible or noticeable inscription on Dinteville's dagger, indicating his age: "ÆTATIS SVÆ 29." While this information is specific to Selve and Dinteville, it is unlikely that the casual observer would have perceived the inscriptions, and even less probable that one would have been able to use that information to identify the men. They are details meant to remain hidden from and cryptic to the observer, not distinguishing symbols of their identities. Given names are not present; in fact, the impersonal possessive adjective (*suae*) is the only tenuous link connecting the men to the inscribed ages. It is more probable, and significant, that the viewer is guided instead to identify the figures as worldly and scholarly statesmen, whose exemplary humanist knowledge and noble courtly positions render their professional appointment and duties both iconic and representative of their time.

The generic title by which the painting is known, *The Ambassadors*, also reinforces the erasure of the individual. The title, assigned to painting at a date and by a person unknown, but certainly well after its completion, reflects the fact that the portrayed ambassadors are not readily identifiable as distinct historical figures.[15] The overwhelming presence of objects of the trade of diplomacy and worldly knowledge are what permits the identification of the sitters as diplomats, yet obscures any further personal identification. Holbein instead casts them as emblematic figures of the general ambassadorial/diplomatic category, prioritizing the representation of "the ambassador" over the identification of any given ambassador. The ambassador was a figure whose very identity lay in its own concealment. This concealment of the ambassador's personal identity, and in this case also his nationality, is a necessity of the position of ambassador. As Lisa Jardine noted, the ambassador and his staff "operated under conditions of obsessive secrecy, and with fierce loyalty to the state to which it was answerable."[16] The secrecy, enigma, disguise, and peril were essential duties and risks of the ambassador, all of which are alluded to masterfully in Holbein's composition.

Personal biographical details were obscured as the Renaissance ambassador cloaked himself as a statesman, an educated man of the world, and—most importantly—a surrogate for his sovereign. His own identity was necessarily put aside in lieu of that of his state and its head of state.[17] The appearance of an ambassador was dictated by the sovereign to whom he was sent and further guided by the sovereign he represents. In Holbein's portrait, Dinteville, the painting's commissioner, is clad in Tudor-style clothing reminiscent of Holbein's iconic portraits of Henry VIII, to whom Dinteville was sent on embassy at the behest of his own sovereign, Francis I.[18] It could represent merely a sartorial decision on behalf of Dinteville; yet it is significant, since he, a Frenchman, chose to be (or at least allowed himself to be) immortalized in English costume by one of the most important portraitists of the age. This decision could be viewed then as a conscious construction of an identity, in other words, a purposeful creation of distance between the truth and the appearance, the depth and the surface. This distance speaks to the fictional space inhabited by the ambassador, who is in between realities, identities, and geographies. The theatrical atmosphere evoked in the composition bolsters this interpretation. The draperies (curtains?), oppressive presence of objects (props?), elaborate garments (costumes?), and ornate mosaic flooring (stage?) all evoke and delineate a performative space. Ambassadors are not truly actors, however, and their space is not the result of textual representation, but a lived experience that is neither truly their own nor truly that of another. This is the paradox of diplomats: They inhabit a space—a utopia, a non-place—of which they are not in control.

The central importance of the appearance of the ambassador, subject to constant scrutiny and interpretation, is indicative of its paradox. Each instance of examination does not lead toward an understanding of the figure beneath the appearance, but instead toward the fictional character of the ambassador. The myriad details included by Holbein compel the viewer to approach the work and scrutinize it intensely. This vantage point, in turn, compels the viewer to appreciate the space within the portrait as an artistic rendering. Stephen Greenblatt speaks to this in *Renaissance Self-Fashioning*: "For the painting insists, passionately and profoundly, on the representational power of art, its central role in man's apprehension and control of reality, even as it insists, with uncanny persuasiveness, on the fictional character of that entire so-called reality and the art that pretends to represent it."[19] For example, one defining element of the attire is the badge of the Order of St. Michael around Dinteville's neck, the only detail that indicates his noble French origin. The image of St. Michael on the medallion signifies membership in this exclusive chivalric order, an honor the French king conferred on a very select group of nobles in recognition of their loyalty and service to the Crown. Given the medallion's small size, in order to interpret the image, one would need to inspect the portrait quite closely.

Holbein's invitation to closely scrutinize the painting leads the viewer to discern that the composition is a "mass of individual details,"[20] which represent and memorialize less the individuality of its sitters than the "mass" of symbols found on their persons and in the composition at large. In fact, besides the obvious differences in garments—one sitter, a layman (Dinteville); the other, a clergy member (Selve)—their other physical attributes are remarkably similar. Their facial resemblance was so appreciable that Selve was thought to be Dinteville's brother. In privileging the mass of details, Holbein suggested that the world of the sitters is composed of a complicated symbolic language that must be interpreted piece by piece, layer by layer, to understand the larger picture. Their identity is, to a large extent, subject to the interpretation of the beholder, out of the subjects' control. This is therefore similar to what Norbert Elias characterized in reference to the symbolic economy of the court of Louis XIV: "intense scrutiny of each manifestation of a person [. . .] to assess everything relating to him in terms of its social valency, its prestige value."[21] The prestige value to which Elias referred is that of the courtier who sought desperately to gain favor for himself at court. The position of the ambassador was, however, distinct and more complex since his loyalty must always remain to his own sovereign, yet he was subjected to scrutiny similar to that of the courtier and was necessarily caught up in the machinations of the court system.[22]

The painting's intricate composition leads one to question the reasons for its commission. Although it is unimportant to discern the real reason for which Dinteville retained Holbein for this portrait, this line of consideration brings to light the dialogue between the portrait's composition and the circumstances under which it was realized. Renaissance portraits featuring anonymous subjects are not rare, yet the subjects of *The Ambassadors* differ in not being identified in generic personal terms, as is the case with other Renaissance portraits where the subject remains unnamed today, such as "portrait of two men" or "portrait of friends." Instead, the sitters were recognized for their professional capacity as ambassadors—"l'un *Ambassadeur* à Venise, et l'autre dans les pays du Nord" (italics added)—and thus Dinteville may have commissioned the portrait to honor his and Selve's professional diplomatic identities.[23]

The significance of the embassy bolsters the notion that Dinteville may have desired to commemorate his participation in the monumental and highly fraught event. Dinteville was representing King Francis I at the court of Henry VIII on the occasion of his secret marriage to Anne Boleyn and at the eve of his split from Rome. Henry was growing impatient in his desire to legitimate Anne, who was pregnant at the time with Henry's eagerly awaited heir, whom he wishfully (and of course incorrectly) referred to as male. Henry refused to risk that the child be born illegitimate, insisting that the bishop of Canterbury pronounce the legitimacy of his marriage and that Anne be imminently coronated, regardless of the pope's authorization of his divorce from Katherine of Aragon.

These major international conflicts at the time of the portrait portended unknown but ominous, military, political, and religious consequences, making it urgent for a head of state to have direct representation at the Tudor court. One can imagine that only the most respected and trusted emissaries would have been selected for such a mission. The honor in having been chosen to participate in such an embassy would be reason enough for pictorial commemoration, and perhaps this is why Dinteville chose to commission Holbein to depict himself and his fellow French envoy, Selve. The rarity of the subject matter—ambassadors—is also intriguing, and perhaps it was this novelty of subject that also prompted the commission: the depiction of ambassadors, functionaries essential to the creation and maintenance of the state, who would otherwise remain nameless and faceless. Allowing for and securing his own depiction is perhaps even an indication of a desire on the part of Dinteville to exercise ownership over his own body, his own likeness, at a time in which he worried openly about his "santé" and, as we will see, his corporeal integrity.[24]

This commission by Dinteville, a career diplomat, could also allude to his desire to be recognized and memorialized for the work he had done and his dedication to his sovereign. This profession proved to be a sacrifice that he worried would claim his very life and even consume his own body, or at least separate it from himself. In a letter to his brother François, bishop of Auxerre and Francis I's ambassador to Rome, dated May 23, 1533, a week before Anne Boleyn's coronation and the same day that her marriage to Henry was deemed legitimate, Dinteville speaks of his displeasure at being stuck in England and how the experience has rendered him "le plus melancolique et fascheux ambassadeur que vistez oncques" (the most melancholy vexed and tiresome ambassador that ever was).[25]

This sentiment is echoed in a similarly urgent and pathetic tone in Dinteville's letter from early June 1533 to Jean du Bellay, bishop of Paris, in which he urgently implored him for assistance in securing his recall to France, expressing exasperation in having endured ill health for most of the long six months he had been in England. He ended the letter dramatically: "Que si je y demores encore gueres, j'ai grand peur de y lassier la peau et les os" (If I stay here any longer, it is my great fear that I will leave behind my skin and bones).[26] Jardine and Britton suggested that the "gloomy emotional state" Dinteville expressed in his letters is replicated in the painting's anamorphic skull and the death's head on the pin in Dinteville's cap.[27] I would like to propose that, additionally, we pay closer attention to the corporeal metaphor to which Dinteville resorted, which, more than only a sour outlook, importantly speaks to the necessary physical involvement and sacrifice required of the diplomat, who was sent as a bodily representative of his sovereign and state. Just as a present gifted from one head of state to another was destined never to return to its place of origin, here Dinteville referred to the sacrifice of his own body in similar terms: his fear that it might never again return home, but instead remain in its ambassadorial "utopia."[28]

In giving metaphorical shape to his predicament, Dinteville alluded to the little control he could exercise over the physical location of his own body. The corporeality of the ambassador had been sacrificed to another, Francis I, and he, its rightful owner, had been necessarily dispossessed. In fact, in the king of France's absence, it was Dinteville who played a remarkably prominent role by representing France at Anne Boleyn's coronation. Dinteville's ceremonial presence was "politically significant" as it signaled France's support for England through its acceptance of Henry's divorce and new marriage, an allegiance that would unavoidably anger Rome, where Dinteville's brother was serving as ambassador.[29] The pressure was also felt more directly. Dinteville and his retinue, whose attire bearing the French colors was initially paid for by the ambassador himself, were "booed and insulted" while leading the procession by the English populace fond of Katharine.[30] The many months Dinteville had spent in London up to this point, as his letters to the king and other ambassadors attest, were spent trying to avoid the very event in which his body was compelled to perform ceremonially the role of France, which in turn was incarnated by its absent king.[31]

The friction between the ambassador's body natural and the roles imposed on it can be seen at the pictorial level as well. We recall that in *The Ambassadors* Dinteville sports Northern/Tudor-style attire, the dress of the country where he served as ambassador, while he also dons the badge of the Order of St. Michael, an honor whose icon, the medallion, indicates loyalty (and subjection) and cannot be removed from the honoree once it is bestowed by the king of France. Dinteville's body thus participated in a historically and politically important event, yet the performance of this pompous and spectacular role conflicted with the pressures exerted on the diplomat's body natural. The suffering, physically construed by Dinteville, evokes the existential strain of diplomacy and the "melancholic" predicament of the ambassador.

This angst corresponds also to the darker side of the political and diplomatic milieu in which these two emissaries found themselves: *The Ambassadors* was painted in London just two years before the execution of Sir Thomas More in that same city.[32] More went from being Henry's trusted advisor to having been accused and convicted of high treason in such a short time. Fickle and dangerous was the political life for those around the regent: The convictions of the advisor or ambassador were only relevant, respected, and safe to declaim if they were aligned precisely with those of the monarch. Thomas More, executed ostensibly for high treason, was guilty of holding and maintaining religious convictions at odds with Henry VIII's plans for England. Cloaking More's personal betrayal as an official one against the state itself allowed Henry to manipulate the legal framework and rid himself of a detractor who was as widely respected as he was vocal. More's infamous demise brings us to our first case, Giovanni Alberto Maraviglia (also known as Meraviglia, or as Merveilles in France, ca. 1485–1533), a Milanese merchant who, through his association with Franco-Italian *condottiere* and *Grand Èscuyer de France* Galeazzo Sanseverino (ca. 1460–1525), rose to the rank of éscuyer at the French court.[33] Maraviglia can be seen as an unlikely and unknowing ambassadorial martyr. Different from More, whose eminence today has less to do with his execution than with his many erudite contributions and eventual beatification, Maraviglia's assassination is what constituted his notoriety.

Considering this contemporary event, Holbein's association of death and diplomacy via the anamorphic death's head seems less arbitrary or cryptic than it may have been initially. Or at least, the two skulls in the painting should not considered only as a representation of memento mori, the reminder of the looming shadow of death even among prosperity, popular in the art of the period; instead, the general figuration of *vanitas* acquires in this portrait topical significance specific to the complex subjectivity of the ambassador. Along with Dinteville and Selve, the assassinated Maraviglia was also a member of Francis's diplomatic corps, active in the diplomatic negotiations of the shifting alliances that characterized the Italian Wars. The fragile situation of the ambassador himself thus comes into relief. The role of the ambassador is essential to the early modern state, yet the physical body of the diplomat emerges as a most vulnerable entity. The importance of the Maraviglia affair demonstrates that the ambassadorial body was a fraught entity in early modernity, contested both physically and in terms of the ambiguities of his office as surrogate for the sovereign. This contested space between the body natural and the body politic displaced geographically disputed terrain to become the new front in the delimitation of the state, as well as in the development of the modern subject.

Mary Hervey suggested an aesthetic link between the Maraviglia affair and Holbein's painting. The inclusion of the lute with a broken string, the object within the painting that most clearly symbolizes strife and discord, was linked by Hervey to Andrea Alciati's emblem entitled "feodera italorum," published in the first edition of *Emblematum liber* (1531).[34] Alciati, who like Maraviglia was also Milanese, accompanied the emblem with a poem dedicated to Francesco II Sforza, duke of Milan, perhaps in commemoration of the 1526 League of Cognac, and thus led Hervey to conclude that Holbein's inclusion of the broken lute contained a significance that was "wholly political," and for reasons specific to the Milanese political landscape.[35] Hervey, however, restricted the influence of Milanese affairs on the composition to the presence of the lute. Beyond the citation of Alciati's lute and its associated political allusions, I propose that the relationship between death and the ambassador is reflected directly in the painting's composition. As is shown herein, Maraviglia's contemporary demise in Milan concretized the physical vulnerability of the supposedly "inviolable" diplomat, and seen in this light, Holbein's double portrait featuring two ambassadors whose pictorial existence is eclipsed by the death's head may offer a visual meditation on the fragility and potential tragedy of the ambassador. Let us now turn to discuss the particulars of the Maraviglia affair.

Giovanni Alberto Maraviglia: Diplomatic (Dis)Member

On the morning of July 6, 1533, Milanese marketgoers were confronted with a sight as gruesome as it was uncommon: a headless body on display in the Piazza Mercanti. The corpse, "whose head was divided from its torso" (la testa divisa dal busto) was soon thereafter identified as having once belonged to Scudiero Giovanni Alberto Maraviglia.[36] He had been apprehended a few days prior, charged, and condemned to death after his alleged confession for the murder of a member of the prominent Castiglione family. Such a display was remarkable because in Milan in this period it was customary for a noble accused and suspected of murder to be banished rather than dangled postmortem as a headless torso in the public market space.[37] The nature of the display, both symbolic and public, indicated that the carnal sight was meant as a message. The mutilated body of a diplomat was, in death, transformed into a text, a message with a discrete recipient: Francis I, king of France.

The political assassination (or murder) of Alberto Maraviglia in Milan proves to be an illustrative example of the potential pitfalls of Renaissance diplomacy and the precarious intermediary role of the ambassador. Though the Italian Wars of 1521 to 1526 and the Sack of Rome (1527) were over by this time, there remained unrelenting political instability in the Italian peninsula. The Duchy of Milan continued to be a mere battleground between two of the most powerful forces in Europe, France and the Habsburg Empire of Charles V.[38] After Spanish reconquest of Milan from the French and the reinstatement of Francesco II Sforza as Duke of Milan, the considerable tension between Charles V and Francis I of France continued. It was Francis's humiliating defeat by Charles V at Pavia in the Italian Wars of 1521 to 1526, during which Francis personally commanded his troops, which led to his subsequent imprisonment, and the political captivity of his sons in exchange for the king's release. Furthermore, Francis was forced to agree to the Treaty of Madrid, which imposed many severely restrictive terms, including the obligation that he would renounce any territorial claims in Italy, particularly in Milan. Francis was eager to vindicate himself after such a devastating personal loss. And Sforza, his leadership of Milan undermined by Spanish occupation and hegemony, surely sensed at some level the precariousness of his rule of the Duchy of Milan. He was unmarried and in ill health (he died in October 1534), circumstances that provoked the open speculation that he would die without a male heir (indeed he did). Physical and imperial frailty thus kindled a diplomatic relationship between these two leaders. Both Sforza and Francis had been and continued to be hamstrung, and humiliated by Charles. This treacherous political terrain required the most competent diplomacy; however, the result was one of the most scandalous affairs in Renaissance diplomatic history, which was still polemical even in post-Unification Italy.[39]

The dismembered diplomatic body, a surrogate for his sovereign, was, in death, transformed into a symbolic and public text, acting as a political message. The transmission of such a message by a diplomat's mutilated corpse supplanted diplomacy: The body of the diplomat *became* the message; he was no longer the bearer, translator, communicator, or negotiator of that message. Though itself horrific, the death of Maraviglia became an international scandal largely because of Francis's incensed and vociferous reaction to it, not necessarily because of the assassination itself. While it is understandable that Francis would be disturbed by the death of his equerry, whom he appears to have known well, that was not the reason he stated for his anger. The death of Maraviglia—the man—was not what proved disturbing to Francis. In letters to Sforza, Charles V, Pope Clement VII, Henry VIII of England, the doge of Venice, and other "princes of Christendom" (*Princes Chrétiens*), Francis declared over and again that his anger was due instead to the fact that Maraviglia was "[his] ambassador" (*mon ambassadeur*) and as such was protected under the ancient statutes of the *ius gentium*, which should have provided him not only with safe passage but, most importantly, exterritorial diplomatic immunity.[40] Consequently, Francis asserted that Maraviglia was unlawfully murdered, not justifiably executed for crimes committed, and hence the Kingdom of France had been wronged. Also, in employing the possessive adjective—"my ambassador"—Francis indicated a sort of ownership over Maraviglia, as well as even implying that the personal affront he suffered because of the murder of "[his] ambassador" was in essence a symbolic murder of the king himself: "Il ne me seroit pas possible de vous exprimer l'indignation que m'a causée *un pareil outrage fait à moimême dans la personne de mon minister*" (It would not be possible to express the indignation caused me by *such an outrage done to myself through the person of my minister*; italics added).[41]

In fact, in his *Mémoires*, Martin du Bellay (1495–1559), noted French chronicler of the Italian Wars and experienced diplomat, reported the comments of the king regarding the death of Maraviglia, in which there is the repetition of the phrase "fait trancher la tête à mon ambassadeur" (had my ambassador's head severed).[42] One quotation is from the king's letter to Francesco II Sforza, the duke of Milan, accusing him of having defied "the most sacred laws, inviolably observed since time immemorial by all of the world's princes" (des droits le plus sacrés, invioblement observées de tems immémorìal par tous les princes du monde).[43] It is intriguing that neither du Bellay nor the king himself resorted to euphemisms—or even a more general phrase evoking the murder of Maraviglia, such as "had my ambassador killed." Instead, they both insist on the mode of death—decapitation—in their comments and recriminations.

If brought into the context of the body politic, this specific and gruesome characterization of the demise of Maraviglia acquires meaning beyond gratuitous detail and alludes to the reason why the manner of death proved so offensive to the king of France. It is Francis, the king, who occupies the head (*la tête*) of the corporate entity of the French body politic. Therefore, severing Maraviglia's head from his body natural, I propose, can be—and, I argue, was meant to be—interpreted as a symbolic murder of the king himself and in turn a symbolic mutilation of France's body politic. I suggest that Maraviglia's body natural acted as a substitution for the body natural of the king and the body politic of France. This surrogate violence toward Maraviglia evinces the ambassador as a sacrificial entity, a sort of scapegoat onto whom falls all the responsibility and who, with his life, unjustly suffers the consequences.

This notion of the scapegoat, or the scapegoat mechanism as René Girard theorized, comes from the matrix of archaic religion.[44] The scapegoat acquires its "sacredness" by being both the origin of violence and the reason for renewed peace, a duality that accounts for its "prodigious power" to diffuse crisis. This notion of the sacred is particularly intriguing if applied to the discussion of violence and the diplomat, who is by very definition "sacrosanct" and "inviolable," as Francis stated in his letter. However, this is not because of the sacrificial nature of the diplomat's role, but because of the ambassador's potential to diffuse crisis through mediation. The ambassador's special status was because the ambassador was a figure both within and outside the law, both privileged and cursed. The ambassador's curse consisted in acting as substitute for his sovereign, and as such the sacrifice of the ambassador as a substitute sacrifice for that of the king, the regicide, was thus a permissible sacrifice in comparison.

This infamous example of diplomacy gone wrong violated every aspect set forth in the *ius gentium*. However, ironically, this was precisely the same legal framework that Francis I evoked in his protests after the death of Maraviglia. First, as most sources agree, the diplomatic arrangements were made specifically to avoid any type of transparency: Sforza initially sent an envoy by the name of Francesco Taverna to France, with the discrete intention of enticing Francis into establishing a secret ambassadorial presence in Milan, an arrangement desirable to Francis, yet one that would have enraged Charles V.[45] Taverna then suggested his own uncle, Maraviglia, to Francis, based on Maraviglia's establishment at the French court and also his Milanese origins. Francis's agreement to appoint Maraviglia to represent him secretly in Milan was due directly to the fact that his dual identity would be less likely to arouse Habsburg suspicion. Second, Maraviglia's undercover status was unofficial and left him unprotected, and thus an envoy dispossessed not only of *ius gentium* protections but also eventually his own life.

Each interested party offered a different version of the events, but the indisputable facts that led to the death of Maraviglia are as follows: Giovanni Alberto Maraviglia, Milanese by birth and a long-time *scudiero* at the court of Francis I, returned to Milan in early 1533. Over six months Maraviglia set up a sumptuous dwelling in central Milan and successfully ingratiated himself with the local nobility. On July 4, 1533, he was arrested, incarcerated, and condemned to death for the murder of a member of the Castiglione family, a charge to which Maraviglia may or may not have confessed. Maraviglia was then executed by decapitation during the night of July 6, and his headless torso was publicly displayed in the marketplace in central Milan.

The timing of the execution proved to be an especially revealing element to Francis I. If Maraviglia was indeed guilty of murder, reasoned Francis, why would it have been necessary to execute him privately at night. Therefore, it was clear to him that Sforza's concealment of the execution from the public revealed an unlawful execution of "[his] ambassador," not of a criminal. This lack of theatrical "spectacle" (to use Foucault's terminology) of execution is conspicuous, since two more centuries would pass before capital punishment ceased being a public event.[46] Some sources indicate that Maraviglia was not charged with murder, but instead with sedition for his attempts at rallying those Milanese subjects still loyal to the French king.[47] Others indicate that, in addition to murder and sedition, he was condemned for the attempted poisoning of the duke of Milan, conspiracy against the state, and espionage on behalf of the French.[48] There is also a fervently nationalistic source dating from the immediate post-Unification period in Italy that defended Sforza's actions, assuming and attempting to prove Maraviglia guilty of ambushing and murdering Castiglione with *archibusi* (arquebuses, early modern muzzle-loaded firearms), citing long-standing animosity and a conflict over a noble woman's love, and/or hand in marriage.[49]

If all the facts mentioned in Francis's argument were indeed true, then this would clearly indicate a violation of the *ius gentium* on the part of the Duchy of Milan, based on accepted standards of international diplomacy. The thorny issue regards the actual status of Maraviglia in Milan. Was he indeed an actual ambassador of France to the Duchy of Milan, or, contrarily, was he a Milanese-born expatriate who returned there to conduct private affairs? Sforza claimed that Maraviglia was never presented officially at court as an ambassador, nor was he ever accepted as such by Sforza himself, and was therefore not entitled to diplomatic privileges. Also, having been born in Milan, Maraviglia was Sforza's subject and hence subjected to his justice. Charles V was intransigent, maintaining that had Maraviglia been an ambassador, he would have been granted his due diplomatic immunities, but he had in fact been a private citizen and therefore due and granted no such privileges. The matter became even more salacious once details emerged linking Maraviglia's presence in Milan to the duke himself.[50] Francesco Taverna, Sforza's ambassador to Francis I, had suggested the arrangement and nominated his uncle, Maraviglia, to fulfill the role, and then had devised the secretive terms of the embassy, citing the emperor's assured disapproval of diplomatic ties between France and Milan.[51]

The fact that this matter became an international scandal is significant to understanding the state of diplomacy and international law at the time. Writers, including Montaigne,[52] treated the matter, as did jurists and theoreticians of international law such as Alberico Gentili[53] and Jean Hotman.[54] Gentili, in *Des legationibus*, maintained that Maraviglia should have been considered and respected as an ambassador regardless of the fact that he neither presented himself nor was received officially at court. This ritual, typical of Renaissance diplomacy, would have entailed a presentation of credentials and perhaps letters from his principal, along with a requisite exchange of gifts, followed by a lavish banquet.[55]

Gentili's treatment of the Maraviglia affair[56] analyzed it from a more general legalistic perspective, known today as international law, and upheld the necessity of equality of the law:

> As the sovereign can order him to depart, he ought not put him to death. Nor can anyone say to me that this ruling of the jurists holds for private individuals but not for kings. The principle of international law holds equally for all, and the principle which controls the relation of private

> individual to private individual is unquestionably the same as that which controls the relation of public personage to public personage, and of ambassador to king, *because an ambassador also is the personal representative of the sovereign* (italics added).[57]

For the purposes of this study, the last sentence is most salient. Hampton modifies the translation of the original Latin text—"quia legatus quoque principis personam gerit"[58]—as follows: "For the legate also bears the person of the prince."[59] Hampton's rendering, as opposed to Laing's above, gives proper attention to the verb *gerit* ("wear"; first person: *gerō*, infinitive: *gerere*) and maintains the term "person," rather than diminishing the corporeal connotation. It modernizes the term by effacing the relatively archaic English connotation of "the living body or physical appearance of a human being" with the more impersonal, less physical phrase "personal representative."[60] Given that *gerere* connotes "to bear," but also "to carry, wear, have, hold, sustain," and that the first direct object listed is "vestem," Gentili interprets the relationship between sovereign and ambassador as one of physical, corporeal representation in which the ambassador donned the "person" of the king, therefore necessarily obscuring his own "person."[61] The body of the king, unprotected by *ius gentium*, was safe because it was represented by that of the ambassador, who, by obscuring his own identity and putting his own body in harm's way, bore the body of the king safely via his own. Francis knew this danger quite well, having been held captive by Charles only a few years prior.

The mutilation and display of Maraviglia's body certainly sent a belligerent message to Francis, but it also sent a horrifying one to Maraviglia's fellow ambassadors.[62] Francis discussed the assassination at length in (at least) two letters to Dinteville, his ambassador to Henry VII and, we recall, the subject-patron of Holbein's *The Ambassadors*. In both letters, Francis repeats that "his ambassador" had his head cut off by the Duke of Milan, interpreted as the Duke's declaration of his "mortal hatred" (iceluy Duc [. . .] declaré la *hayne mortelle* qu'il me porte) for the French king.[63] Francis then implores Dinteville's urgent response to the letter and assistance in disseminating the news of the Maraviglia affair to gain Henry's sympathy and reinforce the alliance between the kings. There is a certain irony here. An ambassador was killed because of the sovereign's poor judgment and hubris, and then a fellow ambassador was called on to advocate and seek remedy for the wrong done to the sovereign, and compelled to disregard or repress the more direct threat to his own person.

Francis read the assassination as a sign of "mortal hatred" toward himself, but Maraviglia's headless body must have read like a different text to the ambassador. Despite the talk of customary diplomatic law and theory, the practice of diplomacy left the envoy alone, powerless, and defenseless in a foreign land, a naked, violable body. The cloak is *ius gentium* and the armor of courtly garb, pomp and circumstance, but the line between sacred and inviolable ambassador and decapitated "private citizen"/"criminal" proves to be thin indeed.

This example of diplomacy is opposed to the stated procedure for an official diplomatic mission, but it is perhaps much closer to the realities of early modern diplomacy, and therefore illustrative in its supposed unorthodoxy. Ambassadorial missions are often ceremonial and ritualistic, and the visual and physical acts can mask, or at least distract from, the actual negotiations. The line between diplomacy and espionage has always been and continues to be a fuzzy border. The ambassadorial body is a richly symbolic entity that could be likened to a gift, and is often treated as an object devoid of agency but full of meaning.

In contrast with the Maraviglia affair, let us consider the situation of Francesco Taverna, Sforza's official ambassador to the king of France. As mentioned before, Taverna is widely considered to be the intermediary responsible for facilitating the covert diplomatic arrangement between Milan and France, going so far as nominating and recruiting his uncle, Maraviglia, for the job. Taverna's involvement in the affair did not end with the death of Maraviglia, however. After the execution of Maraviglia sparked Francis's ire, as well as copious correspondence to fellow "princes of Christendom" in the hopes of uniting them against Charles, Sforza was compelled to send Taverna once again to France in the hopes of placating Francis.

Taverna's task proved much more difficult this time around; given the situation, on this occasion his verbal gifts were now a liability. Famed for being a skilled speaker, it is not surprising that Taverna was sent as representative in this most delicate, if not impossible, diplomatic mission, as Montaigne explained in *Des menteurs*: "King Francis I boasted that he had trapped by this means Francesco Taverna, ambassador of Francesco Sforza, duke of Milan, a man very famous for his skill in talking" (Le Roy François premier, se vantoit d'avoir mis au rouet par ce moyen, Francisque Taverna, ambassadeur de François Sforce Duc de Milan, homme tres-fameux en science de parlerie).[64] Francis's knowledge of Taverna's verbal skills, however, prepared him to transform that strength into a weakness.

In pressing Taverna on the issue of the time of the execution, Francis outmaneuvered him, confusing him enough that he confessed to the reason for an apparently stealthy nighttime execution: "to which the poor man, embarrassed, answered, to play the honest man, that out of respect for His Majesty, the duke would have been very reluctant to have such an execution performed by day" (A quoy le pauvre homme embarrassé respondit, pour faire l'honneste, que pour le respect de sa Majesté le Duc eust esté bien marry, que telle execution se fut faicte de jour).[65] Montaigne's characterization here spoke to the theatrical, if not farcical, meeting of the two men. Both men, having previously arranged the entire secretive arrangement, were well aware of the truth. The fault rested not only with Sforza, who was guilty of ordering an opportunistic murder of a man he knew was an official secret agent, but also with Francis for sending Maraviglia into harm's way. Montaigne explains this predicament as follows: [Maraviglia was] dispatched "avecques lettres secrettes de creance, et instructions d'ambassadeur; et avec d'autres lettres de recommendation envers le Duc, en faveur de ses affaires particulieres, pour *le masque et la montre*" (with secret credentials and instructions as ambassador, and with other letters of recommendation to the duke regarding his personal affairs for *mask and show*; italics added).[66] Francis had dispatched an ambassador "masked" as a private citizen, armed only with conflicting papers and the impossible of task of maintaining an untenable duality.

Maraviglia's private persona served as a "mask" for his public identity as ambassador, but this mask stripped him of the protections of his diplomatic inviolability. Maraviglia's "showing" of himself as a private individual deprived him of courtly pomp and costume, the visual semblance of the ambassador, which may have spared him. As Montaigne's visual language—*le masque et la montre*—emphasized, diplomacy was reliant on a visual and theatrical practice. Therefore, without any external, public confirmation of his identity as ambassador, regardless of his engagement in diplomatic activities, Maraviglia was in effect left unarmed and unshielded.

Taverna was characterized by Montaigne as the quintessential liar, the exemplar of one who tells untruths with the explicit knowledge of the falseness of those statements, whose frequent lies strain the memory, rendering it impossible to distinguish between truth and falsehood. Accepting all of Montaigne's premises, this is a defensible conclusion; however, Montaigne does not distinguish between a private lie and one told for political or diplomatic purposes. Most likely, Taverna lied flagrantly to Francis. This is precisely what he was sent to do. Taverna's capacity as ambassador, whose true personal agency was significantly curtailed, should, however, attenuate Montaigne's charges that frame Taverna as the consummate liar. What Montaigne does not address is the role that Taverna's diplomatic status plays in complicating this conclusion. Sforza sent Taverna to Francis as his representative, and therefore Taverna ceased representing himself as a private citizen and became "the person" of Sforza. Yet Montaigne treated and judged him as if he were a private individual, when he acted as a public agent on behalf of his sovereign, Sforza.

This is not to exculpate Taverna, but instead seeks to underscore the distance between his internal convictions and the role, or self-presentation, he was expected and compelled to personify. To better understand Taverna's situation, it is helpful to recall John Jeffries Martin's concept of the Renaissance self as "layered," at times defined by a social or conforming self when circumstances dictated, and alternatively, when imperative, exhibiting a prudential or performative self (cautious and concealing of personal beliefs).[67] Taverna's compromised role as Sforza's official ambassador necessarily undermined his personal agency and the expression of interiority. Sforza was renowned for his brutality toward his envoys.[68] Failing to defend Sforza's position was thus not an option for Taverna, whose insubordination or failure of diplomacy may have resulted in "death, perpetual banishment, [or] confiscation of [his] possessions."[69]

Though perhaps a rare situation, many early modern ambassadors may have fallen into similar binds. An ambassador was never truly a private individual during his embassy, and in many cases not so even after its conclusion: What he wears, says, and does were representations of the principal and/or state he embodied, and therefore cannot be considered entirely of his own accord or indicative of his private persona. He was subject to judgment by others based upon this mask, and at the same time possibly subject to severe punishment by his sovereign for breaching the official "mask." This is not to mention the danger in which he would have found himself for even being suspected of espionage by the sovereign to whom he was sent.[70]

The doubly dangerous situation in which Taverna found himself must be appreciated and used to interpret his less than honest performance at Francis's court. As mentioned, he almost certainly would have been in danger with Sforza had he (purposefully) admitted any guilt on the part of Milan, but he was also in a hostile court and potentially in danger of retaliation from Francis. In a sense, it could almost be considered a virtuous and earnest exercise of duty, which entailed dishonesty and humiliation. In fact, the tense and potentially dangerous atmosphere provoked Sforza's own ambassador, Giovanni Stefano Robio, at the court of Francis I to abandon secretly his post, with neither Sforza's nor Francis's permission ("senza prendere la debita licenza").[71] Fellow Italian ambassadors at the French court, the Venetian ambassador and Papal nunzio, warned Robio, the Milanese diplomat, that his life was in danger, and he should leave at once with his retinue and all his possessions. Robio took the advice seriously, going as far as covering his tracks by sending his servants on a different route from his own, to guarantee as much as possible his own safe departure. This clear violation of diplomatic procedure speaks to the danger the ambassador must have perceived to have undertaken such a risk to his career and personal safety. This scenario can be interpreted as a form of symbolic communication between the two adversarial sovereigns. On the one hand, had Sforza granted permission to his ambassador to vacate his position at Francis's court, it likely would have been interpreted as a public admission of guilt on the part of Sforza, a disclosure that he had wronged Francis and thus understood that his envoy could be held responsible (or hostage) for his actions. On the other hand, Francis's potential and threatened violence toward Sforza's ambassador indicates a punishment by proxy of Sforza, translating the metaphorical relationship between envoy and sovereign into a literal language.

Sforza used his ambassador and his treatment of his person/body as a symbolic language. In requiring his ambassador to stay at court, his presence in France rather than in Milan would have symbolically communicated Sforza's confidence in justification of his actions in the Maraviglia affair. Conversely, the flight of his ambassador without permission symbolically "sustained the French accusations, and damaged the current diplomatic practices."[72] Even with recognition of Sforza's notoriously harsh treatment of his own ambassadors, the irony inherent in this situation is evident.[73] Unto the ambassador fell all the responsibility for communicating Sforza's innocence, yet the "French accusations" were due to Sforza's actions and assassination orders. Additionally, upholding "diplomatic practices" appeared to be the sole duty of the ambassador in danger at a hostile court. His situation, in this case, was precisely due to Sforza's own rejection of "diplomatic practices," ranging from his arrangement of Maraviglia's secret embassy to his assassination orders of Maraviglia ostensibly based on crimes committed, yet truly due to his role as undercover envoy.

Despite his prolific protests, Francis appeared to be no less at fault than Sforza. First, Francis agreed to the arrangement, certainly comprehending the danger into which he was sending Maraviglia. In fact, rulers did not enjoy the inviolability with which envoys were endowed, prompting them to be wary of negotiating in person.[74] It was Francis, after all, who only a short time before had been prisoner of the emperor and thus fully aware of the lethal seriousness with which Charles held to his possession of the Duchy of Milan. Francis's life was spared probably because his regal status authorized him to make vast territorial concessions to Charles. Second, just as Sforza invoked diplomatic propriety at his convenience, Francis too protested the duke's disregard for the *ius gentium* statutes, yet he willingly agreed to this secretive, and thus improper as well as legally unprotected, diplomatic arrangement, which was directly at odds with the practices stipulated in the *ius gentium*.

The *ius gentium* is exposed here as a legal and political philosophy lacking in concrete application or interpretation. It was not employed in all situations necessitating serious, professional diplomacy—such as the situation leading up to the Maraviglia affair. Conversely, it was invoked cynically and often, by all three rulers involved—Francesco Maria Sforza, Francis I, and Charles V—with little to no regard for the ambassador such statutes were meant to protect. It would, of course, be naive to consider the *ius gentium* diplomatic practices as having been developed solely for the safety of the ambassador. Certainly, the motives behind such legal procedures were due to the mutual benefits each participating sovereign derived from the arrangement. It was understood that there was no hope for active diplomacy if ambassadors were not protected in passage and in embassy. However, although the role of the ambassador was fundamental to the functioning and maintenance of the early modern state, the physical body of the diplomat emerged as a fragile entity caught in the machinery of negotiations, subject at times to unlawful punishment, and not truly or consistently protected by international standards of diplomatic transactions, the touted *ius gentium*.

Holbein's "theatrical design"—its costume-like attire and curated assembly of evocative objects, dramatic draperies, exotic carpets, and exquisite mosaic floors—"exposes that world as a fiction."[75] The fiction to which Greenblatt referred is contained within the composition, and I suggest extending that concept to refer to the larger role and position of the ambassador himself. The *ius gentium* itself is exposed in practice as a convenient legal framework that becomes disconcerting if considered from the point of view of the ambassador. Maraviglia, for instance, was killed to spite his sovereign, rather than spared because of him. The capture, condemnation, decapitation, and display of his dismembered body sent a message of disloyalty to his sovereign, Francis, and one of loyalty to his sovereign's archrival, Charles. The treatment of the ambassadorial body is shown as the symbolic language used to communicate between sovereigns, even in this case in which technically there were no true "ambassadors," only Maraviglia the "private citizen." Although diplomatic status should have spared his life, Maraviglia was killed precisely because he was an ambassador, yet ostensibly because he was a private citizen, just as the mask that his French credentials corroborated.

In the guise of a private citizen, an unofficial ambassador allegedly performed the operations of a public functionary, but he did so in inappropriate garb. While not exclusively sartorial in this case, his guise—his performance—was in effect what facilitated his betrayal and eventual murder. By disguising his public role as that of a private citizen, he stripped himself of any diplomatic protection or privilege.[76]

Ottavio Baldi and Henry Wotton: The Fiction of Lying Abroad

The act of disguising one's intentions as a constitutive element of the ambassadorial office is an appropriate transition to our next case study, Sir Henry Wotton (1568–1639), English author, ambassador, and antiquarian. Izaak Walton, a writer contemporary to Wotton, was his first biographer and included Wotton in his seventeenth-century collection of *Lives*, which also featured John Donne, Richard Hooker, and George Herbert.[77] Wotton is widely credited with having wittily defined the early modern diplomat in this fashion: "An ambassador is an honest man, sent to lie abroad for the good of his country,"[78] an assertion that nearly ended his diplomatic career and destabilized his relationship with his principal, James I. What permits Wotton's inclusion in this study of diplomacy in the early modern Italian peninsula are not only his widely known qualities as "Italian cultural connoisseur"[79] but also particularly his establishment of an Italianate ambassadorial alter ego, Ottavio Baldi.

Before contextualizing and analyzing the above quotation, its effects on Wotton's career, and what it uncovers about the necessary duality imposed on ambassadors, let us first look at the beginnings of Wotton's diplomatic service to the English crown. After his coronation, James I summoned Wotton back to London and publicly regarded him as "the most honest, and therefore best dissembler."[80] This honor was bestowed upon him for having possibly saved the life of the king when he was still James IV of Scotland, during the intense controversies and rivalries that were raging regarding the royal succession upon the death of Elizabeth I.[81] In 1601, Wotton was residing in Tuscany after having fled England following the condemnation and assassination for treason of the Earl of Essex, for whom he had served as secretary. Acting in no formal capacity for the British Crown, but as an English exile of outstanding reputation and also favored at the court of Ferdinand I de' Medici, grand duke of Tuscany, he was selected out of the Englishmen at Ferdinand's court and summoned to fulfill an important mission, which presented Wotton with some unsettling news: Letters intercepted by Ferdinand spoke of an assassination plot threatening James IV of Scotland. A biographer contemporary to Wotton, Izaak Walton, notes that those of "the Romish persuasion" contrived "many endeavours, first to excommunicate, and then to shorten the life of King James."[82] Wotton was then dispatched to Scotland as the de facto envoy of Ferdinand, armed with letters and even "such Italian antidotes against poison,"[83] in order to caution the future King James of the plot and potentially save his life. To avoid English suspicion and dangerous travel, he made his way to Scotland, via Scandinavia, under the disguise of an Italian gentleman by the name of "Ottavio Baldi." The ruse of Ottavio Baldi comprised not only the fictitious name and credentials validating the identity furnished by the grand duke; Wotton completed the disguise by dressing as would an Italian and even adopting the language.

Exploiting fully his persona of Ottavio Baldi, envoy of the grand duke of Tuscany, and maintaining the disguise through his first meeting with the future King James I, Wotton was able to successfully gain access to and deliver his crucially important message to James himself. The only element of his alter ego he had to jettison was his "Italian-like" rapier, which he wore, according to Izaak Walton, to appear indisputably Italian. As Baldi/Wotton's audience with the regent was not completely private, Wotton was prudent enough to speak in Italian. Only James, fluent in the language, could understand the gravity of his message and therefore allow for a private meeting in which it would be possible to reveal the danger in its entirety, as well as to secure James's promise to maintain Wotton's disguise for the entirety of his stay in Scotland. In fact, Wotton was able to maintain his Italian identity in public throughout his three-month stay in Scotland, and "he departed as true an Italian as he came thither."[84]

Although Wotton was not acting officially as an ambassador at the time, his successful mission to inform James of the plot on his life greatly impressed the future king of England and Scotland. Upon his coronation after the death of Elizabeth I, James summoned Wotton from Italy to London in order to knight him and then appoint him official English ambassador to the Republic of Venice, where he served intermittently for almost twenty years (1604–1623). The skills that were so remarkable to James and convinced him to deploy Wotton as his own envoy were those practiced in his skillful dissimulation. Thus, Wotton was appointed a diplomat because he so successfully impersonated one. Dissimulation, the concealment of truth, was the skill that James deemed ideal for his envoy. An ideal envoy was one who was willing and capable of subjugating his individual identity to that imposed for the good of the state apparatus.

An interesting detail emerges from Wotton's diplomatic career: He continued to assume the pseudonym of "Ottavio Baldi" in his official correspondence with James. It is certainly curious that Wotton continued to sign his letters from Italy to King James as "Ottavio Baldi" rather than with his given name, but this was for reasons perhaps either distinct from or at least in addition to that which Melanie Ord states: "an attempt to maintain personal closeness with the King capable of compensating for his physical distance from the English court."[85] Perhaps Wotton did attempt to bridge the physical distance between himself and his home country and its sovereign by signing his letters in the name of the persona he had adopted to initially gain access to King James, and thus maintained an intimate relationship with the sovereign for whom he stands in. Evoking an inside, intimate joke that referred to his first official diplomatic success for the English Crown at large, as well as his personal connection to King James, Wotton, under his Ottavio Baldi disguise, attempted both to save King James's life and secure him the crown.

More intriguingly, in my view, is that this marked a distancing from himself and his true identity and a continuation of his disguise, effectively separating his "professional" persona from that of his personal identity; or perhaps, conversely, it marked a convergence of the two, or even an overtaking of his birth identity by that of his adopted identity (ambassador, Italianate Englishman, etc.). After his theatrical performance as Ottavio Baldi, Wotton exhibited an adoption of a literary pseudonym, the chosen identity of the persona and space under which he assumed the voice, identity, and expertise of Ottavio Baldi. This indicates that the position of ambassador required a certain distancing from one's true identity, an adoption of a separate, foreign one (both in terms of nationality and foreignness from oneself) in order to fulfill the requirement of acting in the best interest of the state and sovereign, thereby perhaps disregarding one's own needs, safety, and best interest.

If his flawless dissimulation is what initiated his diplomatic career, honesty is what nearly ended it. While in Augsburg in 1604, Wotton was asked by his friend, Christopher Fleckamore, to sign his *Album amicorum*. Wotton obliged, and his written statement became what can be considered his first published words. In the 1604 inscription, Wotton chose to meditate on the definition of ambassador, a profession still in the formative stages of its modern iteration, famously penning: "Legatus est vir bonus, peregrè missus ad mentiendum Reipublicae causâ."[86] The original phrase was perfectly clear in meaning: An ambassador is a good, honest man who is sent abroad to lie (to be dishonest) for the good of (on behalf of) his country. The good of the country is thus indirectly proportional to the honesty of its ambassador. In this inscription, Wotton traced an irreconcilable schism between the inherently good man (vir bonus) and his diplomatic office (legatus), which, once assumed, forces the "honest man" into an opposite realm of deceit. To further underscore this distance between man and office, Wotton employed geographically oppositional terms—abroad (peregrè missus) and nation (Republicae causa)—to indicate the foreignness of the act of lying to the "good man" selected to be an ambassador. Just as going abroad confronts the traveler with a foreign reality, the act of lying is just as alien to the honest man. Wotton therefore emphasized the act of lying as an imposition upon the honest man asked (or compelled) to act as ambassador, rather than, as Montaigne in "Des menteurs" would have it, a constitutive quality of the man acting as ambassador.

If the title of "best dissembler" was considered by James to be an accolade, the term "lie" carried with it considerable moral condemnation. Dissimulation was the subject of discussion and scrutiny, and came to be understood not only as an acceptable practice but also a necessary one in both life and politics in early modern Europe.[87] Overt dishonesty, or lying,[88] however, brought with it moral implications.[89] This ambience of moral scrutiny, particularly in the context of the Reformation and Counter-Reformation, cannot be overstated.[90] Had Wotton chosen to deceive by using the more palatable term "dissemble," rather than reveal by using the term "lie," it is unlikely that such an act would have nearly ended his career or that he would have been compelled to publicly apologize both to his sovereign and Europe at large. In exchange for his honesty, Wotton was forced to publicly dissemble what he had revealed. In other words, Wotton was obliged to obscure the truth by transforming it into a dissimulation: His "lie" (read: truth) had to become instead a joke, or as Wotton put it, "a merry definition of an Ambassador."[91]

In defense of himself, Wotton criticizes the Catholic polemicists Kaspar Schoppe (Jaspar Sciopppius in Walton's *Lives*) for using his private words years later to wage a public and political attack[92] not only on him but also on his sovereign, King James I, as well as on James's own 1608 text, *Apologia pro iuramento fideltatis* (*Apology for the Oath of Allegiance*, 1608).[93] Wotton did not consider how the words of an ambassador are never truly private or personal, particularly not the written word. In writing in Fleckamore's *album amicorum* a "deceptively intimate" text, Wotton failed to appreciate that by the time of his inscription, not only had the *album* become a political "tool for international networking," but it also aided in making "international friendship explicitly political."[94]

Wotton's declaration that his words were merely inscribed in jest was a clear attempt at salvaging his job and reputation, an act of deceit made from desperation. The honesty in his inscription, paradoxically, obliged him to then commit an act of deceit. This assumption is confirmed by looking to another quotation attributed to him from his post-ambassadorial years. A friend destined to become an ambassador came to Wotton for advice. At this time, after 1624, when Wotton had returned from his third and final diplomatic mission to Venice, he was acting as provost for Eton College, and thus no longer directly part of the Crown's personnel. Unencumbered by his duty to actively and physically represent the king, Wotton advised his friend on the realities of ambassadorship as follows: "*To be in safety himself*, and serviceable to his country, he should always, and upon all occasions, *speak the truth* (it seems a State paradox) for, *you shall never be believed*; and by this means your *truth will secure yourself*, if you shall ever be called to any account; and it will also put your adversaries—who will still hunt counter—to a loss in all their disquisitions and undertakings" (italics added).[95]

As Wotton experienced personally and publicly, uttering the "truth" can endanger the job of an ambassador; yet he seemed convinced, nonetheless, that doing so could ensure safety as well as be lifesaving. In fact, the safety and security of the ambassador himself were Wotton's first concern; being "serviceable to [one's] country" seems, however, to be a perfunctory addition to his statement. Most of the words were spent discussing how the ambassador, through language and truth, can guarantee his own safety. Wotton portrayed the act of diplomacy in ominous terms, characterizing it as a "hunt" and reinforcing the presence of "adversaries." What was of little importance, however, as an ambassador's gift of persuasion; in fact, Wotton asserted that the ambassador "shall never be believed," and instead what an ambassador stated was understood to be its opposite. Wotton candidly advocated against dissimulation here, underscoring that such a practice was expected, and the ambassador could therefore outmaneuver others by giving them what they would neither expect nor ever believe: the truth.

What is intriguing in the perspective Wotton offered is its impracticality; it most likely is advice that was impossible, or unlikely, to be followed. As Wotton himself stated so succinctly, an ambassador was not expected to advocate for himself or for his own safety; instead, as an instrument of the state, he was expected to subordinate his own identity, physical safety, and particularly his own notion of truth. Wotton's "truth" consisted in articulating publicly that the ambassador was expected to lie. This was offensive because it accomplished precisely the opposite of what was expected of an ambassador: that is, to shield his principal with his own dissimulated persona. Wotton, instead, breached decorum by unveiling the assumed veil, and in doing so, revealed that the honesty of his principal, the king, the country incarnate, was a facade as well. In shifting out from beneath "Ottavio Baldi," master dissembler, Wotton revealed that the "vir bonus" was necessarily concealed by the office of ambassador. He was no longer speaking as this acceptable persona—obedient and subordinate state functionary—but instead as himself, and perhaps this was the ultimate state betrayal.

CHAPTER THREE

Tasso's Messengers
Ambassadors and Poets

Though Tasso was never a diplomatic agent, he demonstrated keen interest in diplomacy and even expressed professional ambassadorial aspirations.[1] Tasso's engagement with diplomacy was therefore not superficial. As a court poet whose livelihood depended on patronage and favor, Tasso, like ambassadors, was also a courtier by default. Tasso's patron, Alfonso II d'Este (1533–1597), just as the dukes of Ferrara before him, commissioned art that served a political purpose. Preceded by Matteo Maria Boiardo's *Orlando innamorato* (1482/1483) and then Lodovico Ariosto's *Orlando Furioso* (1516, 1532), Tasso's *Gerusalemme Liberata* (1581) was the third and final of the "Ferrarese crowns" to sing the mythical origins and exploits of the Estense dynasty in their romance epics.

Tasso's interest in diplomacy is thus evident by virtue of his treatise *Il Messaggiero* (a text I discuss in detail later in this chapter), but it is also prominently portrayed in the *Liberata*. This chapter demonstrates how in the *Liberata*, through ambassadorial figures, Tasso interrogated the role of the poet in society and its political significance by equating it with that of the diplomat. Like the ambassador, the poet was both subject to and representative of his lord, yet both figures had to question, confront, and negotiate the meaning of signs as well as truth itself. In the dogmatic political and religious climate in post-Tridentine Europe, such practices carried significant risk, both personal and professional, for the poet as well as the diplomat. In understanding his role as poet as analogous to that of the ambassador, a courtier, whose responsibility

Tasso defined as "unit[ing] souls in friendship" (congiunger gli animi ne l'amicizia) in *Il Messagiero,* Tasso endowed both figures with an essential autonomy and duty to deceive when necessary and for a righteous purpose, as well as to perceive and present truth as multiple and controvertible.[2] From the outset of the *Liberata,* Tasso characterized his poetical task as founded upon persuasion and deception: "'l vero, condito in molli versi,/i più schivi allettando *ha persuaso*"; "succhi amari *ingannato* intanto ei beve,/e da *l'inganno* suo vita riceve" (The truth in fluent verses hidden has by its charm *persuaded* the most froward; he drinks *deceived* the bitter medicine and from his *deception* receives life).[3] Deception, in Tasso's poetics, is not categorically immoral, but is instead, paradoxically, a life-giving vehicle for truth or its perception.[4] Likewise, deception is key also to the practice of diplomacy, the end of which is peace, as Tasso proposed in his diplomatic treatise *Il Messaggiero.*

The autonomy and duty Tasso ascribed to the ambassador, which I discuss in more detail later, contrasts starkly with his overall negative assessment of the role of courtier and the court,[5] the environment in which he considered himself to have been "born and raised" (nato ed allevato).[6] In *Malpiglio overo de la corte,* a philosophical dialogue first published in 1587, Tasso gave voice to his discontent under the guise of il Forestiero Napoletano, who entertains the questions of an aspiring courtier. Tasso offered a pessimistic revision of *Il libro del cortegiano* that did not coincide with Castiglione's aim of "form[ing] the perfect courtier with words" (formare con parole un perfetto cortegiano), depicting instead the courtier as a servile and "morally neutral instrument of power."[7] The role of Tasso's courtier is simply to act as directed, not to think. Far from Castiglione's idealized courtier, who functions as the moral and political advisor to the prince, the courtier described in *Malpiglio* inhabits a very different and degraded world of increasing political absolutism and corruption, in which the courtier is bereft of both dignity and autonomy.

Professional ethics were not considered in detail in *Malpiglio,* as Tasso reserved that discussion for his *Messaggiero,* a dialogue written around the same period, in which he sought not only to delineate the office of the ambassador but also to define his duty and purpose ("l'ufficio e la fine").[8] The ambassador, like the courtier, was an agent "dependent on the prince" (L'ambasciatore ha dipendenza dal prencipe).[9] However, despite this significant curtailing of autonomy, in Tasso's formulation there is some potential for the ambassador to fulfill a political role. This glimmer of optimism can be seen through Tasso's allusion to Castiglione by seeking to "form the image of the perfect ambassador" (formare l'imagine del perfetto ambasciatore), a pronouncement conspicuously absent in his dialogue on the courtier.[10] Unlike Tasso's courtier, whose exercise of prudence is restricted to executing his prince's demands, the ambassador—an extraordinary man specially selected for the office by a rigorous selection process ("diligente investigazione")—is granted the exercise of judgment and rhetorical license reminiscent of the persuasive, and even deceptive, tasks of the poet outlined in the opening octaves of the *Liberata* referenced above.[11] Beyond simply reporting a received message after discerning its essential truth, the ambassador must employ his gifts of prudence and eloquence to soften and sweeten the message ("l destro e cortese modo di negoziare può ammolirla e raddolcirla") and then deliver the message at the opportune time and place, or alternatively, remain silent should he deem that option preferable ("cercando l'opportunità del tacere e del ragionare").[12]

In 1580, while confined in the Ospedale di Sant'Anna, Tasso began to compose *Il Messaggiero*, one of his most well-known dialogues, which centered on the figure of the ambassador. He first published it in 1582 (Venice, Bernardo Giunti), then continued to rework the text until 1587, perhaps because of its curious choice of topic for a court poet who was not directly engaged in political office during his lifetime. His interest in diplomacy is, however, confirmed by the large presence of ambassadors of all varieties in *Gerusalemme Liberata*, his major literary work. Additionally, Tasso's lack of direct involvement in diplomatic activity did not seem to dull the incisiveness of his observations.[13] On the contrary, Tasso's dialogue proved influential. It was included alongside writings on diplomacy by practicing diplomats in the very first bibliographies of writings on the figure of the ambassador and mentioned in Jean Hotman's treatise *De la charge et dignité de l'ambassadeur* (1603), as well as by other important writers on the ambassador, both contemporary and after Tasso.[14]

Il Messaggiero comprises a dialogue between Tasso and a heavenly spirit. The first part, rooted in Neoplatonism, discusses the nature of demons and spiritual beings, culminating in the assertion that angels link the human and the divine and thus are akin to messengers in their mediatory nature. It is this analogy that lends the dialogue its title and pivots the discussion from a cosmological and philosophical perspective to a political and earthly one concerning the "human ambassador" (l'umano ambasciatore). In the dialogue, despite its title, "messenger" (messaggiero) and "orator" (oratore) are terms that Tasso dismisses in favor of "ambassador" (ambasciatore), a term whose frequency by far outnumbers those of the other two, perhaps because "ambassador" does not explicitly signal the limitation of the role of the diplomat as a vessel that relays predetermined communication. Though unconcerned with specifics regarding the day-to-day practical matters in embassy, Tasso's dialogue offers an important and original contribution to the evolving discussion of the general role of the ambassador, the norms governing diplomatic conduct, and the ethical implications inherent in the office. For example, Tasso departed from a definition of the ambassador as "a gentleman who represents the person of one prince to another with the aim of peace and friendship" (l'ambasciatore sia gentiluomo che appresso un prencipe rappresenta la persona d'un altro prencipe a fine di pace e d'amicizia)[15] before moving on to interrogate the complex nature of this apparently superficial role.

The purpose of an ambassador for Tasso, therefore, should always be to unite princes and maintain their friendly relations within the limits and possibilities of an interrogated diplomatic practice.[16] Central to this practice of mediation between princes are good oratorial and persuasive skills as well as the ability to navigate the ethical implications of message bearing, particularly whether and to what extent an ambassador may alter a message, the potential sanction of dissimulation, the concealment of the truth ("tacere il vero"), and whether deceit ("dire il falso") could ever be permissible. This line of inquiry reveals Tasso's bestowal of a certain agency upon the ambassador in terms of the form and content of the message being communicated. As Timothy Hampton explained, in Tasso's mind the ambassador is more than a "reporter" or message bearer, but "is valuable to the community because he has the capacity *not* to report faithfully, the power to change or add to his message."[17]

In addition to the relationship between oratorial skills and ethical issues such as dissimulation, another relevant point of discussion for Tasso was the parameters and limitations of an ambassador's representation of the sovereign. Diplomacy for Tasso, as an embodied practice that is conducted spatially, forces upon the diplomat the separation of personhood because he must simultaneously carry, or perform, two distinct personae ("l'Ambasciatore due persone sostiene"), "one from nature" (l'una che dalla natura) and the "other of the prince imposed upon him" (l'altra che del Prencipe che gli è stata imposta).[18] Furthermore, this separation of personhood was problematized by Tasso when considering the emerging figure of the resident ambassador, which he saw as the ambassador "per eccelenza," as it is unclear whether the ambassador can or should remain equidistant from both princes or instead owes a greater fealty to the prince who sent him or to the one who receives him, given his authority to bear goodwill as well as negotiate on the sovereign's behalf on a variety of matters.

The body of the ambassador is thus a major preoccupation throughout *Il Messaggiero*. However, interestingly, this body is not a unified "corpus," but instead a kind of conglomerate, a recomposition of different "bodies"—comprising both the prince's representation and the ambassador's own "natural" body—in addition to other attributes from various models. Tasso addressed the physical body of the ambassador and the reassembly, or "re-memberment," of the perfect ambassadorial body. I use the term "body" purposefully to emphasize the curious fact that instead of citing authors of treatises on diplomacy and the ambassador, such as Ermolao Barbaro, whom Tasso mentions once in *Il Messaggiero* but with whose treatise he does not engage further, he chooses to liken his task, "fashion(ing) the image of the perfect ambassador" (formar l'imagine del perfetto ambasciatore) to that of the ancient visual artist Zeuxis (fl. fifth century BCE), to whom he refers as "the painter from Crotone" (il pittor di Crotone). The portrayal of Helen, whose beauty was otherworldly, presented a predicament for the painter, who was unable to realize his vision by basing his depiction on any one human model. Instead, to successfully illustrate her "supreme perfection" (sovrana perfezione) it was necessary for Zeuxis to commit a pictorial dismemberment of five models, removing from each her most beautiful feature in order to compose perfection via aggregation and recomposition.[19]

In the employment of this analogy between Zeuxis's depiction of Helen and his own portrait of the perfect ambassador, Tasso implied three essential elements of the diplomatic figure and consequently the practice of diplomacy. First, the "perfect ambassador," just like the depiction of Helen's "supreme beauty," was a work of fiction. Whether there existed a perfect ambassador, a possibility Tasso seemed to reject in his treatise, or whether it was even possible for a perfect ambassador to exist at all, is called explicitly into question: "Le quali condizioni tutte perché forse in alcuno non si ritrovaranno giamai, resta che colui più al perfetto s'avicini il quale d'esse avrà maggior parte" (Since all of the aforementioned conditions will perhaps never be found in one person, it remains that he who most approximates perfection is the one who possesses the majority of them).[20] Thus it remains the job of the artist, not the politician, to formulate (and eventually deconstruct) the composition of this essential, yet flawed and compromised, figure of Renaissance politics.

Second, it is curious that Tasso stressed the visual quality—"the image" (l'imagine)—of his discussion of the ideal ambassador, about which he stated "*formar l'imagine* del perfetto ambasciatore" (*to fashion the image* of the perfect ambassador; italics added).[21] As the inclusion of a visual artist and the precise pictorial depiction of Helen attest, there is a strong visual and corporeal component to the office of the ambassador. Beyond mere decorum, the sartorial and physical languages that make up the appearance of the diplomat are at least as significant as the rhetorical virtuosity and prudent oratorical skills that underscore the undeniable verbal component of the office of the ambassador, as revealed by the early term for the diplomat, "orator" (oratore).

Leaving aside for a moment the emphasis on the visual composition of the perfect ambassador, to which Tasso alluded obliquely through his mention of "the painter from Crotone," the third noteworthy element is the inherent erotic message in employing Helen as his archetypal figure of composition. As Christopher Marlowe famously stated in *Doctor Faustus*, it was her "face that launch'd a thousand ships," which makes explicit that she was a figure whose incitement of erotic desire resulted in her subsequent captivity and infamously started war. Zeuxis's use of living models, maidens of Crotone, from which to create the nude image of Helen as a representation of absolute beauty, was controversial. Zeuxis is also rumored to have charged patrons to view the art, resulting in charges that the work itself was pornographic, and the artist a pimp. In fact, germane to this study, among Zeuxis's contemporaries the painting was dubbed "Helen the Hetaira."[22] Whether or not Tasso was aware of this does not diminish the fact that, by utilizing the figure of Helen, Tasso made the essential link between erotics and politics explicit.[23]

In this chapter, through a close analysis of scenes featuring diplomacy in the *Gerusalemme liberta* in conjunction with a reading of *Il Messaggiero*, I demonstrate that Tasso's thoughts about the practice of Renaissance diplomacy explored in *Il Messaggiero* are present in the *Liberata*, and additionally how reading the two texts in dialogue allows for the emergence of essential questions about the office of the ambassador itself and its relation to poetics. Specifically, through the analogy of the depiction of Helen, I derive three fundamental elements regarding diplomacy and the role of the ambassador that Tasso addressed in both texts. Diplomatic practice is not only a verbal one, but the symbolic language—both visual and corporeal—are just as fundamental in diplomacy as is rhetoric.

Second, in stating explicitly the nonexistence of the perfect ambassador as well as the artistic dismemberment necessary for the fictitious portrayal of the ideal ambassador, Tasso questioned the basis of and the possibility for successful diplomacy. And last, as a practice based on seduction and persuasion, Tasso established the fundamental contamination between erotics and politics inherent in diplomacy, which underscored the schism between body and office, as well as between the personal and the professional. This last element allows us to extend this discussion to the figure of Armida, in chapter 4, by considering her as a diplomatic, or mediatory, figure who is both eroticized and politicized in the *Liberata*; it is precisely this union of body and politics that allows her to move beyond the strictures imposed upon the Renaissance diplomat and become a political actress in her own right.

Archangel Gabriel: Embodiment of Embassy

The poem's first action is a diplomatic one. After God expresses his frustration regarding the protracted crusade, which, entering its sixth year, is no closer to liberating Jerusalem, he surveys the consciences of the crusaders and selects Godfrey to be the crusaders' unifying leader since he "makes no account of any mortal glory, empire, or treasure" (ogni mortale/gloria, imperio, tesor mette in non cale, *GL* 1.7–8), thus embodying the genuine religious zeal necessary to expel the infidels from Jerusalem. To inform Goffredo of both his election and his charge of subordinating his companions into a united front, God summons Archangel Gabriel to act as his "faithful interpreter and messenger of good tidings" (interprete fedel, nunzio giocondo, 1.11). Though Tasso made it clear that Gabriel's embassy was heavenly, it is significant that the poet used a diplomatic event to initiate the poem's action. Centering diplomatic practice and communication indicates both the poet's interest in diplomacy and how instrumental the ambassadorial agent is in realizing the will of the sovereign. Tasso's depiction of Gabriel goes beyond mere plot device (i.e., a theologically appropriate vessel by which God's law is communicated to humans) and serves to highlight the role and agency the poet granted the messenger, foregrounding the more "earthly" diplomatic episodes in the *Liberata* discussed later in this chapter. Through Gabriel's embassy, Tasso dedicated a significant amount of attention to the preparatory phase of diplomacy, commenting saliently on the physical transformation the messenger must undergo, which in turn parallels the rhetorical transformation of the message he bears.

The angelic ambassador, first situated within the heavenly hierarchy—"Gabriel, who was second among the first" (Gabriel, che ne' primi era secondo, *GL* 1.11)—is informed by God of the general content of his message, which

Gabriel is then responsible for modifying in order to "move souls" (muove gli animi), inspire, or even seduce Goffredo, his target, into action, as Tasso defined the goals of diplomacy in *Il messaggiero*. The "art" of the ambassador happens to be surprisingly similar to that of the pimp (ruffiano) in that both professions require that their practitioners be "experts of souls" (conoscitori de gli animi).[24] The ambassador's movement of souls is, however, an embodied practice, as the messenger's physical body is the entity that serves as the human link between the two "souls." In fact, after being summoned by God to embark on his embassy, the first action Gabriel undertakes is a transformation of his ethereal form into one corporeal and human in appearance:

> Gabriel s'accinse
> veloce ad esseguir l'imposte cose:
> la sua forma invisibil d'aria cinse
> ed al senso mortal la sottopose. (1.13)
>
> (Gabriel girded himself quickly to execute the affairs laid upon him. His form invisible he clothed with air and made it subject to mortal sense.)

The "subjection" (sottopose) of Gabriel's angelic form to the human body (senso mortal) offers an important lexical link between this moment in the *Liberata* and *Il Messaggiero*, in which Tasso discussed the ambassador's predicament of having to negotiate between two "persons" or "personae," his "natural" one and the one "superimposed" (sovraposta) on him, or the image, the persona, he must perform as diplomatic agent representing his sovereign:

> Perché la persona e le persone de la natura son tali che non si possono più spogliar per altra persona sovraposta, dee l'ambasciatore in tutte le azioni così private come publiche ricordarsi de la persona naturale e de la sovraposta, ne le private più de la naturale e ne le publiche più de la sovraposta, così in quel ch'appertiene a la bellezza come ne l'ordine e ne l'ornamento atto a l'azione; ne le quali cose principalmente consiste il decoro (italics added).[25]
>
> (Because the person and the natural personae cannot be stripped away [to reveal] another superimposed persona, the ambassador must account for both his natural and superimposed personae in all public and private affairs; in private affairs, he must account more for the natural

[persona], and in public affairs, he must account more for the superimposed [persona], as it pertains to beauty, the order, and the ornament suitable to the given occasion; it is in these things that decorum principally consists).

Like this theoretical description of the ambassador's management of his "personae," Gabriel too must subject his "natural persona," invisible to the human eye, to one discernable to Goffredo. To act as an effective messenger, Gabriel's appearance must conform to Goffredo's expectations of an angel bearing God's message; his identity, and thus his authority, depends on the ability of Goffredo to identify him visually as such. As Walter Stephens indicates, Gabriel "undergo(es) an 'imitation' of the Incarnation by putting on a fictive body visible to humans in order to announce to Goffredo that he will be elected" (*GL* 1.13–17).[26] Additionally, and particularly appropriate to diplomacy, Gabriel's process of embodiment is likened, lexically and metaphorically, to the act of clothing the body, "la sua forma invisibil d'aria cinse" (his form invisible he clothed with air, 1.13). "Cinse," from the verb *cingere* (to gird, to wrap around), from which the term for the accessory *cintura* (belt) derives, is defined as "legare il vestimento nel mezzo della persona"[27] (to fasten a garment at the waist). The reference to clothing is then reprised in describing the angel's earthly descent—"Così *vestito*, indirizzossi a l'ime/parti del mondo il messaggier celeste" (So *clad* the heavenly messenger made his way to the low portion of the universe, 1.14; italics added). Gabriel creates himself visually so that his form coincides with his content, or identity. Gabriel's appearance—youthfulness, fair complexion, blond locks crowned with a golden halo, and wings tipped in gold ("ornò di raggi il biondo crine/Ali bianche vestì, c'han d'or le cime," 1.14)—confer earthly beauty and heavenly majesty while also indicating his mediatory status as celestial messenger. A hybrid of human and angelic features, Gabriel's form represents his status as negotiator between heaven and earth, God and human.

Moreover, in discussing Gabriel's physical transformation from invisible to visible, Tasso adopted language indicative of artistic creation: "Umane membra, aspetto uman *si finse*/ma di celeste maestà il *compose*" (human limbs, a human face he *feigned*/but he *composed* it of heavenly majesty, *GL* 1.13; italics added). *Fingere,* "to feign, or to create using the imagination," is the same term Tasso used in his *Discorsi dell'arte poetica* (1594) to differentiate artistic license, "la licenza di fingere"—something "most necessary to poets" (è necessarissima a i poeti)—from the historian's adherence to "those particulars" (que' particolari) of chronicle.[28] Similar to the poet's strategy of embellishment of the truth in order to persuade even "the most froward" (i più schivi) discussed in the very first octaves of the *Liberata,* Gabriel's self-fashioning has a captivating effect on Goffredo, from his first apparition as even more splendid ("più lucente") than the sun, to the overwhelmingly pleasurable effect evoked in Goffredo upon his departure: "Resta Goffredo a i detti, a lo splendore/d'occhi *abbagliato, attonito* di core" (Godfrey remains—by the words, by the shining splendor/in his eyes *bedazzled, astonished* in his heart, 1.17; italics added).

Tasso included the direct quotation of God's words to Gabriel in addition to Gabriel's subsequent words to Goffredo. This choice on the part of Tasso, an eminently thoughtful and disciplined poet, is significant considering the apparent redundancy of presenting both the full contents of God's charge as well as the messenger Gabriel's version of it.

God's restrained message to Gabriel comprises one octave containing two rhetorical questions—"Perché si cessa?/perché la guerra omai non si rinova/a liberar Gierusalemme oppressa?" (Why is the war given over? Why is it this moment not renewed/to liberate oppressed Jerusalem? [*GL* 1.12])—followed by direct orders for Goffredo to gather the other leaders of the Crusade, to announce himself as God's elected captain, to subordinate his former companions, and then to spur them toward the "lofty enterprise" (alta impresa, 1.12).

However, Gabriel's version of God's message to Goffredo comprises twelve verses, fifty percent more words than God's economical original. Gabriel announces himself, in a phrase whose rhetorical arrangement reflects his intermediary status: "Dio *messaggier mi* manda" (God sends me as *His messenger, GL* 1.17; italics added). He also clarifies that the precise nature of his duty is as the conveyer of God's mind: "Io ti rivelo/la sua mente in suo nome" (In His name I reveal to you His mind, 1.17). This phrase at once confirms his privileged status as God's chosen and trusted messenger, yet also delimits his authority over the content of the message. Gabriel transmits the content of God's "mind," but his words are not a verbatim replication. Instead, as Gabriel reveals God's message through his own body and mind, what he communicates is, in fact, a translation, an interpretation.

Some modifications are inconsequential, such as the swapping of words for their synonyms ("Gierusalemme *oppressa*" becomes "Gierusalem *soggetta,*" for instance), but there are other more significant changes that demonstrate a certain license on Gabriel's part. A different lexical change lends more moral gravity to the message: "Chiami i duci a consiglio, e *i tardi mova*/a l'alta impresa" (Let him call the chiefs to council and *stir up the sluggish* to the lofty enterprise, *GL* 1.12; italics added) becomes, in Gabriel's rendering, "Tu i principi a consiglio omai raguna/tu al fin de l'opra *i neghittosi affretta*" (Assemble the princes at once in council, *hurry the slothful* on to the end of the task, 1.16; italics added). The change from "i tardi" (the sluggish) to "i neghittosi" (the slothful) adds moral condemnation, even the accusation of sinful negligence of the princes' Christian duty. Additionally, Gabriel's message ends with an exhortative statement meant to inspire, persuade, and compel Goffredo to action while also engendering confidence in his newly gained authority and in the mission at large:

> Oh quanta spene
> aver d'alta vittoria, oh quanto zelo
> de l'oste a te commessa or ti conviene! (1.17)
>
> (O how much hope you ought to have now of the noble victory! O how much zeal for the army entrusted to you).

The role of the messenger goes beyond that of a reporter and is tasked with leveraging both visual and rhetorical aesthetics that "bedazzle" and "astonish" the message's receiver into action.

"Così di messaggier fatto è nemico": Impossible Embassies

Let us now look at the two most official ambassadors in the *Liberata*, the "messaggi" of the king of Egypt, Alete and Argante. The fact that they are introduced as "messaggi" (messages) rather than "messaggieri" (messengers) or "ambasciatori" (ambassadors), or even "oratori" (orators), is curious. Perhaps this lexical choice could be justified based on the rhetorical demands of the octave since "messaggi" rhymes with "paggi" in the next verse. I would like to draw attention, however, to the evocative nature of referring to the ambassadors as "messaggi."[29] Such a choice draws attention to the meaning of the term *messaggi* and evokes the notion that message and messenger are not two distinct entities. In other words, the messenger—the one who bears the message—is not fully separable from the message. The message is embodied by the messenger, an objectified entity, meant to be read and interpreted as a highly symbolic figure, a message in itself, not merely its bearer.

This visually symbolic notion is reestablished in the description of the arrival of Alete and Argante at the Christian encampment. The messengers arrive at dusk, and the low position of the sun is established—"Oltra il meriggio il sol già scende" (But because the sun is already declining below the meridian, *GL* 2.56). This is then underscored in the following octave—"Poco era remota / l'alma luce del sol da l'oceano" (The lifegiving light of the sun was but little removed from the ocean, 2.57)—so as to impress upon the reader the light's uncertain quality. The obscured visibility as these two strangers are introduced places the reader in the same state of scrutiny as the Christian crusaders, inviting the reader also to visually interpret the ambassadors as they enter the scene. While the natural timing is inopportune for receiving visitors, it is not the only inscrutable aspect of the scene; the messengers themselves come into view—"venir sono visiti" (are seen approaching, 2.57)—and yet their appearance is still indecipherable, "duo gran baroni in veste ignota" (two great barons in dress unfamiliar), "portamento estraneo" (their manner foreign). The doubly suspicious nature of their exterior—"unfamiliar" (ignota), and "foreign" (estrano)—is then immediately juxtaposed with the disarming description of their manners, "Ogni atto lor pacific dinota / che vengon come amici al capitano" (Their every peaceful gesture / shows that they are coming as friends to the captain, 2.57). The language of courtly encounters, manners, is what allows the visitors to be interpreted as official and friendly envoys who pose no threat to Goffredo, the Christian captain.

In contrast to the excessive entourage, replete with squires and pages, and ostentatious costumes worn by Alete and Argante, the "two great barons" (duo gran baroni), Goffredo is found in his quarters sitting "on a low seat and in plain attire" (in umil seggio e in un vestire schietto, *GL* 2.60) rather than ostentatiously dressed on a throne. Just as his humble physical appearance and austere surroundings denote, Goffredo is a participant in neither the visual diplomatic language of constructed appearances nor the insincere ambassadorial rhetoric that employs, alternately, flattery and threats:

> Chieser questi udienza ed al cospetto
> del famoso Goffredo ammessi entraro,
> *e in umil seggio e in un vestire schietto*

fra' suoi duci sedendo il ritrovaro;
ma verace valor, benché negletto,
è di se stesso a sé fregio assai chiaro.
Piccol segno d'onor gli fece Argante
in guise pur d'uom grande e non curante. (2.60, italics added)

(These men sought audience and being admitted into the presence of the famous Godfrey. They found him seated among his barons, *on a low seat and in plain attire*: But true valor, though neglected, is of itself to itself bright ornament enough. Argantes made him a little sign of courtesy, in the manner of the great man who cares for nobody.)

Goffredo does not reciprocate the courtly rhetoric of Alete. Instead, after allowing Alete to offer flattery and threats, he offers a contrasting tone of discourse. Goffredo's speech, characterized as free of both simulation and dissimulation, sincerely represents the "true valor" (verace valor) to his identity, and in speaking so "simply" (in semplici parole), so he effectively removes himself from the indistinct rhetorical realm of diplomacy: "Risponderò, come da me si suole,/liberi sensi in semplici parole" (I shall answer [as is my custom] with frank sentiments in simple words, *GL* 2.81).

The narrative voice assures the reader that each gesture connotes peace as the ambassadors arrive to the Christian encampment: "Ogni atto lor pacifico dinota/che vengon come amici al capitano" (*GL* 2.57). Yet, in addition to the assurance of peaceful intentions, Tasso also suggested a theatrical insincerity upon closer scrutiny of the messengers' diplomatic performances. Alete embodies *sprezzatura* and represents a parody of Castiglione's perfect courtier, or in the words of Timothy Hampton, "Alete is a parody of the humanist rhetorician."[30] His affected manner demonstrates an insincerity that is acknowledged by Goffredo when, overlooking the superficially flattering nature of Alete's rhetoric, he interprets the duplicitous message as simultaneously "courteous" and "threatening":

Messaggier, dolcemente a noi sponesti
ora cortese, or minaccioso invito.
Se 'l tuo re m'ama e loda i nostri gesti,
è sua mercede, e m'è l'amor gradito.
A quella parte poi dove protesti
la guerra a noi del paganesmo unito,

> risponderò, come da me si suole,
> *liberi sensi in semplici parole.* (2.81, italics added)
>
> (Ambassador, pleasantly have you set forth for us an offer sometimes courteous, sometimes threatening. If your king has love for me and praises my deeds, it is kindness in him, and his love is welcome to me. To that part following, where you propound a war of pagandom united against us, I shall answer [as is my custom] *with frank sentiments in simple words.*)

Piece by piece, member by member, Tasso offers a description of Alete's corporeal language of diplomacy, which speaks to the physical and visual practice of the ambassador, as well as its theatrical basis:

> Ma *la destra* si pose Alete al *seno,*
> e chinò *il capo,* e piegò a terra *i lumi,*
> e l'onorò con ogni modo a pieno
> che di *sua gente portino costume.*
> Cominciò poscia, e di sua *bocca* uscieno
> piú che mel dolci d'eloquenza i fiumi;
> e perché i Franchi han già il sermone appreso
> de la Soria, fu ciò ch'ei disse inteso. (2.61, italics added)
>
> (But Alete placed *his right hand over his heart* and bowed *his head* and fixed *his eyes* on the ground and paid him full honor in *every fashion that the customs of his people might allow.* Then he began, and rivers of eloquence sweeter than honey issued from *his mouth*; and because the Franks have already learned the Syrian language, what he said was understood.)

Here we have a "dismembered" ambassadorial body, in which each separate member acts independently of the (seemingly) integral persona of the ambassador, which is itself, as we have seen, but a composite of two separate personae. Alete's right hand ("la destra") is placed on his breast ("al seno"); his head is bowed ("chinò il capo"); his eyes turned toward the earth ("piegò a terra i lumi"); and finally, from this mouth exit "rivers of eloquence sweeter than honey" (più che mel dolci d'eloquenza i fiumi). Each part of Alete's body must conform to compose the physical image of the "perfect" ambassador. Just as in Tasso's analogy in *Il Messaggiero* of the depiction of Helen by Zeuxis, Tasso's depiction of Alete here is disconcerting in its artifice. Although each element appears perfect in isolation, the entire composition is unsuccessful. Goffredo is ultimately unconvinced, perceiving Alete's performance as an insincere contrivance, rather than revering it for its perfection. This comportment appears however so formulaic, more like a precise performance taken from a conduct manual on how to behave during an embassy. Or, better, what Alete offers here is an obvious performance of the theatricality necessary in the exercise of diplomacy.

While Alete's performance was insincere and unimpressive, perhaps even offensive to Goffredo, it is more complex than that of a stage actor. It is doubtful that Alete himself would have derived any personal benefit, and Alete's performance entails a violent separation between self and portrayal, a body acting independently of his "persona privata," instead acting in accordance with the imposed persona of the prince:

> Il decoro, rispose, si considera ne le due persone de l'ambasciatore, l'una impostagli da la natura, l'altra dal principe e dal suo giudicio medesimo a se stesso accomodata. [. . .] dee ricordarsi de la sua propria e natural condizione e *la convenevolezza de la publica persona in guisa accompagnare con quella de la privata* ch'egli si mostri piacevole con gravità (italics added).
>
> (Decorum, he replied, is understood in the two personae of the ambassador, one imposed upon him by nature, the other by the prince, the latter of which he adapts to himself according to his own judgment [. . .] he must bear in mind his natural and proper condition as well as *the suitability of his public persona, which must be done in such a way that his public persona coincides with his private one* and he appears pleasantly dignified).[31]

Thus, though Alete would not personally benefit from any potential success of his embassy, he acted to the advantage of his sovereign, the king of Egypt, and quite likely to his own disadvantage.

In contrast to Alete, Argante is rendered as fundamentally anti-diplomatic. He refuses to accommodate this fictional persona, which would necessitate the subjection of one's "private persona" to that persona imposed upon the envoy by his sovereign. Whereas Alete's "legge" (law) is that of simulation, Argante's is that of war:

> L'altro è il circasso Argante, uom che straniero
> se'n venne a la regal corte d'Egitto;
> ma de' satrapi fatto è de l'impero,
> e in sommi gradi a la milizia ascritto:
> impaziente, inessorabil, fero
> ne l'arme infaticabile ed invitto,
> d'ogni dio sprezzatore, e che ripone
> *ne la spade sua legge e sua ragione.* (*GL* 2.59, italics added)

> (The other is Circassian Argantes, a man who came a stranger to the royal court of Egypt but was made one of the satraps of the empire and enrolled in the highest levels of the army. Impatient, unrelenting, fierce, in arms unwearying and invincible, a despiser of every God, and one who *bases on the sword his reason and his law.*)

Contrary to Alete's studied demeanor and polished languages, both rhetorical and corporeal, Argante, is *fero* (savage). His nearly bestial, "unwearying" body—"ne l'arme infaticabile"—can be neither trained nor forced to submit to decorous courtly niceties. Even upon meeting Goffredo, Argante's disdain—"impaziente, inessorabil, fero"—becomes readily apparent physically: "Picciol segno d'onor gli fece Argante/in guisa pur d'uom grande e non curante" (Argantes made him a little sign of courtesy, in the manner of the great man who cares for nobody, *GL* 2.60). Argante, rarely verbal, communicates most often physically and thus comprises the metaphorical "body" of the diplomatic pair, the corporeal, savage element of warfare that plays foil to Alete's studied poise and polished intellectual character.

This flawed duo emphasizes the impossibility of an organic perfect ambassador: It is always a fictional composite. Alete and Argante together form an imperfect but not unrealistic envoy. Although each member of the pair is an exception in his own right, together they form a partial ambassador. Alete is a fine rhetorician, and Argante a skilled and courageous warrior, yet together they still amount to less than the sum of their parts. Alete is clearly more successful in the creation and maintenance of his diplomatic persona than is Argante, who refuses the endeavor outright. The duo of Argante-Alete, and their failed embassy, personifies the friction between the two "personae" of the ambassador: Alete's theatrical performance, imposed upon him by the sovereign, on the one hand; and Argante's private, "irascible" expression of the self, on the other.

However, Alete and Argante's embassy is not the only aspect of diplomacy problematized by Tasso in this episode. The diplomatic mission itself is an unrealistic task that fails even within the fictional world of the *Liberata*. As Tasso revealed in both the *Liberata* and *Il Messaggiero*, embassy and diplomatic practice required attempted seduction on the part of the ambassador, which was often met with suspicion on the part of the sovereign.[32] The dichotomy between seduction and suspicion was yet another obstacle for any one ambassador to embody the "perfect ambassador." Just as the function of the poet entails the sweetening of a medicinal message—"Porgiamo aspersi/di soavi licor gli orli del vaso:/succhi amari ingannato intanto ei beve" (So we present to the feverish child the rim of the glass sprinkled over with sweet liquids: he drinks, deceived, the bitter medicine, *GL* 1.3)—the role of the ambassador necessitates seduction via flattery of the sovereign to whom he is sent. It is thus this need for balancing ethical elements, such as dissimulation, with rhetorical elements, such as (apparently) sincere flattery, that made Tasso relate the task of the ambassador to that of the poet.

As in the case of Gabriel discussed above, his wings and human form, for example, were created to satisfy Goffredo's expectation of what God's messenger should look like. Even for an angel, a simple apparition was insufficient; it was necessary to appear as a convincing angel as well. In that sense, Gabriel's creation of his own appearance not only represents artistic license inspired by well-known iconography, but it is also fundamental for the conveyance of God's words, and thus the successful completion of Gabriel's ambassadorial mission. Tasso, in his capacity as poet, is tasked with uniting two disparate forces, the conciliation of seemingly irreconcilable "enemies" of poetic genres—epic and romance—as well as history and fiction; an enterprise that requires the contamination of each part with its opposite: truth with adornment, for example, to which Tasso famously refers as "fregi al vero" (the truth I interweave with embroiderings, *GL* 1.2). The ambassador, similarly, is tasked with an equally difficult, if not impossible, task to fulfill the "perfect" completion of an embassy. This idea of completing his mission "perfectly" is only feasible under almost impossible circumstances, or as Tasso's *Messaggiero* reminds us, by God himself: "[Il messaggiero] non si può qua giù fare alcuna perfetta unione, [. . .] in Dio solo adunque gli animi de' principi possono perfettamente unirsi" ([The messenger] can make no perfect union down here [. . .] it is thus only within God that the souls of princes can perfectly unite).[33]

The two most official ambassadors in the *Liberata*, Alete and Argante, are sent by the king of Egypt to Goffredo and the Crusaders precisely to attempt "to unite" (unire) the souls of the Christian capitan, Goffredo, with that of the king of Egypt. Alete's polyptotonic repetition of the term *amore* is proof that, at the very least, he would like to impress upon Goffredo his desire to unite the Christian and pagan souls.

> (Il mio re) *amando* in te ciò ch'altri invidia e teme:
> *ama* il valore, e volontario elegge
> teco unirsi *d'amor*, se non di legge. (*GL* 2.63, italics added)
>
> ([My king] *loving* in you that which another envies or fears. He *loves* valor and willingly chooses to unite himself with you—*in love*, if not in law.)

Goffredo, as we have seen, shows himself to be thoroughly uncompelled by this "amorous" rhetoric and praise. He feels no obligation to reciprocate this linguistic gesture, choosing instead to minimize it as simply the prerogative of the king of Egypt that demands nothing on the part of the receiver: "Se 'l tuo re m'ama e loda i nostri gesti,/è sua mercede, e m'è l'amor gradito" (If your king has love for me, and praises my deeds, it is kindness in him and his love is welcome to me, 2.81).

Goffredo professes appreciation but remains unpersuaded to reciprocate, and his response amounts to a near refusal of Alete's "gift" of flattery. Alete's antiphrastic name, which means "without simulation" in Greek, is employed ironically, contradicting his honest namesake and alluding instead to vulgar dissimulation in the form of excessive and insincere adulation. In introducing him, the narrator spends an entire octave in order to discredit him:

> Alete è l'un, che da principio indegno
> tra le brutture de la plebe è sorto;
> ma l'inalzaro a i primi onor del regno
> parlar fecondo e lusinghiero e scòrto,
> pieghevoli costumi e vario ingegno
> al finger pronto, a l'ingannare accorto:

gran fabro di calunnie, adorne in modi
novi, che sono accuse, e paion lodi. (*GL* 2.58)

(The one is Alete, who because of his low birth was raised amid the meanness of the common people; but he was exalted to the chief honors of the kingdom by a flowing and feigning and prudent speech, by compliant manners and a shifty nature, ready at pretense, experienced at deception. A great fabricator of slanders, he decks out in novel terms what appear to be praises and are accusations.)

In the case of Alete, Tasso interjects in the guise of the omniscient narrator briefly to tell the story of Alete's low birth and how he came to be appointed the official messenger of the king of Egypt. Chances of a triumphal story of a self-made courtier quickly dissipate upon our learning that Alete overcame his humble origins not via merit, but instead because of his talents for "pretense" (finger) "deception" (ingannare) "slander" (calunie) and making "what appear to be praises and are accusations." The voice of the narrator intervenes to guide the reader toward a negative assessment of Alete's talents, employing morally questionable terms to catalog Alete's activities and skills. Yet close attention to the octave reveals that the terms that modify the abovementioned criticisms also speak to his astuteness, prowess, and inventiveness: "accorto" (ready), "gran fabro" (great fabricator), and his "modi novi" (novel terms) are complimentary terms that destabilize the accusations of deceit and defamation.[34]

The censure becomes even more complex upon noticing that the poet himself engages in precisely the same "deceitful" rhetoric of which Alete is accused. Tasso's accusations of Alete also "appear to be praises" (paion lodi) or perhaps even more interestingly, Tasso does precisely the opposite, his admiration (lodi) are disguised as accusations (accuse). Alete is thus invested with a rhetorical license, "finger pronto" or a certain "licenza del fingere," similar to that which Tasso grants himself in the poem's opening octaves:[35]

tu rischiara il mio canto, e tu perdona
s'intesso fregi al ver, s'adorno in parte
d'altri dialetti, che de' tuoi, le carte. (*GL* 1.2, italics added)

(illuminate my song, and grant me pardon if *with the truth I interweave embroiderings, if partly* with pleasures other than yours I ornament my pages.)

The textile metaphor used often in the *Liberata* here establishes a thread between the poet himself and a character toward whom, via the narrative voice, he demonstrates scorn. The verbs *intesso* (from *intessere*, "to weave"), and *adorno* (from *adornare*, "to embellish"), respectively, refer to the words of the poet that ornament both truth (ver) and history (le carte) and thus deceive the reader into ingesting truth ("il vero [. . .] ingannato ei beve") and receiving life ("vita riceve," 1.3).

Particularly in his *Discorsi dell'arte poetica*, Tasso maintained that certain rhetorical liberties—particularly the "licenza del fingere"—must be reserved for literary creation. This matter is, however, complicated by Tasso's characterization of the deceit of several characters, most importantly Alete, in rhetorical figures (metaphor) within a work of fiction (the *Liberata*). Even though endowed with rhetorical skill akin to that of the poet himself, in addition to a certain degree of metaliterary authority, the figures are not poets, but most often political actors (e.g., Alete is a messenger; Vafrino, a spy; Armida, a politically active and savvy seductress; Sofronia, the willing martyr to save the Christian community) whose deceit thus should require the discussion of ethics, not poetics. The narrator often intervenes to guide the moral and ethical assessment of the character in question, yet these interventions are almost always undermined, often quite subtly, by contingencies or situations in which the character finds him or herself; these provoke, if not pathos, at least comprehension on the part of the reader, leading to a reconsideration of the so-called act of deceit.

Just as the narrator intervened to guide the reader toward a disapproval of Alete's "gift" of flattery to Goffredo, the reader is similarly guided, although more discreetly, to question the gifts for the ambassadors. It is worth citing the complete passage:

> Soggiunse allor Goffredo: —Or riportate
> al vostro re che venga, e che s'affretti,
> che la guerra accettiam che minacciate;
> e s'ei non vien, fra 'l Nilo suo n'aspetti.—
> Accommiatò lor poscia in dolci e grate
> maniere, e gli onorò di *doni eletti*.
> *Ricchissimo ad Alete un elemo diede*
> *ch'a Nicea conquistò fra l'altre prede.*
> *Ebbe Argante una spada*; e 'l fabro egregio
> l'else e 'l pomo le fe' gemmato e d'oro,
> con magistero tal che perde il pregio
> de la ricca materia appo il lavoro.

> Poi che la tempra e la ricchezza e 'l fregio
> sottilmente da lui mirati foro,
> *disse Argante al Buglion:—Vedrai ben tosto*
> *come da me il tuo dono in uso è posto.* (*GL* 2.92–93, italics added)
>
> (Then Godfrey added: "Now report to your king that he may come, and that he should make haste, for we accept the war that you are threatening; and if he does not come, let him expect us there amid his Nile." Then he bade them farewell in sweet and pleasant fashion, and *honored them with choice gifts. To Alete he gave a most magnificent helmet that at Nicaea he had made his own among other booties.*
>
> Argantes had a sword, and the clever swordsmith had made the hilt and the pommel gilded and bejeweled with such mastery that the worth of the rich material was sunk in the workmanship. When he had admired in detail its temper and richness and ornament, *Argantes said to Bouillon, "You will soon enough see how your gift is put to use by me."*)

The "dolci e grate/maniere" (sweet and pleasant fashion) contrast violently with the unambiguously bellicose message uttered by Goffredo and the luxurious materials and impeccable quality of the gifts that he presents to the ambassadors. The distinction of head and body (discussed in the previous section) between the two ambassadors is further emphasized by the choice of gift presented to each messenger by Goffredo. To Argante, Goffredo presents a sword to be held by the hand and wielded by the power of his dominant arm; Alete is gifted a helmet to underscore his intellectual talents, willingness and ability to subjugate his own physicality to the desires and reasonings of his mind.

The highly embellished sword Goffredo gifts to Argante, as with the Nicaean origins of the helmet he just previously gifted to Alete, was seized by Goffredo along with "altre prede" (other booties) in a prior crusader military campaign in the East. It is easy to judge Argante as "haughty"[36] and his response as ostensibly ungrateful with regard to Goffredo's generous and "prized" (eletto) present, but the inherent symbolism in Goffredo's gift highlights the imperialism of the act. As a weapon seized from a pagan warrior during a previous battle against different Eastern others, it was claimed as a precious spoil by Goffredo and his crusaders. The choice to regift such a fraught object to another pagan ambassador in the guise of a "gift" after having refused that same ambassador's efforts at negotiation, uncovers a Christian imperial attitude in its treatment of the Eastern "others."[37] Argante thus interprets perfectly the subtext of Goffredo's gift: It is not an omen of peace, nor a merely decorous ambassadorial gift, but a sign of enmity and war. And in verbalizing this symbolic language, Argante intends on, and succeeds in, removing the sword from its symbolic and aesthetic realm and returning it to its original purpose, an instrument of war: "Vedrai ben tosto/come da me il tuo dono in uso è posto" (You will soon enough see how your gift is put to use by me). In *Il Messaggiero*, through the *character* of "lo spirito," Tasso asserted that an ambassador who takes up arms commits "a very grave and most detrimental error, and (offers) a terrible example" (errore gravissimo e dannossissimo e di pessimo essempio), which also violates the *ius gentium* (called "la ragione de le genti" in the *Liberata*).[38] Therefore, this gift from sovereign to ambassador, a decorous and obligatory step in the diplomatic process, is effectively revealed as the termination of the embassy and an end of negotiation, rather than an hospitable and civil parting gift. Argante removes himself from diplomatic discourse, which requires the suppression of his true identity and sincere thoughts and emphasizes both his individuality as well as ownership over his own beliefs all the while, and most importantly, he succeeds in exposing the decorum of diplomacy as a farce.

This abrupt end to the most official diplomatic episode in the *Liberata* is emphasized by Tasso immediately following the episode of the gifts:

> *Così di messaggier fatto è nemico,*
> sia fretta intempestiva o sia matura:
> la ragion de le genti e l'uso antico
> s'offenda o no, né 'l pensa egli, né 'l cura. (*GL* 2.95, italics added)
>
> (*So from an ambassador he is made an enemy,* whether it be untimely haste or mature: whether or not he offends the law of nations and ancient custom, he gives it neither a thought nor a care.)

"Così di messaggier fatto è nemico" is a rich but ambiguous verse.[39] There is no expressed subject, and thus the reader is left without a clear indication of whom to assign blame for the failure of the diplomatic mission, or who is responsible for the creation of a new enemy in Argante, who goes on to kill the first Christian in the text, Dudone (3.44), thus making good on his promise of restoring the bellicose function to Goffredo's prized ("eletto") diplomatic gift. There is also the implication that it was Goffredo's gift itself that finally provoked the transformation of Argante from an irascible and impenitent messenger who merely flouts ancient and established diplomatic protocol ("la ragion de le genti e l'uso antico") into a deadly "enemy." Goffredo's epic destiny, God's mandate of the reconquest of Jerusalem, becomes nonnegotiable. Argante's exposure of farcical decorum and Alete's insincere performance expose that their embassy, irrespective of the skill of the ambassadors, would not have achieved a successful diplomatic conclusion, for any victory short of the conquest of the walls of Jerusalem would have contradicted God's direct command and been impossible by the laws of epic.[40] Alete and Argante's mission in the poem thus also exposes the intransigence during the Counter-Reformation, which attempts to disallow the inherent uncertainty in both the artist's and the ambassador's performance.

The Poetics of Persuasion

In addition to Alete and Argante, the *Liberata* also represents the mission of Carlo and Ubaldo, two Christian messengers sent to retrieve Rinaldo from Armida's "dolce albergo" (sweet abode, 16.35) on her Fortunate Islands (Isole Fortunate). The messengers are prepared and then dispatched by the Magus of Ascalon, a converted pagan practitioner of white magic, whose unique background qualifies him to educate Carlo and Ubaldo regarding the dangers awaiting on Armida's island: monstrous beasts such as pythons, wild boars, lions, and tigers, in addition to sensual temptations, as well as equip them with tools to protect them (a magic wand to scare away the beasts, 14.73) and a diamond mirrored shield (to rouse Rinaldo by reflecting back to him his effeminate state, 14.77). Although their mission contains significant differences from that of Alete and Argante, a comparison between these two sets of messengers allows me to highlight further the fundamental similarity of the poet and the ambassador suggested by Tasso.

A first important difference is that with Carlo and Ubaldo's mission, the reader assumes their point of view as they travel to and, importantly, once they arrive at Armida's island. These two characters are thus a bridge between geographical and generic spaces within the text, linking the epic narrative of war with that of the romance between Rinaldo and Armida. Unlike Armida and Rinaldo, or Tancredi and Clorinda, for that matter, the "nobil coppia" (noble couple) of Carlo and Ubaldo are messengers, and therefore by definition they are visitors, observers, transitory figures meant to carry out a mission and then return to where they belong; yet here, significantly, they carry the reader with them. Though seemingly peripheral characters in the *Liberata* at large, at the plot level their mission is essential for a Christian victory because the crusaders cannot win without Rinaldo's return to the battlefield. Tasso, accordingly, dedicated significant space in the text to the messengers: Their selection and information gathering begins in canto 14; canto 15 is entirely dedicated to their voyage; and additionally, they have a significant presence in canto 16, all of which demonstrates Tasso's interest in their diplomatic role and the perspective it adds to the romance epic. Like the sovereign who entrusts his messengers to bear faithfully his own words, to fulfill the mission's mandates, and so on, Tasso the poet entrusted the perspective of these cantos to the messengers. What is interesting, and novel, is that the messengers are not simply dispatched bearing a message, but instead the entire process—from departure to voyage, to arrival, to mission fulfillment—is given ample space within the text.

Their mission opens an interstitial space and perspective through which Tasso expressed both the privileged point of view of the messenger and the knowledge that accompanies it. It is, after all, the messenger, not the sovereign, who undertakes a long, arduous journey through which he amasses firsthand information. He is then burdened with the duty of recounting what he sees, hears, and accomplishes; or, alternatively, fails to accomplish. It is here, in the narration, where the adjacency between the messenger and the poet can be clearly appreciated. As Carlo and Ubaldo ride on the boat helmed and navigated by Fortuna through space, from the Mediterranean Sea to beyond the pillars of Hercules, over the ocean still unknown (in the fiction of the text), the voice of the poet transverses time and assumes a tone at once bitter and triumphant when addressing the past and present of the lands through which the messengers travel.

When they eventually come upon the "rich and honored seat" (ricca ed onorata sede, *GL* 15.19) of Tunis, Fortuna points out to the messengers "the place where Carthage had been" (il loco ove Caragin fue, 15.19), the great lofty seat of a bygone empire that is now hardly visible—"scarcely does the shore preserve the signs of her noble ruins" (a pena i segni/de l'alte sue ruine il lido serba, 15.29). Space, time, and literature converge here, and the poet intervenes to comment on the bitter ravages of time and the fickleness of fortune: "Cities perish, kingdoms perish" (muoiono le città, muoiono i regni, 15.20). The architectural "signs" (segni), have been reclaimed by nature, scarred over with sand and weeds ("copre i fasti e le pompe arena ed erba," 15.20), and the vision of the poet is responsible for making the invisible once again visible, or at least recognizable enough to remain in the collective imaginary.

Through the voyage of the ambassadors, Carlo and Ubaldo, the poet showed the process by which historical fact transforms into more profound truths regarding empire and war, the subjects of epic poetry. The journey of the messengers is brought to life, depicted by Tasso the poet, as profound knowledge that traverses the contingencies of time and the particularities of geographical space. Tasso emphasized, as discussed in previous chapters, that simultaneous to the knowledge or experiences acquired during the journey, the ambassador must also embody and exploit those experiences during the diplomatic mission. As with Alete and Argante, it is not sufficient to just "show" humble servitude, irascible threats, or caring love; these sentiments transmitted through gesture or demeanor must also be supported by words that confirm their sincerity. Once the messengers arrive on Armida's island and after spying on Rinaldo and Armida—once Rinaldo is alone, Carlo and Ubaldo reveal themselves to him "proudly" and conspicuously suited in full armor, "scoprìrsi a lui pomposamente armati" ([the two] disclosed themselves to him, all proudly panoplied, *GL* 16.27). The messengers' warlike appearance, which contrasts starkly with the image of the magical diamond shield they bear, eventually reveals Rinaldo to himself. In fact, the messengers' ceremonial and almost theatrical military attire serves as an example and reminder of how Rinaldo should appear.

The shield, according to the Magus of Ascalon, is supposedly capable of awakening Rinaldo from his stupor and bringing him back to the battlefield by revealing to him his emasculated state. Yet, although the mirrored shield is instrumental for Rinaldo to fully picture his reduced state, despite the Magus's promise it is not sufficient to fully convert Rinaldo back into a virtuous, vigorous warrior and coax him back to the battlefield. The Magus predicted (in *GL* 14.77) that once Rinaldo's gaze met the image of his own face in the shield, reflected back toward him, the sight ("ch'a tal vista") of his countenance and "soft raiment in which he is enswathed" (l'abito molle onde fu involto) would be sufficient to incite both shame and disdain (vergogna e sdegno), in turn expelling the "unworthy love" (l'amor indegno) for Armida from his breast.[41] In practice, Rinaldo's vision of his image in the shield was effective in rousing his senses from a slumber and allowing him to perceive himself as effeminate, but this image resulted only in a crippling shame:

> ma se stesso mirar già non sostiene;
> giù cade il guardo, e timido e dimesso,
> guardando a terra, la vergogna il tiene. (16.31)

> (but truly he cannot bear to look at himself; his gaze sinks low; and dejected and abashed, staring at the ground, he is possessed by shame.)

The power of the mirror lends him a visual sense of his state—adorned and bearing a decorative sword that serves as nothing more than an accessory—a realization that provokes a profound, binding, but ultimately inert shame—"la vergogna il tiene." Gazing upon his own image was so painful to Rinaldo that he could not bear his own countenance, and the thought of showing himself to the world made him wish instead to retreat even farther from the battlefield and hide himself under the sea or burrow himself within the earth: "Si chiuderebbe e sotto il mare e dentro/il foco per celarsi, e giù nel centro" (He would have shut himself under the sea and with the flame/to be concealed, and deep within earth's core, *GL* 16.31). Importantly, the mirror image alone did not elicit the "sdegno" (disdain, indignation) the Magus of Ascalon predicted: "so that at such a sight Shame and Disdain will be able to drive the unworthy love from his breast" (ch'a tal vista potrà vergogna e sdegno/scacciar dal petto suo l'amor indegno, 14.77). Once the magnitude of Rinaldo's shame became apparent, one of the messengers, Ubaldo, began a rousing inspirational speech:

> Va l'Asia tutta e va l'Europa in guerra:
> chiunque e pregio brama e Cristo adora
> travaglia in arme or ne la siria terra.
> Te solo, o figlio di Bertoldo, fuora
> del mondo, in ozio, un breve angolo serra;
> te sol de l'universo il moto nulla
> move, egregio campion d'una fanciulla.
> Qual sonno o qual letargo ha sì sopita
> la tua virtute? o qual viltà l'alletta?
> Su su; te il campo e te Goffredo invita,
> te la fortuna e la vittoria aspetta.
> Vieni, o fatal guerriero, e sia fornita
> la ben comincia impresa; e l'empia setta,
> che già crollasti, a terra estinta cada
> sotto l'inevitabile tua spada. (16.32–33)

(All Asia and all Europe are going to war; whoever hungers for reputation and worships Christ is toiling now in arms in the Syrian lands: You alone, O son of Bertoldo, away from the world, in idleness, a little corner of the earth shuts in; you alone are nothing moved by the universal movement, the gallant champion of a girl.//What slumber or lethargy has so lulled your manhood? Or what commonness allures it? Up, up!

The army is calling for you, and Godfrey calls; fortune and victory are awaiting you. Come, soldier of destiny, and let the enterprise so well begun be brought to completion; and the wicked sect that you have already shaken fall to the earth, perished beneath your inevitable sword.)

Ubaldo's speech is rhetorically effective, peppered with anafora, anastrophe, erotema, and polyptoton, and composed predominantly in the imperative mood. The messenger's carefully crafted words speak to Rinaldo's identity—son of Bertoldo, a "soldier of destiny," loyal to Christ and hungry for reputation ("pregio")—and remind him that his glorious fate as a "soldier of destiny" wielding an "inevitable sword" is still within his grasp. Additionally, Ubaldo adheres to the rhetorical principles of persuasion—ethos, logos, and here particularly pathos—to appeal to Rinaldo's chivalric duty to aid his fellow Crusaders in this most righteous cause. The shame the mirror evokes was not only insufficient to bring Rinaldo back to battle but also demonstrably counterproductive by having nearly caused his definitive retreat "deep within earth's core" (*GL* 16.31).

It was instead Ubaldo's speech that succeeded in inciting "sdegno," "disdain" as translated, or "indignation," an emotion crucial to spurring action. In the "Allegoria del poema," Tasso refers to the "irascible faculty of the soul" as "sdegno," and identifies it as both flaw in Rinaldo's character, the "intrinsic obstacle" (intrinsec[o] impediment[o]) that led Rinaldo to stray from the collective mission ("lo sdegno che desvia Rinaldo dall'impresa"), as well as the "faculty of the soul that holds the second rank of dignity" (potenza dell'animo che tiene il secondo grado di dignità).[42] Tasso employed "sdegno" judiciously and purposefully, adhering to the significance he assigned to the term in his "Allegoria":

Tacque, e 'l nobil garzon restò per poco
spazio confuso e senza moto e voce.
Ma poi che diè vergogna a sdegno loco,
sdegno guerrier de la ragion feroce,
e ch'al rossor del volto un novo foco
successe, che più avampa e che più coce,
squarciossi i vani fregi e quelle indegne
pompe, di servitù misera insegne; (*GL* 16.34)

(He ceased; and the noble youth remained a little while confused, and without speech or motion. But after shame gave place to anger—anger,

> fierce warrior of reason—and to the blushing of his face succeeded a new flame that blazes stronger and boils more, he ripped off his idle trims, and those unworthy gauds, the wretched insignia of slavery.)

Ubaldo's speech accomplished an essential task in offering a truer mirror of Rinaldo's essence. Ubaldo's words sketched for Rinaldo an aspirational portrait of a better self; the actual mirrored shield, despite its magical provenance, was limited in to reflecting only Rinaldo's shame-inducing superficial state. Ubaldo's speech sarcastically minimized Rinaldo's status as "the gallant champion of a girl" (egregio campion d'una fanciulla), inciting his "sdegno," while offering an alternative portrait of the champion for whom "fortune and victory" await.[43] The messenger's words are what empower Rinaldo to relinquish his present shame, to cede its space to anger and "disdain" ("diè vergogna a sdegno loco," 16.34), and such a transformation in turn enables Rinaldo to regain his masculine, warrior identity and reassume his place as subordinate to Goffredo within the body politic.

This categorization of Rinaldo seems at first antithetical since ferocity, a nearly animalistic rage, is opposed to the intellectual quality of reason. Ferocity, part of the irascible or sensitive part of the soul, is stirred by sensation and in turn stirs movement; reason is part of the superior, intellective part of the soul and is responsible for the cognitive processes of thought and volition. In his "Allegoria," Tasso, following Plato, characterized anger as such: "Among all the other faculties of the soul, the irascible is that which is least distanced from the nobility of the mind" (E quella la quale fra tutte l'altre potenze dell'anima men s'allontana dalla nobiltà della mente),[44] which is echoed in the *Liberata* in reference to Rinaldo, whose anger is described as the "fierce warrior of the reason" (sdegno guerrier de la ragion feroce, *GL* 16.34), the defensive force that assists reason in guarding against harmful and distracting desires.

The messenger's function is hardly peripheral. In this case it is essential for Christian victory, but as Tasso further suggested, it is also necessary for the proper functioning of society, as symbolized by Rinaldo's readmittance into the body politic. In appealing to logic, ethos, and pathos, Ubaldo's discourse succeeds in rekindling Rinaldo's reason and, by inciting *sdegno*, redirecting his rage toward a productive end. Thus *sdegno*, rather than being a fatal flaw or simply an "impediment," is a powerful emotion that must be reawakened for Rinaldo to tame and then redirect it toward collective harmony. The mirror image, accessed by the visual sense, brought about shame but was not able to appeal to Rinaldo's intellect. It was instead Ubaldo's persuasive words that led to an intellectual awakening of Rinaldo's executive faculty of reason, which was essential to bridle his indignation.

Diplomacy and poetry, for Tasso, shared a goal of negotiation of meaning, and thus truth. The ambassador—his body and his voice—is the material embodiment of this negotiation. Through this intermediary figure of the ambassador, Tasso's *Liberata* succeeds in offering a more complex representation of truth. The reflection in Rinaldo's shield represents objective, unvarnished, and ultimately unacceptable truth. This example of a single, unnegotiable version of truth is then supplemented, contextualized, and perhaps even exaggerated and distorted by Ubaldo's speech, reminiscent of how Tasso tasked the poet with softening the truth with "fluent verses" ('l vero, condito in molli versi, *GL* 1.3). The bitter truth ("succhi amari") is sweetened by poetry's deceptions, which, through a Lucretian simile, Tasso likened to a life-giving remedy ("da l'inganno suo vita riceve," 1.3). Ubaldo's rendering succeeds in altering Rinaldo's own visual perception of the image in the shield, which initially he believed to be an indisputable "truth." It was Ubaldo's words that reshaped Rinaldo's perception of himself as irredeemably shameful and had the effect of bringing Rinaldo "back to life" and then reincorporating him into the Christian collective; no longer (only) a champion of a girl (romance; individual), but a champion of the crusaders (epic; collective).

Through the several scenes in which diplomacy is represented, enacted, and referenced in the *Liberata*, Tasso expressed diplomacy's value as a practice as well as an ethos, while also demonstrating its potential failure. The failure of diplomacy, however, is not due to its inherent flaws; instead, Tasso suggested that diplomacy is unsuccessful because of the intransigence and "militan[cy]" promoted by the Counter-Reformation Church.[45] Perhaps this is best represented by the character of Goffredo, whose personal dogmatism, mixed with his divinely derived political power, precludes him from neither entertaining any doubt nor allowing any compromise or negotiation.[46] The emerging prevalence of a moral framework was described by Francesco Erspamer as a form of "pensiero forte," "an ethics assured of its own validity and legitimacy" (un'etica sicura della propria validità e legittimità), which inevitably imposes strain on both the office of the ambassador and the process of negotiation, of which doubt and deception figure prominently in diplomatic practice.[47] Diplomacy and poetry, two practices Tasso equated, inspire doubt, invite an adjustment of perspective, and promote dialogue and negotiation, all of which, ideally, could "move souls" (muove gli animi) and engender peace and friendship (a fine di pace e d'amicizia), goals he espouses theoretically in *Il Messaggiero* and poetically in the *Liberata*.

CHAPTER FOUR

Armida's Mission

Reconciling Body and Language

In *Stately Bodies* (*Corpo in figure*), Adriana Cavarero examined how the body natural, opposed and inferior to *logos*, has been excluded from the political sphere since the beginning of Western civilization because of its inextricable link to the "unyielding alterity" of the female sexed body.[1] Paradoxically, however, it is the body that is entrusted to represent figuratively the same incorporeal institutions (law, politics, the state) that repress it. The bodily metaphor (male, sterile) that represents the *polis*'s primacy of reason and order excludes the generative female body because of its disorderly "murky carnal recesses of female power," which, in their engendering of love through the familial bonds of the domestic sphere, threaten the logic of the political order.[2] Departing from Cavarero's insight, in this chapter I argue that in the *Gerusalemme Liberata*, Tasso attempted to dismantle the opposition between the corporeal and the political through the legitimization of the female body. Traditionally considered "naturally illogical and therefore unpolitical," in the *Liberata* the female body acquires political significance through the eroticization and rhetorical skill of Armida.[3] Tasso reconciled the body natural within the body politic through Armida, and thereby reasserted the link between language and the body.[4]

Tasso sketched out the analogy of the body politic at the poem's outset, which was inspired by Platonic philosophy yet corresponds to prevailing political and social values of the "new Catholic militancy of the day, calling for a new crusade, preaching the subordination of individuals to the totality and to the divinely appointed civil and religious authorities":[5]

> Deh! fate un corpo sol de' membri amici,
> fate un capo che gli altri indirizzi e frene,
> date ad un sol lo scettro e la possanza,
> e sostenga di re vece e sembianza. (*GL* 1.31)[6]
>
> (Oh! make but one body of your cooperating limbs; make but one head that may direct and restrain the others. Give to one man alone the scepter and the power, and let him hold the place and the semblance of a king.)

Additionally, Thomistic doctrine imbues Tasso's corporate metaphor, with the upper limbs allocated to individuals whose sensitive appetites correspond to the concupiscible and the irascible, while the "pious," though essentially bloodless, and sterile, Goffredo, occupies the "head," the pure intellect unaffected by sensorial distraction. The other chief crusader heroes are Rinaldo, the mythical progenitor of the Estense dynasty of Ferrara, Tasso's patrons; and Tancredi, the Christian paladin. Both must overcome serious personal obstacles due to their immoderate sense appetites before their reconciliation within the Christian unity, a prerequisite for the retaking of Jerusalem, which in Tasso's overt allegory represents the difficult achievement of "political peace" (felicità politica).[7] Unsurprisingly, but worth underscoring, the bodily metaphor excludes (or represses) the female body, which instead is evoked only as an obstacle to military and political victory.

Although recent criticism has emphasized Tasso's more general project of reconciliation, I would like to stress the role of the female material body in the development of the body politic through the character of Armida. Timothy Hampton notes, for example, in *Fictions of Embassy*, "It [*Gerusalemme Liberata*] is a diplomatic message of reconciliation in the form of an epic [. . .] Tasso's poem is about the reintegration of Europe."[8] Similarly, Douglas Biow stresses how "Tasso's lifelong project was to bring together disparate elements, whether it be romance and epic, chivalric behavior and Christian piety, or early humanist praise for multiplicity and individualism and the late sixteenth-century emphasis on unity and centralized authority."[9] For Hampton and Biow, Tasso's relevant attempt at reconciliation is framed within the abstract construct of European states or within literary genres and rhetorical traditions. Tasso's integration of corporeality and politics in his poetics, by way of Armida's female body, however, has not been specifically examined by critics.[10] I aim to demonstrate that in the *Gerusalemme Liberata,* underneath the story of Christian ideological project of the Crusades, and in the interstitial space between the logocentrism of the body politic and the body natural itself, we find Armida, a figure representing the union of the erotic and the diplomatic—the corporeal and the civic—as well as the significance of such a union.

An invented character with no historical basis, Armida, the beautiful Damascene sorceress and niece of Idraote, ruler of Damascus, is introduced in the *Liberata* as she is being conscripted as a secret weapon in the pagan war effort against the Crusader military might, "il valor franco" (the Frankish valor, *GL* 4.22). Uncertain of battlefield victory, Idraote "fears the costs of bloody victory" (di sanguigna vittoria i danni teme, 4.22), yet is desirous of spoils for himself and his people. He is persuaded to utilize Armida, a nontraditional combatant because of her sex, beauty, and keen knowledge of the dark arts (4.23). These female-gendered qualities are privileged precisely because of their incongruence with the male-dominated theater of war, in the hopes they will facilitate, through Armida's body, a pagan infiltration of the unsuspecting Christians. Aided by her physical beauty, Armida's successful seduction hinges on the skillful narration of a pitiable story of oppression and dispossession that preys upon the crusaders' chivalric impulses and negative preconceptions about their enemy. I discuss how, through Armida's adjacency to structures and bodies of power, she gains awareness of her political subordination, exclusion, and exploitation. This recognition awakens Armida politically and facilitates her assumption of the subject position and entrance into, and fundamental modification of, political discourse and order. Armida's subjectivity, which disrupts expectations for feminine speech, is reminiscent of that of the Renaissance courtesans,[11] whose speech ("parole lascive" [lascivious words]) and eroticized physical presence ("mali esempi con molti atti" [bad examples with many acts]) were publicly and notoriously censured, as examined in the next chapter, through repeated legislation.[12]

Defying Dido's Destiny

To better illustrate Tasso's conscious modification and modernization of the female figure through the character of Armida, it is important to spend some time discussing the character of Dido as portrayed in the *Aeneid,* one of the *Liberata*'s foundational texts. In my view, Tasso carved out a space for female sexuality within politics and state formation that was precluded in Virgil's seminal work. Tasso strove to reconcile sex and war, love and politics, and eventually the masculine and the feminine. Virgil, in contrast, left little space allocated for desire (appetitive faculty) in general, and essentially none for female desire or sexuality, as exemplified by Lavinia's silence and passivity, and by the ultimate price Dido pays for gratifying her bodily desires. Unlike "pious Aeneas" who can forgo desire in the name of duty, thus fulfilling his innate male capacity, Virgil suggests that Dido represents not only the perils of female desire and sexuality but also the notion that women are incapable of ruling effectively precisely because of their inability to eschew personal desire in the name of political and civic duty. Through the following examination of the ways in which Tasso's characters of Rinaldo and Armida are founded on, but also significantly diverge from, their Virgilian models, I seek to demonstrate both how Tasso reconciles sexuality and politics through these characters, returning the body natural to the body politic, and the significance of such a gesture.

Tasso's direct engagement with the *Aeneid* is clear from the outset of *Gerusalemme Liberata* (*Jerusalem Delivered*). "Arma virumque cano" (Arms I sing and the man, *Aeneid* 1.1) begins Virgil's famous opening verse, which Tasso echoed as "Canto l'arme pietose e 'l capitano" (I sing the reverent armies and the captain, *GL* 1.1).[13] Tasso's opening verse contains two significant modifications, however. First, the adjective "pietose" (reverent) was added to modify "arme" (armies), indicating that the war at the epic's center is a holy war. Second, Virgil's "virum" (man) became "'l capitano" (the captain), the leader of a religious army rather than the founder of a race from which the Roman Empire develops: "genus unde Latinum/Albanique patres atque altae moenia Romae" (whence came the Latin race/the lords of Alba, and the walls of lofty Rome, *Aeneid* 1.6–7). Goffredo, Tasso's "captain," is chosen by God for his "full[ness] of faith and zeal" (pien di fé, di zelo, *GL* 1.8) and precisely because his only desire is to "drive the wicked pagans from the holy city" (scacciar desia/de la santa città gli empi pagani, *GL* 1.8). Unlike Aeneas's destiny as imperial originator, Goffredo "makes no account of any mortal glory, empire, treasure" (ogni mortale/gloria, imperio, tesor mette in non cale, *GL* 1.8).

These distinctions between the two texts thus disallow the expectation that Goffredo, the stated hero of the *Liberata*, will follow the model of Aeneas by shunning amorous distraction in order to fulfill political and imperial goals. Goffredo's chastity and Christian piety are never challenged, as opposed to the piety of Aeneas, which is best described as dutiful fulfillment of obligations assigned to him by the gods. Goffredo's job is not to found an empire, but instead to lead his fellow Christian princes back toward the collective religious goals of the Crusades, which requires the subordination of personal desire. He is even described by the metaphor of the body politic as "one head that may direct and restrain the others" (un capo che gli altri indirizzi e frene), its "cooperating limbs" (membri amici, *GL* 1.31).

One of the "cooperating limbs" particularly germane to this study is Rinaldo. Like Aeneas's destiny, Tasso created Rinaldo as mythical progenitor of the Estense dynasty, rulers of Ferrara and eventual patrons of Tasso himself. The trajectories of the two characters then diverge significantly, however. Aeneas's amorous entanglement was a distraction that had to be overcome to fulfill his destiny, resulting in Dido's abandonment and suicide. Rinaldo's destiny, announced by Pietro l'Eremita, is to be the creator of the Estense dynasty:

> Ben di lui nasceran degni i figli
> De'figli dei figli [. . .] così verrà che vóle
> l'aquila estense oltra le vie del sole" (*GL* 10.75–76)
>
> (And sons well worthy of him will be born. Sons from those sons [. . .] So it will come that the Eagle of the Este flies beyond the roadways of the sun).

This fertile destiny, however, could only be fulfilled by indulging his libido with Armida, the Damascene enchantress, and then subsequently legitimizing that affair through marriage. While all of these "sons" are overtly Rinaldo's and thereby subsumed under the wings of the Estense dynasty, covertly they are Armida's as well, thanks to her actions as autonomous agent. This modification to the epic genre by Tasso modernized the female role through the character of Armida by challenging and reworking the inherited authority of poetic precursors.

Virgil, for example, used two different women, Dido and Lavinia, to personify Aeneas's struggle between desire and destiny. Lavinia, the silent and nearly invisible[14] daughter of Latinus and Amata, and destined bride of Aeneas, comprises an important contradiction. As a character, she is essentially a cipher, appearing physically in only a handful of verses and speaking none.[15] What is known about her is in connection to men: daughter of Latinus, object of the affection of Turnus, her suitor, and the fated consort of Aeneas. Despite a complete lack of character development, the crucial significance of Lavinia to the plot[16] is clear from the poem's start: "Troiae qui primus ab oris/Italiam fato profugus Laviniaque venit/litora" ([The man] who first from the coasts of Troy, exiled by fate, came to Italy and Lavine shores, *Aeneid* 1.1–3). These verses constitute an indirect reference to Lavinia—"Lavine shores"—as the namesake of the city Aeneas will found. Lavinia is both Aeneas's destiny and destination, essential to the fulfillment of the Roman empire and the procreation of the Latin race. Additionally, she is the only heir to Latinus's kingdom and therefore the sole vessel through which a new people, the Latin race, is generated.

Yet Lavinia is also rendered irrelevant and passive: She utilizes no verbal language (her minimal communication is limited to blushing and weeping)[17] and expresses neither desire nor opinion, instead accepting her fate as inevitable. Lavinia is merely a means to fulfill the destiny of others, particularly Aeneas's, and then more generally that of the Roman Empire. The conflation between land ("Lavine shores") and female body in the figure of Lavinia reduces her to a symbol of empire and conquest, who is not even credited semantically for her generative role. Virgil instead assigns sole credit to Aeneas for begetting both a people and empire, erasing Lavinia's generative body once more. It is Aeneas who rhetorically assumes both maternal and paternal roles in a description that approximates asexual reproduction: "Arma virumque cano [. . .] genus unde Latinum/Albanique patres" (Arms and the man I sing [. . .] whence came the Latin race, the lords of Alba, 1.6–7).

Aeneas's own sexuality in these proemial verses, which appears comprehensive in its generative powers, not only reinforces the effacement and exclusion of female sexuality but also underscores the hero's maturation as a process of overcoming the appetitive faculties (specifically sexuality) and obtaining, or perhaps reclaiming, political authority through his rightful role as male ruler. Aeneas's openly sexual and romantic relationship with Dido is thus at odds with his destiny as founder of the Roman polis, which could never have come to pass had he remained in Carthage, where Dido ruled as queen. While in Carthage, for instance, Aeneas's masculinity is denigrated; he is accused of being a wife-stealing Paris who associates with "eunuch[s]" (semiviro comitatu; literally "a retinue of half-men") by King Iarbas, Dido's previously spurned suitor, upon learning of their relationship:

Et nunc ille Paris cum *semiviro comitatu*,
Maeonia mentum mitra crinemque madentem
subnexus, rapto potitur. (*Aeneid* 4.215–217; italics added)

(And now that Paris with his *eunuch train*, his chin and perfumed locks bound with a Lydian turban, grasps the spoil.)

Aeneas's effeminate appearance—his perfumed, glossy hair and Lydian turban—coincide with the traditionally female role as consort rather than king. But once Aeneas sets sail for "Lavine shores," his previous pleasure indulgence is superseded by his obedience to the will of the gods and the adherence to duty, attested by his epithet, "pious Aeneas."

Whereas Lavinia, who represents the vehicle for the fulfillment of the Latin race, appears in the narrative to be significant only as an absence, Dido represents the opposite; she is the obstacle to Aeneas's destiny and destination. Yet, unlike Lavinia, she is fully rendered in Virgil's text through a poignant, both ambiguous and nuanced elaboration of her personal history, motivations, strength, and fragility. Though Dido dies tragically by suicide in the fiction, it is she who lives on beyond the confines of the text by becoming the literary prototype of the lamenting woman who was seduced and abandoned.[18] Tasso, too, was clearly moved by Virgil's story of Dido and inspired to rework her story as a basis for his most significant female character, Armida. He consciously bases Armida's response to Rinaldo's abandonment on Dido's words to the departing Aeneas:

Né te Sofia produsse e non sei nato
de l'azio sangue tu; te l'onda insana
del mar produsse e 'l Caucaso gelato,
e le mamme allattar di tigre ircana.
Che dissimulo piú? l'uomo spietato
pur un segno non diè di mente umana.
Forse cambiò color? forse al mio duolo
bagnò almen gli occhi o sparse un sospir solo? (*GL* 16.57:1–6)

(Sofia did not give birth to you, and you are not born of the blood of the Azzi; the raging ocean wave and frozen Caucasus gave birth to you, and the dugs of the Hyrcanian tigress gave you milk. Why do I pretend any longer? The heartless man gave not a single sign of human emotion. Did he change color, perhaps? Did he at least for my sorrow bathe his eyes perhaps, or drop a single sigh?)

Armida, upon discovering Rinaldo's attempt at furtive abandonment, denies him his royal lineage because of his pitiless ("spietato") treatment of her. Instead of descending from nobility, son of Bertoldo and Sofia, Armida insists, Rinaldo must have bestial or inanimate forebearers, namely, the frigid Caucasian lands, the harsh ocean as father, and a cruel tigress as mother.[19]

The distinction Armida draws between nobility of lineage and morality echoes Dido's recrimination of Aeneas, whom she also denies both royal pedigree and the human characteristics of mercy and faithfulness ("perfide"):

> Nec tibi diva parens, generis nec Dardanus auctor,
> perfide; sed duris genuit te cautibus horrens
> Caucasus, Hyrcanaeque admorunt ubera tigres.
> Nam quid dissimulo, aut quae me ad maiora reservo?
> Num fletu ingemuit nostro? Num lumina flexit?
> Num lacrimas victus dedit, aut miseratus amantem est? (*Aeneid* 4.365–370)
>
> (False one, no goddess was your mother, nor was Dardanus founder of your line, but rugged Caucasus on his flinty rocks begot you, and Hyrcanian tigresses suckled you. For why hide my feelings? For what greater wrongs do I hold myself back? Did he sigh while I wept? Did he turn on me a glance? Did he yield and shed tears or pity her who loved him?)

However, despite certain deliberate similarities between her character and that of Dido, Armida refuses the tragic fate, inevitable for her literary predecessor, and forges a new, more active and independent female figure. Through the exercise of agency and the communication of her own desires, she succeeds in shaping her own destiny and even seeking her own revenge. Essential to this independence is a reconciliation of mind and body, which allows her to force her way into the polis, Armida offering the prime example.

Like Aeneas, Rinaldo ordered Armida to stay behind, confined in her "dolce albergo" (pleasant abode, *GL* 16.35):

> Rimanti in pace, i' vado; a te non lice
> meco venir, chi mi conduce il vieta.
> Rimanti. (16.56)

(Stay here in peace; I am going; you are not allowed to come with me; she who is guiding me forbids it. Stay here.)

Despite Rinaldo's invocation of patriarchal authority, as well as that of Fortune herself ("chi mi conduce") to restrain her, Armida refuses confinement or containment. While Dido sees no choice but to accept her fate, Armida surpasses the role Tasso prescribes to her in his "Allegoria" as "minister of the devil" (ministr[o] del Diavolo) and "temptation" (la tentatione).[20] Instead of accepting Rinaldo and Fortune's attempt at containing her ("a te non lice/meco venir"), she destroys her own pleasure islands and then seeks "other arms, other arts" to avenge herself, beyond the female ones she previously wielded (beauty, lamentations, tears). Armida's open expression of her sexuality and resultant questionable morality are essential for her integration into the body politic and for her evasion of Dido's fate. The romantic and public association of Dido, a widow and professed *univira*, with Aeneas, a "Trojan wanderer" (Troia profectus), sets her up for a tragic end:

Neque enim specie famave movetur,
nec iam furtivum Dido meditatur amorem:
coniugium vocat; hoc praetexit nomine culpam). (*Aeneid* 4.170–172)

(For no more is Dido swayed by fair show or fair fame, no more does she dream of a secret love: She calls it marriage and with that name veils her sin!)

Dido was overcome by passion, resulting in misguided actions, Virgil suggested, by failing to guard her reputation and honor ("neque enim specie famave movetur"); instead, she imprudently regarded her affair with Aeneas as a true marriage ("coniugium vocat"). Conversely, Armida's refusal of Dido's fate is permitted *because* of her questionable reputation. Free from the strictures of decorum, she can commit herself to the pursuit of restitution until her "destiny" coincides with the establishment of a powerful house, in this case, the Estense dynasty.

Dido's reputation, in contrast, is irreparably sullied as the news of her relationship quickly spread. Her public disgrace leaves her openly concerned about the potential of violent responses from men she previously spurned. She wonders whether Pygmalion, the brother she fled upon learning he killed her husband, will soon destroy her and her city, and whether King Iarbas, a suitor Dido had previously rejected, would take her captive ("aut captam ducat Gaetulus Iarbas?" *Aeneid* 4.326). Once King Iarbas hears of her affair, he is incensed that Dido refused his marriage proposal yet received Aeneas into her kingdom and home ("conubia nostra/reppulit ac dominum Aenean in regna recepit," 4.213–214). Through Iarbas, Virgil demonstrated the patriarchal resentment of the exercise of female choice and desire. Iarbas believes that his desire should have been enough to secure what he wished for, ownership of Dido's home and kingdom, along with her person and her power. The fact that Dido rejected his proposal ("conubia nostra/reppulit") and instead allowed Aeneas to possess her person, her home, and her kingdom proved particularly offensive to Iarbas because Dido dared to exercise choice and act on her own desire by refusing him and receiving Aeneas. Although Aeneas claims neither to have agreed nor intended to marry Dido—"nec coniugis umquam/praetendi taedas, aut haec in foedera veni" (I never held out a bridegroom's torch nor entered such a compact, 4.338–339)—she is keen to point out to him the consequences of the affair as they relate to her. Whether or not their union was official, it nonetheless resulted in her becoming an abandoned woman (deserta) without a male protector and deprived even of her chaste reputation: "Te propter eundem *exstinctus pudor,* et, qua sola sidera adibam, fama prior" (Because of you *I have also lost my honor* and that former fame by which alone I was winning a title to the stars, 4.321–322; italics added). These words to Aeneas draw a direct connection between Dido's eventual death and the extinction of her honor ("exstinctus pudor"), which was her saving grace.

Dido's tragedy rests on the fact that upon her loss of honor, she had no option for survival; her sexual behavior, or the perception of it, became a matter of morality, which directly and irreparably diminished her public image and social worth. The success of Dido, reigning Queen of Carthage, in building her city was dependent on the respect she commanded from her subjects. That respect is founded on the *pudicitia* she embodied, particularly on her vow to remain *univira* (a woman faithful to only one husband), which in practice demanded her complete dedication to state formation at the cost of the abandonment of her own body and sexuality. Her pursuit of a relationship with Aeneas and allowing herself to revel in the "former flame" of concupiscence (adgnosco veteris vestigia flammae, *Aeneid* 4.22) signaled Dido's unsuitability as regent because she was privileging personal desires over political duties, the precise opposite of Aeneas's "piety":

> illum absens absentem auditque videtque;
> aut gremio Ascanium, genitoris imagine capta,
> detinet, infandum si fallere possit amorem.
> Non coeptae adsurgunt turres, non arma iuventus
> exercet, portusve aut propugnacula bello
> tuta parant; pendent opera interrupta, minaeque
> murorum ingentes aequataque machina caelo. (4.83–89)

> (Though absent, each from each, she hears him, she sees him; or, captivated by his looking like his father, she holds Ascanius on her lap in case she may beguile a passion beyond all utterance. No longer rise the towers begun, no longer do the youth exercise in arms or toil at havens or bulwarks for safety in war; the works are broken off and idle—great menacing walls and cranes that touch the sky.)

Dido exhibits a sort of cognitive dissonance in which her dutiful commitment to the maintenance of her *pudor* conflicts with her passionate love for Aeneas and a desire to marry him and establish a family with him. Virgil underscores this conflict by juxtaposing her feminine and maternal desires with her negligence as ruler, thereby evincing the impossibility of her fulfilling simultaneously the roles ascribed to women (as both lover and mother) and those of a ruler.

Dido herself, in her confrontation with Aeneas before his departure, states that her own Tyrian subjects hate her ("infensi Tyrii," *Aeneid* 4.321). Dido's unfaithfulness to her dead husband is in effect equated to her unfaithfulness to her city, thus rendering her undeserving of the faith of her subjects. This, of course, is treatment to which a male ruler would never be subjected. A prime example is the case of Aeneas. His destiny as founder of the Roman Empire was never, and would never, be questioned, regardless of his dalliance with Dido and his lack of fidelity to Creusa, his first wife, who perished in Troy. In fact, the entire plot of the *Aeneid* is predicated upon these two "infidelities." Dido, on the contrary, was beholden to the morality that compelled her to remain faithful to her dead husband. Dido's faithfulness places her in a double bind in which any action that violated her high standards of *pudor* warranted her death. Dido understands and accepts that the maintenance of her honor, her *pudor*, depends upon her remaining a faithful widow. Marriage demanded that Dido relinquish a significant aspect of her life, the right to love another, since her dead husband, Sychaeus, had taken part of her, "her heart" (amores) with him "in the grave" (sepulchro, 4.28).

"Quid moror?" ("Why do I linger?" *Aeneid* 4.325) asks Dido in full comprehension of her predicament when Aeneas departs and she becomes an "abandoned woman" (deserta, 4.330). It is tempting to read this simply as desperate heartbreak at having been deserted by her beloved, as many male authors do; however, there is more at stake.[21] Virgil depicts Dido as "a woman of the highest moral character" who equates her own *pudicitia* with her worth, "a religious and moral duty."[22] In vowing to remain *univira* upon the death of her first husband, Dido underscores her own moral rectitude by upholding the sanctity of marriage, and maintaining her *pudor*:

Sed mihi vel tellus optem prius ima dehiscat,
vel Pater omnipotens adigat me fulmine ad umbras,
pallentis umbras Erebi noctemque profundam,
ante, *Pudor*, quam te violo, aut tua iura resolvo.
Ille meos, primus qui me sibi iunxit, amores
abstulit; ille habeat secum servetque sepulchro. (4.24–30, italics added)

(But rather, I would pray, may earth yawn for me to its depths, or may the Almightly Father hurl me with his bolt to the shades—the pale shades and abysmal night of Erebus—before, *O Shame*, I violate thee or break thy laws! He who first linked me to himself has taken away my heart; may he keep it with him and guard it in the grave!)

Limiting the cause of Dido's suicide to emotional upheaval resulting from her abandonment is problematic in its implications. First, such an interpretation suggests that women are purely emotional creatures, irrational, and incapable of stoicism and strength; in short, conventional misogyny. More problematic, however, is that it completely ignores (or is blind to) the distinct societal, cultural, and political factors that contribute to the despair underlying Dido's suicide. It could not have only been the loss of her beloved, though surely distressing, that provoked Dido's desperate action. Aeneas's abandonment of Dido was not merely a personal loss to her; it was an action that nullified Dido's existence by offering no viable path for survival because her cultural, political, and social worth had also been revoked, leading inevitably to her own extinction, a fate Dido understood instinctively and to which she immediately alludes in her confrontation with Aeneas upon realizing his plan to abandon her: "Nec te noster amor nec te data dextera quondam/Nec mortiura tenet crudeli fundere Dido?" (Does neither our love restrain you, nor the pledge once given, nor the doom of a cruel death for Dido? (4.307–308).

Armida's Vendetta: Agency and the Rejection of Imposed Patriarchal Limitations

Upon Rinaldo's abandonment of her, Armida also declaims a rhetorical question that echoes both Dido's "Quid moror?" and her final lines: "Ed io pur ancor l'amo, e in questo lido *invendicata* ancor piango e m'assido?" (And do I love him yet, and sit me down to weep along this shore, yet *unavenged? GL* 16.63:8; italics added). In contrast with Dido's final words—"I shall die unavenged, she cried, but let me die" (moriemur inultae, sed moriamur ait, *Aeneid* 4.660)—Armida's query does not carry an assumption of defeat. The presence of the word "invendicata" (unavenged), instead indicates her intention to pursue revenge to salvage her honor and punish Rinaldo. In fact, Armida's call for revenge ("vendetta") is repeated here three times in the space of a few octaves.[23] Dido's question is existential and acknowledges her unavoidable death, whereas Armida's is geographical: Why am I still sitting here crying on this island ("in questo lido [. . .] ancor piango e m'assido?") when revenge is to be sought elsewhere? Her refusal to remain geographically fixed and accept as destiny her abandonment and defeat while her absconding lover is on the move is an acknowledgment and an assumption of agency, both political and personal.

Armida's evident sexuality and generative capacity, I argue, allows for reading her as a hybrid figure of the courtesan and the ambassador, a female agent whose corporeality reconciles—albeit ambiguously—the personal body with the body politic. Through her consummate narrative and rhetorical abilities, she gains freedom by carving a place for herself, her history, and her body within a system in which she was previously exploited, excluded, or abandoned. Politically, she is the only female character who is explicitly enlisted as an agent of the state, thus breaking with the ancient tradition of warrior virgins (Camilla, Clorinda, Bradamante) who all obscure their sexuality by donning armor and assuming the phallus via the sword. In the case of Armida, contrastingly, her uncle Idraote, the lord of Damascus, utilizes her body and its sexuality openly for his own purposes and advantage. Armida has been convincingly read, via Marian and Petrarchan echoes, as a figure who transforms from Petrarchan dominatrix into an example of Marian humility in her wifely submission to the Christian warrior Rinaldo, her once lover and future husband in the final canto of the *Liberata*.[24] The subjugation of Armida has, however, not been read for the political implications of her trajectory in the *Liberata*, which I propose here.

In order to elucidate the political implications of Armida's character, it is worth returning briefly to *Il Messaggiero*, where Tasso explicitly connected erotics and politics. In this dialogue, both rhetorically and literally, Tasso attempted to reconcile the body with the soul. The "celeste messaggiero" (the celestial messenger), in the form of a beautiful human body, appeared to our author just at the point at which night gave way to dawn. The essence of his material substance is the point of departure for a discourse that negotiated bodies celestial and terrestrial, material and spiritual, in both theology and poetics.[25] The last section of the dialogue focused concretely on the figure of the ambassador, his duties, his history, and his perfect form. A curious moment is Tasso's comparison of the pimp ("ruffiano") and the ambassador ("ambasciatore"), or more generally as he put it in the same dialogue: "paragone certo assai strano, ma nondimeno tale che può dimonstrare che le arti umane, quantunque nobili, sono assai a l'ignobili somiglianti" (a very strange comparison for certain, but nonetheless such that it can demonstrate that the human arts, no matter how noble, are really quite similar to the ignoble ones).[26] The figure of the pimp, squarely within the "ignoble" corporeal domain, is nonetheless similar to that of the ambassador, a courtly figure representative of the operations of the body politic and the logocentric rudiments of political practice, in that they both have the skills that "move souls" (muove gli animi). The movement of souls requires the knowledge of their complexity, an entity covered by "questo manto de l'umanità" (this cloak of humanity) that therein contains "mille passioni" (a thousand passions).[27]

These passions of the material body, stirred by corporeal desires, are not to be excluded from body politic, but to be reconciled within it, as Tasso declared in his "Allegoria della *Gerusalemme Liberata*": "Superati agevolmente tutti gli esterni impedimenti, l'uomo conseguisce la felicità politica" (Once all of the external impediments are easily overcome, man achieves political peace).[28] I draw attention to Tasso's use of the term "overcome" ("superati"), not excluded or vanquished; reconciled, in other words, not repressed. Tasso thus made the case for the inclusion of the material body—and all its passions—within the body politic. As has been discussed in previous chapters, this role of the material body in service of the body politic is a constant negotiation and source of anxiety for ambassadors well before Tasso's treatise.

Nevertheless, in the *Liberata,* and in Armida's character in particular, the reconciliation between the body natural and the body politic acquires an explicitly female corporeality. Armida's female body, however, also linked to the Renaissance courtesan both visually and literarily. Armida's eroticization in the text, her obvious and ostentatious sexuality characterized by her exposed breasts, in addition to her vanity as exemplified by her mirror gazing (*GL* 16.20–21) signal the visual semantics of the Renaissance courtesan in painting contemporary to Tasso, as Titian's *Venus with a Mirror* (1555) (see Figure 4.1) is a prime example.[29]

Armida's rhetorical skill and erudition are reminiscent of courtesan poets, particularly Veronica Franco, a contemporary of Tasso. Yet, Tasso juxtaposed this admirable skill with derogatory male-originated tropes, representing the courtesan as a deceitful, mercenary sorceress whose spellbinding eroticism is a force that is destructive to both men and empire. Through the complexity of Armida's characterization—admired and feared—Tasso also demonstrated a certain awareness of, and ambivalence toward, his participation in the misogynous discursive and figurative practices that confine and blame the desired female body for the passion it provokes in men.

We are presented with a dual image of Armida right from her introduction into the poem, with her body and intellect represented by way of conflicting codes: "donna a cui di beltà le prime lodi/concedea l'Oriente" (woman to whom the Orient yielded first honors for beauty, *GL* 4.23:3–4). Her exceptional physical beauty is juxtaposed with the traditionally masculine, logocentric attribute of wisdom and virility, characteristic of the politically active man, "canuto senno e cor virile" (manly heart and gray-haired wisdom, 4.24). This is immediately contrasted with Tasso's daring and original portrayal of her eroticized body, to which he dedicated several verses—nearly two entire octaves—in admiration of her bosom, described without the veil of metaphor: "il bel petto"; "le mamme acerbe e crude" (her lovely bosom; her breasts unripe and unready, 4.31).[30] Her beauty, however, is accompanied by rhetorical talents that the narrator described similarly to those of Alete. Her status as a beautiful and young woman, along with her words, are enough to convince all the crusaders to take up her cause, with the noteworthy exceptions of an "irrational" Goffredo.[31] Armida's eroticized appearance disarms the warriors and dulls their interpretative skills. Her

Figure 4.1. Titian. *Venus with a Mirror* (1555). Oil on canvas, 124.5 × 105.5 cm. Accession Number 1937.1.34. National Gallery of Art, Washington, DC, Andrew W. Mellon Collection. Photo courtesy of National Gallery of Art, Washington, DC.

official mission was veiled—"vela il soverchio ardir con la vergogna / e fa' manto del vero alla menzogna" (your overmuch boldness veil with maidenly modesty, and make of the truth a mantle for your lying, 4.25)—in contrast with the symbolic language of pageantry that characterizes Alete and Argante's approach to the Christian camps—"duo gran baroni [. . .] molti intorno avean scudieri e paggi" (two great barons [. . .] and had about them a large number of squires and pages, 2.57)—which was meant to signal clearly their courtly importance and the official nature of their visit.

Armida arrives alone at the Christian camps, without any of the obvious diplomatic ceremony typical of arriving envoys, yet is treated rhetorically as an envoy/messenger: "E traggon tutti per veder chi sia / sí *bella peregrine*, e chi l'invia" (And they all draw round to see who she may be, so *beautiful a pilgrim*, and who sends her, *GL* 4.28; italics added).[32] Unlike the eventually triumphant Armida, Alete, regardless of his earnestness, is ultimately unsuccessful in rhetorical seduction and thus fails in fulfilling a key ambassadorial responsibility. He is a "perfect" ambassador, to the point of parody, yet Alete was nonetheless ineffective. Alete offers a double fiction: He is a character within Tasso's fiction, as well as an example of the depiction of the "perfect ambassador" Tasso compiled, we recall, in his diplomatic treatise *Il Messaggiero,* in which can be found the work of an artist who can select the best attribute from several imperfect ambassadors to assemble a platonic ideal. Armida, like Alete, is granted exceptional rhetorical powers of persuasion and even seduction, talents that in the *Liberata* are possessed only by those who occupy a mediatory role. In other words, in the *Liberata,* the poet grants powers of narration and rhetorical skill to "errant" figures, figures at odds with the Christian telos, figures in movement, much like the "me peregrino errante" (myself a wandering pilgrim, 1.4), as the poet describes himself via an antithesis in the opening octaves of the poem. This is an antithetical phrase since a pilgrim, by definition, departs with a predetermined and fixed destination and follows a well-worn route to arrive at the destination, and therefore does not, or cannot, wander errant. The stories of these "surrogate author(s)"[33] are the most dynamic of the entire poem: Their destinies either progress and acquire meaning, like Armida's, or at least remain open-ended and subject to the reader's interpretation in order to fulfill their fates, like those of Erminia, Alete, and Vafrino, a spy and unofficial ambassador.[34] These are in stark contrast to static figures, such as Goffredo and Sofronia, whose destinies, like the quintessential pilgrim's, are predetermined and linear.

Armida's Conversion: Beyond Faith and Fatherland

When the reader is introduced to Armida, the narrator states, "E piú occulte frodi/ch'usi o femina o maga a lei son note" (Well known to her are the subtleties and the most hidden frauds that witch or woman can practice, *GL* 4.23). Thus her talents are well within the stereotypical seductress/witch category of narrative poetry, such as those exemplified by Melissa and Alcina in Ariosto's *Orlando Furioso* and Circes in both Homer and Virgil. In carrying out her mission on behalf of Idraote, her uncle and sovereign, this frank eroticism is contrasted with her assumption of a bashful maidenly role at this point in the narration, masterfully adopted to infiltrate the Christian camp in order to deprive it of its greatest warriors. This ruse is performed in fulfillment of that strategic political mission, and she proves a mistress of her physical image: openly seductive yet reassuringly modest enough to appear a virtuous "wandering maiden" (vergine peregrina, 4.36). This role of dispossessed princess in distress, which Armida narrates with the diplomatic and rhetorical skills of *pathos*, *ethos*, and *logos*, is, however, reminiscent of a bygone poetic genre, the chivalric *romanzi*. Yet unlike the damsels of Ariosto and Boiardo, Armida is not only active sexually but also politically. Tasso repurposes this *topos* as a dissimulated facade, facilitating Armida's execution of Idraote's instructions: "Vela il soverchio ardir con la vergogna, e fa' manto del vero a la menzogna" (Your overmuch boldness veils with maidenly modesty, and makes of the truth a mantle for your lying, 4.25).

This is one of many episodes in which the reader is encouraged to interpret the actions of Armida as immoral: "Menzogna" (lie) is juxtaposed with "vero" (truth).[35] Tasso established a dissonance between the expected moral condemnation of Armida and the subtle clues that justify, if not absolve, her actions. Following is another key verse whose beautiful alliteration establishes Armida's subordinate status as "agent" (essecutrice), not originator: "Tessi la tela ch'io ti mostro ordita,/di cauto vecchio essecutrice ardita" (Weave the web that I show you all laid out, a bold-hearted agent for a cautious old man, *GL* 4.24). Idraote, a representative of the political and familial patriarchal orders as lord of Damascus and Armida's uncle, exploits her through flattery ("essecutrice ardita") and vulnerability ("cauto vecchio") to embolden his "agent." This preestablished plan ("tela/ordita") is predicated on the appropriation of Armida's body and intellect but also weaponizes the female body. Idraote's militant plan centers on the irresistibility of Armida's sexuality to mortally wound the enemy. Idraote employs the language that in epic is typically associated with female domesticity, *tessere* (weaving); however, unlike Penelope, Armida does not pass her time weaving and waiting, but employs her body actively. Idraote instead stays back and minds Damascus while Armida acts politically and militarily on his and Damascus's behalf. Idraote's plan is inconspicuous, hidden under the dissimulated cloak of Armida's female, and thus seemingly apolitical and unbelligerent, body.

As established, Armida is lexically presented as an official state "agent" (essecutrice) much like Alete, an official envoy of the king of Egypt to Goffredo.[36] With these figures, Tasso integrated Renaissance diplomatic procedure into the *Liberata*.[37] In rereading Armida, it is important to take into consideration the political and diplomatic framework under which she operates. Armida is labeled a "ministro del diavolo" (minister of the devil) by Tasso himself in his "Allegoria della *Gerusalemme Liberata*."[38] The term "minister," political in connotation, also reminds us that Armida is subordinate to a commanding power. This subordination is lexically reinforced by the term "essecutrice." In terms of political philosophy, her actions must be interpreted according to the final words spoken to her by Idraote after detailing his plan and before dispatching her: "Al fin le dice:/Per la fé, per la patria il tutto lice (For the Faith, for the Fatherland, all is permitted, *GL* 4.26). Here Idraote—in the *rima baciata*, the most privileged position of the octave—addresses Armida like a man, in the sense that he invests her with the same responsibilities that a sovereign would a male agent of state, warrior, spy, or ambassador. To motivate her into "battle," as it were, he utters a phrase that underscores the parties for whom Armida would sacrifice herself: the faith and the fatherland, two rigid patriarchies. Machiavelli's pragmatic political theory is apparent here and provides a justification that not only allowed for, but effectively demanded, actions whose ethics are distinct, and perhaps distant, from accepted morality. This modern, nationalistic notion of statehood is conspicuous in the premodern setting of the First Crusade. Its modernity signals that Armida represents a different time, which coincides with her refusal to accept societal expectations and limitations imposed on her, and her rhetorical virtuosity links her to courtesan poets contemporary to Tasso. She represents the future, the modern historical and political context of the poet, rather than the poem's historical context.

I refrain here from discussing some of the most celebrated episodes in the *Liberata* that focus on Armida, and eventually Armida and Rinaldo, the Christian warrior with whom she unexpectedly falls in love. Most of the actions she executes in these cantos are ostensibly deceitful, and readers, guided by interventions of the narrator characterizing her over and again as "falsa," "rea," and "ingannatrice" (false, wicked, and deceptive), are encouraged to interpret them as immoral. Armida, the "essecutrice," was sent on a mission precisely to complete those actions that the reader is guided to judge as immoral. I seek here to probe the implications of this contradiction, particularly regarding gender and politics.

Armida's morally questionable political mission not only ends in failure but also leaves her alone and distraught on the shores of her paradisiacal island, somewhere near the Fortunate Isles in the Atlantic Ocean, after Rinaldo abandons her to return to the battlefield. This unfortunate situation causes her to rethink her role as an instrument of faith and fatherland. Out of dejection, at one point, Armida shouts to Rinaldo as he is leaving:

> Vattene, passa il mar, pugna, travaglia,
> struggi la fede nostra: anch'io t'affretto.
> Che dico nostra? ah non piú mia! fedele
> sono a te solo, idolo mio crudele. (*GL* 16.47)

> (Go your way; pass over the sea, fight, struggle, destroy our faith; I even urge you to do it. Why do I say our faith? Ah no more mine! I am faithful only to you, my idol cruel!)

In contrast with Virgil's Dido, who was moved to suicide after Aeneas abandoned her, Armida makes a different choice. Instead of self-destruction, she makes a conversion, but not to another religious faith, pledging instead faith to her own personal "idol" of love. "La fede nostra," referring to Armida's religion of Islam, is here revealed to be but another patriarchal system, a revelation that spurs her to claim personal agency. In declaring "che dico la nostra? ah non piú mia!," Armida abandons both her religious affiliation as well as her status as official state agent ("essecutrice") of the Damascene theocracy, which demanded submission and immorality in the name of patriarchal state order from which she was excluded and dispossessed. In losing faith in both her religion and her country, Armida thus ceases to be held to the expectations of those institutions on her body.

This loss of faith is a source of personal freedom. Armida, unburdened by allegiance to structures (political and religious) that would exploit her body and sexuality for their own ends, is free to act upon her own desires, create her own destiny, and act as her own agent. It also establishes her loyalty to her own political order. She is still "faithful" (fedele/sono); however, no longer to the collective religious and theocratic bodies, but instead to Rinaldo, the object, "idol," of her own choosing and to whom she desires to submit, no matter what the risk.

Shortly after this episode, Armida implicates Idraote, her protector and sovereign:

> Non accuse già me, biasmi se stesso
> il mio custode e zio che cosí volse.
> Ei l'alma baldanzosa e 'l fragil sesso
> a I non debiti uffici in prima volse;
> esso mi fe' donna vagante, ed esso
> spronò l'ardire e la vergogna sciolse:
> tutto si rechi a lui ciò che d'indegno
> fei per amore o che farò per sdegno. (*GL* 4.74)
>
> (Let him make no charge against me, let him blame himself, my uncle and guardian, who willed it thus. He first directed my bold spirit and frail sex to offices not befitting them. He made me a wandering damsel, and he set the spur to Daring and gave free rein to Shame. Let it all be set to his count, whatever worthy thing I did for love, or yet shall do for hatred.)

Just as she previously denied her faith, here Armida denies her fatherland, represented by Idraote, lord of Damascus. These two episodes, read together, form what I see as Armida's true conversion. Armida is now free to reclaim her own body and the authority to use it toward her own ends, her own faith, and politics. In this episode, the accusations and implications she makes against her uncle reinforce her lack of agency as a (reputedly) deposed heiress and certainly as an exploited envoy/agent. This accusation of Idraote could be interpreted as a spiteful attempt to absolve herself of her own immoral actions. Instead, I argue that this amounts to Armida's political awakening.

Some critics have read this episode exclusively in sexual terms, as a mere expression of regret for having given away "il virginal suo fiore" (her flower of virginity, *GL* 16.46).[39] I find that the octave, which commingles political and corporeal references, contains an ambiguity consistent with Armida's dual identity as sexual and political actress. Talk of her "fragil sesso" (frail sex) and referring to herself as a "donna vagante" (wandering damsel, 4.74) allude to a sense of sexual exploitation; while the phrase "i non debiti uffici" (offices not befitting, 4.74) is interesting in its bureaucratic register, intimating that Armida and Idraote both viewed her enterprise to be a mission on behalf of her "fatherland" (patria, 4.26). "Uffici" (offices, duties, or obligations) also provides a lexical link with *Il Messaggiero*, in which Tasso spoke of the "uffici" of the diplomat.[40]

The rhetorical virtuosity and persuasiveness of her account to the Christian troops in canto 4 could be attributed to her immoral art of deception. In this case, however, Armida does not have an audience. This monologue is performed to the reader alone and thus makes it less convincing to doubt her sincerity. There is no textual evidence to sustain or refute Armida's narrative of her origins in canto 4, yet the tone she takes in vilifying her uncle and sovereign aligns with that original story. In the original (potentially false, potentially true) narrative, Armida also implicates her uncle and denounces his usurpation of, and his selfish designs on, her "realm" (regno) and her body: "e farlo [Idraote's son] del mio letto e del mio regno/consorte" (and make him [Idraote's son] consort of my bed and my kingdom, *GL* 4.47).

In condemning patriarchies of faith and fatherland, Armida has acquired the theoretical basis from which to assert true authority over her own body. Just as Rinaldo returned to the crusade battlefield, Armida too decides to fight for her faith, which entails the demise of her new lover-cum-enemy and idol, Rinaldo. Instead of allowing herself to be further procured by Idraote in the name of the state—"per la fé e per la patria" (for the Faith, for the Fatherland, *GL* 4.26)—Armida inverts that logic in canto 17 and wages her own private war. In employing the same rhetoric that a head of state would, as Idraote did in canto 4, to recruit her own army, Armida effectively sells her own body for personal gain. In her earlier attempt to infiltrate the Crusaders, Armida follows Idraote's orders by veiling her "overmuch boldness with maidenly modesty" (Vela il soverchio ardir con la vergogna, 4.25), thus simulating a maiden-in-distress appearance, partly modest, partly seductive: "Parte appar de le mamme acerbe e crude/parte altrui ne ricopre invida vesta" (A portion appears of her breasts unripe and unready/a portion the envious vesture hides from others, 4.3). In contrast, she presents herself to the Caliph of Egypt, wearing a short skirt, "succinta in gonna" (17.33). She then addresses him as follows:

> O re supremo—dice—anch'io ne vegno
> *per la fé, per la patria* ad impiegarmi.
> Donna son io, ma regal donna: indegno
> già di reina il guerreggiar non parmi.
> Usi ogn'arte regal chi vuol il regno. (17.43, italics added)

> (O Monarch Supreme, I too come to make myself of use *for the Faith, for the Fatherland.* Woman I am, but a royal woman: Warfare seems to me in no way unworthy of a queen. She who desires a realm, let her practice every royal art; italics added)

In quoting the exact same words Idraote uses as he dispatched her, "per la fé e per la patria" (for the Faith, for the Fatherland, 4.26), here Armida dissimulates her sincere meaning—"faith" refers to her personal desire, and "fatherland" to her personal revenge mission—and cloaks both in the language of politics, not in chivalric modesty as she did before. In doing so, Armida usurps the role of sovereign and procuress, becoming sovereign over her own body and desires. This amounts to a refusal of her state's corporeal control, allowing her to act independently.

This newfound independence and agency are taken further when, in the same canto, Armida also appropriates the words of another sovereign, the Roman tetrarch Herod Antipas:

> io vuo'vendetta.
> E la procurerò [. . .]
> ma s'alcun fia c'al barbaro inumano
> *tronchi il capo odioso e me 'l presenti,* [. . .]
> a grado sí che gli sarà concessa
> quella ch'io posso dar maggior mercede:
> me d'un tesor dotata e di me stessa
> in moglie avrà, s'in guiderdon mi chiede. (*GL* 17.46–48; italics added)

> (I want revenge. . . . And I will get it [. . .] But if it shall be some other that *cuts the hateful head from that inhuman barbarian and presents it to me* [. . .] so welcome that the greatest gift will be granted him that I can give. He shall have me as his bride, endowed with a treasure and with my person if he asks for me as his reward.)

Here Armida directly employs the words that Herod Antipas used when he ordered the head of John the Baptist on a platter, while she also embodies Salome with her eroticized body and revealing costume ("succinta in gonna," 17.33). The biblical versions of Salome's story, in the Gospels of Mark, Matthew, and Luke, all indicate that it was her mother, Heroidas, who eventually succeeded in persuading Herod Antipas to order the execution of John the Baptist by asking Salome to promise Herod that she would dance at his birthday party in exchange for his ordering of John's decapitation. Armida, however, does not require that her message be mediated or authorized. She calls for Rinaldo's execution directly while revealing her eroticized body to titillate the mercenaries into following her orders. Effectively Armida is seductress and sovereign in one: Salome in body, and Herod Antipas in political authority.[41]

These instances of rhetorical appropriation by Armida, examples of Tasso's *imitatio*, are evidence of the process through which Armida acquires political agency and bodily sovereignty. The last of these, which we look at next, has received the most critical attention. After her plans to slay Rinaldo are unsuccessful, and having thus lost her religion ("fede"), Armida desperately flees alone into the woods to bloody her own arrows. Rinaldo, having seen and followed Armida, interrupts her suicide attempt, bathes her in tears, and then swears to restore her to the royal throne"—"Nel soglio, ove regnar gli avoli tuoi/riporti giuro" (I swear to restore you to the royal throne where your forefathers reigned, *GL* 20.135)—on the condition that she will convert to Christianity.

The following verses, containing Armida's positive response, are her last of the poem: "'Ecco l'ancilla tua: d'essa a tuo senno/dispon,' gli disse 'e le fia legge il cenno'" ("Behold your handmaid; dispose of her at your discretion," she said, "and your command shall be her law," 20.136). Armida's response is an adoption of Marian rhetoric—an almost verbatim quotation of the Virgin in the Gospel of Luke—which problematically likens her to the archetypal figure of chastity and Christian female subjugation, who gives her body willingly for procreation: "Dixit autem Maria: 'Ecce ancilla Domini, fiat mihi secundum verbum tuum' (And Mary said, "Behold the handmaid of the Lord; be it unto me according to thy word," 1 Luke 38).[42] Through the appropriation of words of the Virgin, Armida rhetorically reclaims virginity, converting from deflowered seductress to a fertile, virginal, and generative body. Additionally, Armida seemingly converts to Christianity, and in doing so, assumes the figure of motherly and wifely submission.[43] Yet, as Jo Ann Cavallo convincingly argued, Armida's words do not truly indicate her conversion to the Christian collectivity, as did the Virgin's in declaring, "Ecce ancilla Domini" (Behold the handmaid of the Lord).[44] In contrast, Armida's declaration, "Ecco l'ancilla *tua*" (italics added) specifies that her submission is to the man she loves, not to an abstract deity.

Armida's manipulation of this biblical text, however, does not end there. In redeeming herself as a handmaiden (l'ancilla), Armida sells herself by privileging the virginal, and thus marriageable, qualities associated with a chaste handmaiden, and in doing so transforms into this archetype sanctioned by Christian ideology.[45] She also erases her poetic and pagan past in the sorceress tradition of Circe and Calypso as well as that of the tragically rejected heroine, Dido, all of whom were excluded from the epic narrative genre and thus the body politic.

There is also an additional semantic distinction between the Virgin's utterance and Armida's self-reference. Armida includes a third person pronoun "essa" (her)—"Ecco l'ancilla tua: d'*essa* a tuo senno/dispon, gli disse" (italics added)—as well as the feminine indirect object pronoun, "le" (to her)—"e *le* fia legge il cenno" (italics added). Except for one self-reference in the third person (where Armida indicates herself by her proper name, "Armida"), there are no other instances in the *Liberata* where Armida creates a semantic distance between herself and her self-reference. Furthermore, I am inclined to view this moment as particularly significant because it comprises the last appearance of Rinaldo and Armida in the text.

The meaning of the verse, like Armida herself, is twofold. First, if we extend Walter Stephen's persuasive reading in which Armida lexically and through an allusion to St. Paul "declares herself the body of Rinaldo,"[46] I view this not as an act of submission, but effectively an action that makes a space for herself and her body *within* the body politic, of which Rinaldo is the "head," and she the body. Together they form *their* body politic, and thus Armida moves beyond the traditionally (and exclusively) generative role granted to the female body; hers is now activated politically and corporeally. Armida demonstrates an awareness of the potential for her objectification and instrumentalization by the state. In other words, Armida is cognizant that she was used by the state for its own ends, with no regard for her fate, interests, or survival. Armida embodies a fundamental comprehension of politics. Through experience, she comes to understand that in a politics in which "il tutto lice" (all is permissible, *GL* 4.26), morality is subjugated to the political interests of the state, which entails the disregard for its agents and their bodies.

Second, in light of this reading, one could also argue that "essa" ("her") also alludes to Armida as a rhetorical creation, an interpretation that the other, in this case Rinaldo, has made of the "texts" she has offered him. These "texts" amount to different versions of herself and her history. Rinaldo's response conveys this when he admonishes her to "pacify [her] turbulent heart." In this declaration Rinaldo tells Armida's of his plans to place her back on the throne:

> Armida, il cor turbato omai tranquilla
> non a gli scherni, al regno ti riservo;
> nemico no, ma tuo campione e servo [. . .] ove regnàr gli avoli tuoi
> riporti giuro" (*GL* 20.134–135)
>
> (Armida, now pacify your turbulent heart. I am not preserving you for mockeries, for my rule—no enemy I, but your champion and your servant [. . .] I swear to restore you to the royal throne where your forefathers reigned.)

Rinaldo's words repeat Armida's convincing origin story that she provided to the Crusaders as she commenced her mission to sabotage the Christian effort (4.36–64). At that point in the poem, the narrator guides the reader to dismiss the story of her origin as fraudulent—"fa' manto del vero a la menzogna" (make of the truth a mantel for your lying, 4.25]—or embroidery on Idraote's "web" (*tela*). Yet, as Marilyn Migiel argued, Armida's origin story remains "irrefutable" in the text as she remains "in control of all such information about her origins" and thus "controls the text."[47] In fact, even at the poem's end, we see that Rinaldo still believes her and vows to "replace her on her regal throne" (Nel soglio, ove regnar gli avoli tuoi/riporti giuro, 20.135), which is precisely what Armida had requested. Migiel argued that Armida is never unmasked because "[she] is not only she who *deceives*, but she who *perceives*," and therefore she proves not only an admirable creator of texts but reader and interpreter of them as well.[48] These exemplary skills are, not coincidentally, those that Tasso ascribed also to the poet.

Is Armida's achieved emancipation and sovereignty up to this point thus for naught? Or is this all too rhetorically convenient and abrupt? Is it but another dissimulation by Armida for her own benefit? This ambiguity underscores her modernity. The deception at the heart of Armida's conversion is authorial: She "rewrites" (through *imitatio*) her own destiny, just as the poet authored the characters' fates. Male writers often assumed the female voice poetically to represent vulnerability, and Tasso played with that tradition. His female characters perform vulnerability and utilize ambiguous rhetoric to gain power and exercise authority, taking full advantage of the existent expectations regarding female vulnerability. Tasso revealed some ambivalence about the rhetorical power he assigned to his female characters, particularly Armida. Nonetheless, the power to control discourse and manipulate responses assigned to female characters, most formidably in Armida, is also inherently diplomatic, and together with authorial agency clearly indicates an embrace of an ethos of ambiguity emerging in Tasso's historical period.

The freedom of her diplomatic and mediatory body allows her, in the end, to assume "lo scettro regal"/"la nobil sede," in accordance with the story she told Goffredo in canto 4 upon first meeting the Christian camp: "Per te spero acquistar la nobil sede/e lo scettro regal de' miei parenti" (I hope to acquire through you the noble seat and the princely scepter of my parents, *GL* 4.40). Armida earns precisely what she claims to desire: a kingdom of her own, which transforms her body into the politically significant progenitress of the Estense dynasty. This exercise of agency is what saves Armida. It is true that she still submits to a patriarchy, and though she does so willingly, she also does so conditionally by rhetorically making space for herself not only within that patriarchy, but at its very center. Armida thus escapes a system in which she was manipulated and dispossessed of her kingdom and where her body was sacrificed to, and exploited for, the good of the state. Now she chooses to integrate herself into a body politic that will beget her dynasty rather than hold her body hostage as one merely passively procreative. Rinaldo's words emphasize this union:

> Armida il cor turbato omai tranquilla
> non a gli scherni, al regno ti riservo;
> nemico no, ma tuo campione e servo [. . .]
> ove regnàr gli avoli tuoi/riporti guiro. (20.134–135)
>
> (Armida, now pacify your turbulent heart. I am not preserving you for mockeries, for my rule—no enemy I, but your champion and your servant [. . .] I swear to restore you to the royal throne where your forefathers reigned.)

Through his words, Rinaldo exhibits an understanding of Armida and her awareness of the potential for her objectification and instrumentalization by the state.

Robert Durling argued that "autonomy and submission, inspiration and Christian orthodoxy, variety and unity, love and death—all the great themes of Tasso's poetry hinge on the crucial relation of the individual to the collectivity. The Catholic collectivity maintained centralized and mediated unity at the expense of cutting off from itself what it thought of as heretical, following the council of Jesus (Matthew 26). So Tasso's most living characters—Tancredi and Armida—must undergo what amounts to a spiritual mutilation before being reintegrated in the Christian totality."[49]

I propose, in contrast, that Armida's spirit is not mutilated, or at least I am not convinced that hers undergoes a complete mutilation. Armida survives, and does so by choice, meaning that she is in control of her persona even as she submits (or perhaps feigns submission) to Rinaldo, the man she loves, not to the collective Christian body. Rather than spiritual mutilation, Tasso's character of Armida could instead be seen as the only successful representative of autonomy in this epic of collectivity. Armida regains the "regno" (kingdom) that she sought and is the only character to declare fidelity to her own law of desire—"fedele/sono a te solo, idolo mio crudele" (I am faithful only to you, my idol cruel! *GL* 16.47). This amounts to an intriguing subversion of authority represented by the autonomous, fertile, female figure of Armida, whose "unyielding alterity,"[50] to reprise Cavarero's formulation, should preclude its reconciliation within the body politic, but nonetheless generates the Estense dynasty in Tasso's fiction.

As David Quint discussed in his important essay on political allegory in the *Liberata*, it was widely speculated at the time that Alfonso II d'Este, duke of Ferrara and the patron with whom Tasso experienced a tormented relationship, was sterile; he had failed to produce an heir, either legitimate or illegitimate.[51] A Venetian diplomat relayed to the Senate in 1575 that "La commune opinione è che sia inabile a generare" (The common opinion is that he is unable to procreate).[52] The continued existence of the Estense line in Ferrara was very much in doubt. And this biological problem was compounded by politics masquerading as faith: In 1567, Pope Pius V issued a bull that forbade "illegitimate family lines from inheriting feudal titles in papal domains," specifically tailored to preclude the perpetuation of the Estense line.[53] Although Tasso, who died in 1595, could not have known for certain, he seemed to have anticipated the demise of the Este in Ferrara, which occurred almost immediately upon the death of Alfonso II in 1597, at which point the Duchy was promptly subsumed into the Papal States.

The Estense Duchy of Ferrara produced all three of Italy's great Renaissance chivalric romance/epics: Boiardo's *Orlando Innamorato* (1483, 1495), Ariosto's

Orlando Furioso (1516, 1521, 1536), and finally Tasso's *Liberata*. The Estense instrument of power, political and otherwise, was not military might, but poetry. This is critical to appreciate Tasso's position as court poet whose work was instrumentalized as a tool for power and politics. In addition to political pressures, poetry was subjected to Tridentine restrictions of the Counter-Reformation, both of which threatened a "sterilization" of his poetics.[54] In a letter from 1576 to Luca Scalabrino, Tasso alluded to the effects of political and religious pressures on his poetry, to which he responded by adopting the "shield" (scudo) of allegory to "protect the love stories and the enchantments" (assicurare ben bene gli amori e gli'incanti), the moments of potential fertility (as well as potential heresy) in his poem.[55] Tasso characterized this strategy by using the corporeal metaphor "farò il collo torto" (I will bow my head), meaning to capitulate unwillingly, feigning reverence or devotion.[56] Tasso suggested that the performance of submission was generally a means by which to safeguard oneself from authority, something that was particularly necessary for the court poet, for whom humility and compliance is a demonstration of how the poet "serv[es] the political" (serve il politico).[57]

With these words—"farò il collo torto"—Tasso demonstrated that dissimulation as a practice—both physical and rhetorical—is necessary at times for survival, particularly during the Counter-Reformation, wherein reigned a "pensiero forte," "an ethics assured of its own validity and legitimacy" ("un'etica sicura della propria validità e leggitimità"), which excluded the possibility of negotiation.[58] Hence, dissembling was not merely a rhetorical device confined to poetry, or only a question of morality, but a tactic for both political and literal existence. The period during which Tasso was writing the *Liberata* was one characterized by political, and particularly religious, schism and instability. We are reminded of these very real dangers in canto 2, through the figure of Sofronia, a willing martyr who is nearly burned at the stake and barely escapes this fiery martyrdom because of the deus ex machina intervention of the virgin warrior Clorinda. Sofronia uses her head/intellect to lie convincingly and righteously for death—her famous "magnanima menzogna" (noble lie, *GL* 2.22). It is her "capo altero" (her proud head, 2.22) that offers her body to the stake. During the Inquisition and the Counter-Reformation, many other victims may also have been innocent, yet far less willing than Sofronia. Tasso displayed ambivalence toward the confessional purity represented by Sofronia and Goffredo, which could be considered unsuitable to the contemporary historical period during which religious differences divided Counter-Reformation Europe.

Goffredo, the head ("il capo") of the Crusaders is all head, all conviction, in terms of both the poem's allegory and its character development. He is a one-dimensional character, willing, able, and obliged to sacrifice his body, just like Sofronia, for the greater religious cause. They both are crystallized in the text's historical setting: Goffredo, for instance, is a symbol of priestly sterility; there is no talk of his dynasty or even his life after the crusade.[59] He is essentially already dead in the text. Goffredo's direct communication with God suggests it, and his entrance into a tomb, the Holy Sepulcher, at the end of the *Liberata*, where he fulfills his vow ("scoglie il voto," *GL* 20.144), and therefore his destiny, confirms this stasis. He is head of a crusading spirit that won this battle but will eventually lose the Crusades. The temporary Christian victory recounted in the *Liberata*, as the historical record attests, will be tempered by the eventual loss of Jerusalem and the Holy Lands, which will soon fall again to Islamic forces. This acknowledgment of the transience of things that appear eternal is reinforced, as discussed in chapter 3, through the perspective of the narrative, whose vantage point, distant and wide, coincides with that of the ambassador: "Cities perish, kingdoms perish" (Muoiono le città, muoiono i regni, 15.20).

Armida, however, breaches the text's borders. In astutely manipulating her personae based on the requisite contingencies she faced, Armida ensured her survival and triumph within the narrative arc of the *Liberata* and beyond: She lives on through her dynasty, Tasso reminded us.[60] Her body will found a dynasty to which the poem itself owes its existence. As the progenitress of the Estense dynasty, her entrance into the body politic is a testament to her malleability, rhetorical ability, and keen understanding of the character she must adopt at the opportune moment. Her modernity is confirmed by her ability to survive and triumph politically and corporeally in an era that demands such skills.

Armida represents survival in a political atmosphere in which her body is disposable to a state interested only in its own existence. Her body was used as a pawn in the war against the Crusaders, but possibly worse, if we take her at her word, her sovereign also had (incestuous) reproductive designs on her body. In forcing her to be consort to his son, he would have reduced her to an apolitical and subjugated existence, a purely generative maternal body, like that of Virgil's Lavinia. Armida's body would have figuratively suffered the fate of Sophocles' *Antigone*: She would have essentially been "buried" alive, outside of the *polis*.[61] Armida instead successfully transforms herself, and in doing so, creates a space for herself—and, importantly, her female body and its sexuality—within a modern and increasingly complex political system. The modernity of this survival is incarnated by the agent (essecutrice) who refuses to act in accordance with the orders of the sovereign, the "head" of the metaphor of the body politic, whose relevance seems diminished among the shifting alliances, expanding horizons, and the emergence of authoritarian, centralized nation-states.

Tasso's Armida, conspicuously modern in the Crusader context of the *Liberata,* represents a female figure whose obvious sexuality disencumbers her from the traditional expectations of female chastity and decorous behavior, pressures that serve to exclude women from the public sphere. In fact, her eroticism is represented as a source of power, granting her access to the male milieux of war and politics, which in Tasso's fiction eventually permits their reconciliation within the female-gendered domains of love and sex.

The inspiration on which Tasso based the figure of Armida, the character through which the political and the sexual, the masculine and the feminine are integrated, may have been the courtesan writer Veronica Franco, the subject of the following chapter. Though Veronica Franco's renown as a courtesan would have likely reached Tasso regardless, evidence suggests their many common points of contact, through which Tasso may well have become acquainted with Franco and her writing.[62]

Like Armida, Franco reestablished the link between language and body. A woman writer who embraced her sexuality and her professional courtesanry, she actively used her poetic platform and humanist literary tools to advocate both for herself and her fellow women, denounce political hypocrisy, and seize a place for herself within the same body politic that aggressively excluded the prostitute. Franco's representations of herself, novel in women's writing, are far from that of a passive figure who languishes at home in silence. Franco, as Diana Robin described, fashions herself in her poetry as "the hunter of the man who has wronged her, whom she stalks through the streets. At other times she is the seeker of violent revenge to be exacted with weapons and terror against him who has defamed her."[63]

The courtesan represented a powerful role for women in early modern society, which "satisfied new social imperatives," as Guido Ruggiero stated,[64] and "distinguished themselves primarily through their speech and language," as Elizabeth Horodowich asserted.[65] Tasso's fiction reflects this through the figure of Armida. Similar to courtesan writer Veronica Franco, who adopted bellicose and martial figurative rhetoric with her pen, Armida takes up literal arms to fight for herself and her dignity in Tasso's poetry. She also rejects Rinaldo's empty chivalric rhetoric as he abandons her (*GL* 16.54) and refuses to conform to the role of the powerless abandoned lover (Dido), Petrarch's silent Laura, or the distant beloved of the *amore cortese* tradition.

As discussed, Armida denounces Rinaldo, her cruel lover, and wages war upon him in the hopes of killing him and vindicating herself. Furthermore, Armida adopts aggressive retorts, at once intelligent and erudite, which reveal the emptiness of male chivalric rhetoric—"S'offre per mio, mi fugge e m'abbandona" (He offers himself as mine; he flees and abandons me, 16.58)—and ridicules hypocritical attempts at chastity and morality—"Odi come consiglia! odi il pudico / Senocrate d'amor come ragiona!" (Hear how he gives advice! hear how the chaste Xenocrates marshals his reason concerning love! 16.58). This authoritative, even irreverent, female voice, through which Tasso offered a modernization of the epic genre via its feminization, was not the invention of male poets. A fusion of body and language, this voice instead reflects the response of women writers, particularly of the courtesan poets contemporary to Tasso, who fundamentally disrupted an ancient, yet still pervasive, symbolic and political order, as well as a literary canon that excluded them from political and intellectual spheres and tethered them to domesticity and corporeality.

CHAPTER FIVE

Controlling Her Corpus

The Courtesan as Political Writer

In 1577, Veronica Franco wrote a petition to the Venetian government, proposing the establishment of the Casa del Soccorso, a house for unwed mothers and women otherwise perceived as unvirtuous, conditions that made them ineligible for refuge in the other charitable institutions for women in Venice, the Casa delle Zitelle (for maidens at risk for prostitution) or Casa delle Convertite (for repentant prostitutes). In her petition, the absence of a place in Venice for these women ("da questo mancamento di provisione") was the cause not only of licentiousness but also for the greater sin of the exploitation of innocence: "questa altra abominanda sceleratezza ancora, che le proprie madre ridutte in bisogno vendeno secretamente la virginità de le proprie innocenti figliole" (this further abomination of mothers who, being destitute, secretly sell the virginity of their innocent daughters).

This horrible, dehumanizing chain of victimization could be remedied, Franco argued, if only this forsaken, demeaned, and ridiculed segment of Venetian society had a space of refuge: "se avessero *luoco onesto* dove potessero ripararsi" (if they had some *reputable place* to repair to; italics added).[1] Advocating for the literal establishment of the Casa del Soccorso—a "luoco onesto"—I suggest, originated from the same impulse as Franco's creation of a metaphorical space within her writing from which she could comment politically on the concerns of the prostitute in society. In doing so, Franco integrated—at least rhetorically—the body of the prostitute into a "luoco onesto" within Venetian discourse, a place of dignity, respect, and care, as well as legitimate indignation. To appreciate the significance of Franco's project, it is first necessary to broadly assess the status of the prostitute in Venetian society.

Res pubblica: The Courtesan's "Public" Body and the Health of the Body Politic

In Tasso's *Gerusalemme Liberata*, Armida abducts Rinaldo and holds him under her erotic spell on her *Isole fortunate*, a space of impossible abundance and overwhelming sensorial pleasure, which at once reflects paradisiacal male fantasies and the fear of the feminine. This labyrinthine, irrational, and unnatural space intoxicates Rinaldo into secluding himself from civic, patriarchal, and Christian duties and values, and devoting himself exclusively to serving Armida. Once his spell is broken by the intervention of Carlo and Ubaldo, Rinaldo absconds furtively from the "dolce albergo" (pleasant abode) of Armida's island—"e 'l vide (ahi fera vista!) *al dolce albergo*/dar, frettoloso, fuggitivo il tergo" (and she saw him [ah bitter sight!] hasty and fugitive turning his back on their *pleasant abode*, *GL* 16.65; italics added). Then he orders Armida to stay behind, because she is unauthorized to accompany him off of the island: "Rimanti in pace, i' vado; a te non lice/meco venir, chi mi conduce il vieta. Rimanti" (Stay here in peace; I am going; you are not allowed to come with me; she who is guiding me forbids it. Stay here, 16.55). The "dolce albergo" of sensual pleasure is a place Rinaldo is free to leave behind, but it becomes for Armida a place of confinement, and thus a figurative representation of the desired "isolation," or "brothelization," of sexually promiscuous women from respectable society.

The first part of this chapter examines the myriad strategies meant to isolate and discipline the prostitute, with a focus on early modern Venice in particular, yet legislation limiting the movement of prostitutes and confining them to certain areas was widespread in early modern Italy.[2] The types of confinement ranged widely in terms of their conditions and amenities. Thomas Coryat (1577–1617), the pioneering tourist and travel writer (discussed in more detail later), described in sumptuous and desirous detail the dwelling of the elite courtesans in Venice, a "Paradise of Venus," in his accounts of Venice's social life and festivities, in *Coryat's Crudities* (1611).[3] The confinement of prostitution to quarters of the city where sex work was tolerated, and eventually institutionalized, had been in effect generally since the late Middle Ages, though repeated attempts to reinforce such restrictions indicate their inefficacy.[4] In Venice, starting in 1360, legislation was imposed to restrict prostitution to Castelletto in the Rialto district. Historians have drawn attention to the 1502 reinstatement of these laws, which demanded that prostitutes residing in the thirty parishes (contrade) listed return to the Rialto, the location of the Republic's sanctioned brothel ("al postribolo de Rialto").[5] The remarkable number of parishes where prostitution was pervasive enough to warrant legislation indicates the inadequacy of the attempts to contain prostitution to certain spaces. In fact, this is confirmed by the Council of Ten's establishment of harsh, even disfiguring, punishment (the amputation of the nose) for prostitutes who refused to leave Venice, which was justified because "one cannot go to any part of this city where there are not so many of them" (non si po andare in parte alcuna di questa Città che non ve ne siano molte).[6] Just how many prostitutes constituted "molte" (many) is difficult to establish, but contemporary sources claim huge (and likely exaggerated) numbers. Venetian historian and diarist Marino Sanuto (1466–1536) estimates there were nearly twelve thousand prostitutes in Venice, or over ten percent of the whole population.[7] Coryat remarks that the fame of the courtesans was not limited to the inhabitants of Venice, or even of the Italian Peninsula, but instead "the name of a Cortezan of Venice is famoused over all Christendome." Now disregarded as an exaggeration, the figures that Coryat cited are nonetheless telling of their importance vis-á-vis Venice's image, particularly to a foreigner: "As for the number of these Venetian Cortezans, it is very great. For it is thought there are of them in the whole City and other adjacent places, as Murano, Malomocco, etc., at least twenty thousand."[8]

The founding of institutions for "converted," or repentant, prostitutes (convertite),[9] as well as public, yet isolated, shelters for young maidens (zitelle), who were both poor and beautiful, and thus considered at particular risk for prostitution, are examples of attempts, often punitive but also rehabilitative, to contain sex work and prostitutes.[10] These spatial measures are one example of the consistent desire throughout early modernity to control the female body. The anxiety over the public presence of the female body becomes most apparent in the case of the prostitutes precisely due to their high visibility and the ambiguity of sex work. Morally condemnable, yet sex work was tolerated on social and economic grounds as a necessary compromise to safeguard female chastity, marriage, and inheritance, as well as to deter men from homosexual practices.[11] Legalized prostitution was therefore contemporaneous to legislation that attempted to control and contain that same prostitute's body. Three Venetian institutions that contributed to the regulation and containment of prostitution, directly or indirectly, were formed in the late fifteenth and early sixteenth centuries: Provveditori alla Sanità (public health); Provveditori alle Pompe (sumptuary laws); Esecutori contra la Bestemmia (regulation of speech and crimes of speech). This restructuring of the body politic in response to the body of the prostitute betrays an anxiety founded on her ambiguous corporeal status. She was mobile both physically and socially, and capable of earning her own income and establishing connections with the signorial class. These were but a few reasons that the body of the prostitute threatened the established social and political hierarchy.

The laws that tried to contain these mobile and ambiguous bodies, however, did not differentiate between different classes of prostitutes, regardless of their status, which ranged from the lowly *meretrice publica* to the lofty *cortegiana honesta*, from public brothels (postribuli) to palatial "Paradise[s] of Venus." Despite the different economic classes of prostitutes, it is instead my intention to focus on the aspects common to all female practitioners of the sex trade, all of whom "were desirable and despicable, appealing and appalling," and thus all suffered from confinement and blame.[12] In fact, a brief look at an excerpt of Venetian legislation from 1571 reveals precisely this equalizing notion of prostitution:

> Che *alcuna meretrice over Cortesana sia di che conditione esser si voglia, non possano ne debbano de cetero andar in chiesa alcuna* il zorno della festa et solenità principali di quella, acciò non siano causa di *mali esempi con molti atti et parole lascive* a quelli over quelle che vanno a buon fine in ditte giesie con vergogna di questa città et in dihonor et dispregio delli lochi sacri et offesa della maiestà di Dio. [. . .] ma *debbono star separate et lontane* da quelle acciò non diano scandalo alle altre persone da bene et di buona vita (italics added).[13]

> (*Any prostitute or courtesan, whatever her condition may be,* henceforth may not, and must not, enter any church on feast days or important celebrations so that those well-intentioned men and women who frequent those churches are not confronted by the bad examples of their [prostitutes'] *many lascivious words and deeds,* which shame this city, dishonor and demean sacred spaces, and offend God's majesty. *They must remain separate and distant* from churches so that they do not scandalize the other decent and respectable people.)

In terms of spatial restrictions within the city, whether a woman was identified as a "meretrice" or "cortesana"—the two poles of the sex work spectrum—the Provveditori alla Sanità, the civic body charged with controlling movement in the name of public health and beyond, placed equal restriction on any class of prostitute: "sia di che conditione esser si voglia" (whatever her condition may be). This ostracization was justified ostensibly on moral grounds due to the potential that their "bad examples" (mali esempi) would infect honorable residents. The statute also restricted prostitutes from religious practice during feast days, holidays, and other parish celebrations. This moral and spiritual isolation created a subclass of female citizens who were, at least by virtue of the language of the law, allowed to be neither seen—instructed to hide their "many acts" (molti atti)—nor heard because of their "lascivious words" (parole lascive). While courtesans were often on public display, inducing "marvel" in foreigners, they were forced to become invisible when respectable Venetian society was publicly participating in rituals performing and reinforcing Venice's collective religious and civic identity.

The attempt to remove the body of the prostitute from the collective body of Venice is akin to rhetorical efforts to cast them as "foreign" or subhuman. The othering of the prostitute is exemplified in a witty line from Pietro Aretino's *Ragionamenti,* in which Nanna, an older prostitute, tells a less experienced one that "le puttane non son donne, ma sono puttane" (whores are not women, whores are whores).[14] The label of *puttana* or *meretrice,* or even *cortegiana,* displaced the identity of *donna* (woman), a rhetorical mechanism by which the prostitute was denied her female body.[15]

In this social and political context, in which "whores are not women," I read the *Lettere familiari* of Venetian writer and courtesan Veronica Franco as evidence of her attempt to integrate the body of the prostitute within the Republic's body politic. A remarkable representative of the tense and ambiguous attitude toward the prostitute's body and its place in society, Veronica Franco attempted in her writing to extend the legal, political, and social limits of a courtesan's mobility. She did this not only by her repeated presence in the art and literature of the period, and not just by simply exorcising fears and obsessions, but also by reclaiming her bodily sovereignty and her identity, and by relinquishing the vast blame assigned to her by society at large. Before analyzing Veronica Franco's writing in detail, however, it is necessary to specify how the prostitute's body managed to be seen—and was seen—within a context that tried to exclude its gender and presence from political life.

Dangerous Bodies

The disruption of the gendered identity of prostitutes was documented by the Venetian writer and artist Cesare Vecellio in *De gli habiti antichi et moderni di diversi parti del mondo*, his vast costume book depicting and describing clothing from all over the known world.[16] The image illustrating the "Prostitutes in Public Places" (meretrici publiche) and its accompanying text indicate this liminal status of the prostitute that disrupts the male–female binary. The woodcut (see Figure 5.1) portrays a prostitute in an overtly feminine rendering; her exposed cleavage comprises the focal point of the image, while the textual description of her costume focuses on her adoption of male attire:

> Hanno con tutto ciò in uso un'habito, che pende più tosto al virile, perche portano giubboni di seta, ò di tela, ò d'altro secodo che ciascuna può havergli più o meno ricchi: & questi sono forniti con frange larghe & piene di bombagia, come à punto gli portano i giovani, & più simili al portamento de' Francesi. Ma su le carni portano la camicia da huomo [. . .] Le pianelle, ch'elle portano, sono più alte d'un quarto di braccio [. . .] & anco alcune braghesse come gl'huomini [. . .] & à questi segni, & altri di tondini d'argento, di manili, sono facilmente riconosciute.[17]
>
> (All of them have a garment tending toward men's clothing: They wear a doublet of silk or linen or some other fabric, more or less rich depending on what they can afford; and these are decorated with wide strip=s of trim and padded with cotton, exactly as young men wear them and much like the French style of dress. Next to their skin they wear a men's *camicia* [. . .] The *pianelle* they wear are more than half a foot high [. . .] Many wear *braghesse* like men [. . .] and by these signs and by their round beads of silver and their bracelets, they are easily recognized.)[18]

The dress of the prostitutes (meretrici), as described by Vecellio, marks their alterity in three key ways. First, their female-gendered bodies were covered by male-gendered clothing, even at the layer closest to their skin: "Next to their skin they wear a men's *camicia*." Additionally, their adopted styles breached national and historical borders by their use of both French and Roman costume, almost denying them their Venetian-ness. Their exceedingly high platform shoes, *pianelle* (chopine, or "chapineys," as Thomas Coryat refers to the footwear),[19] allowed them to distinguish themselves vertically from respectable

Figure 5.1. Cesare Vecellio. *Meretrici pubbliche* (*public prostitute*). In *De gli habiti antichi et moderni di diversi parti del mondo* (Venice: Damian Zenaro, 1590). Bibliothèque Nationale de France, Paris. Photo courtesy of Bibliothèque Nationale de France, Paris.

women, or alternatively, to disguise themselves as those same virtuous women. On the other hand, their jewelry, silver beaded necklaces and bracelets, helped to brand them definitively as prostitutes as opposed to ladies.

The importance of being recognizable is understandable given the necessity of alluring clients, yet the government revealed its anxiety about the potential of the prostitute being confused for a respectable lady. Venice adopted sumptuary laws in 1514 via the formation of a new government entity, Provveditori alle Pompe, which monitored, controlled, and disciplined the appearance of prostitutes. Though originally created to enforce dress codes for all Venetians during a period in which increasing emphasis was placed on decorum, it was also evident that a principal goal of this apparatus of control, claimed Guido Ruggiero, was "to keep prostitutes in their place by controlling their public appearance."[20]

The erasure of the prostitute's gender was also attempted by denying her capacity to bear and raise children. In his "Observations of Venice," Coryat observed that

> there is one notable thing more to be mentioned concerning these Venetian Cortezans [. . .] If any of them happen to have any children (as indeede they have but few, for according to the old proverbe the best carpenters make the fewest chips) they are brought up either at their own charge, or in a certaine house of the citie appointed for no other use but onely for the bringing up of the Cortezans bastards [. . .] And from henceforth the mother is absolutely discharged of her child.[21]

The prostitute's body, biologically speaking, can reproduce and bear offspring. Coryat, however, implied that prostitutes possessed an arcane knowledge and skill in limiting conception, but did not elaborate on how this was accomplished, citing only a crude "old proverbe" by which he likened the prostitute to a carpenter. This strange analogy implied that, like the best and most experienced carpenters, the prostitute too possessed knowledge that made her body an efficient machine, capable of satisfying male desire while limiting the production of "waste" byproducts (chips, sawdust—or children, in the case of the prostitute). Unlike the carpenter, however, who sold his product, the prostitute's body was both an agent of craftsmanship as well as its product. Her body's sexual commerce required the relinquishment not only of her humanity but also her maternity. The biologically generative female body was effectively replaced, in the prostitute's body, by an institution, "a certaine house of the citie," that "discharged" the prostitute of her child(ren). A fundamental female characteristic, the ability to bear and nourish children, was denied to the prostitute, for she was actively or passively encouraged, and at times compelled, to relinquish maternity and have the "bastard" children be raised by the state.

Yet another way in which the body of the prostitute was isolated and removed from the collective body was by her frequent designation as "foreign." Laura McGough established that in 1539 the Venetian Provveditori alla Sanità directed their punishments toward "foreign" prostitutes owing to the "disorder" and disease, particularly plague, they were thought to transmit.[22] It is true, as McGough noted, that prostitutes of foreign origin were in Venice at the time, yet this notion of foreignness is certainly exaggerated given that the majority of "foreign" prostitutes were from either other parts of Italy or the Venetian republic. This legal insistence on the foreignness of prostitutes participating in the Venetian sex trade seems instead more attributable to a generalized anxiety provoked by "the patriarchal male fear of the feminine," particularly the unbound female body, as Ian Moulton claimed in regard to the Aretine Lorenzo Veniero's mock epic, *La Puttana errante* (ca. 1531).[23] This vehemently misogynous work, published in Venice, "chronicles the progress through Italy of an unnamed whore—a monstrous parody of epic warrior women such as Ariosto's Bradamante and Marfisa."[24] The errancy of the figure of the *puttana* was threatening because of the ease with which her body crossed borders, infiltrated society, and caused "disorder." Veniero's mobile "puttana" was likened via simile to the "executioner" (boia), and her conquering success was reputed to have been accomplished more with her "cunt" (potta) than had been Orlando's with his "sword" (spada) and "lance" (lancia).[25]

The wandering and triumphant whore (puttana) in Veniero's mock epic, who travels the entire Italian peninsula conquering the innumerable "dicks" (cazzi) she encounters, acts as an allegory of the long association between prostitution, disease, and mobility, on the one hand, and societal deterioration, on the other.[26]

This unscientific yet pervasive association had real ramifications in terms of the body politic: Provveditori alla Sanità was founded in Venice in 1485, and in the 1490s its authority was expanded because of the introduction of and spread of syphilis. Linking prostitution to disease authorized this entity to control the movement of prostitutes, ostensibly for the sake of public health. The Provveditori alla Sanità therefore became a major player in the growing complex of Venetian institutions seeking to contain and discipline prostitution.[27]

The supposed "foreign" character of the prostitute feeds into the anxiety provoked by excessive and unsanitary mobility. Othering the prostitute's body as foreign to the body politic situates the threats it poses as alien to the political and social life of the republic. During the sixteenth century, legal restriction and government control of the body of the prostitute developed synchronously with a medical theory of contagion. This new "science," though not exclusively biological in scope, authorized further restriction of the mobility of the "dangerous" female body, in particular that of a beautiful prostitute, or a young girl whose beauty alone deemed her vulnerable to prostitution and consequently a more capable instrument for the transmission of disease.[28] In fact, beauty was a requirement of admission for entrants into the Casa delle Zitelle in Venice. The likelihood of becoming a prostitute had little to do with the desire of the young girl to prostitute herself, but instead with the dangerous, lascivious desires that female beauty provoked in men. In fact, "scientific" texts of the period do not address the more pertinent reason that leads a young girl into carnal commerce: poverty. This, instead, is only addressed from the "inside," as I discuss later, notably by Venetian poet and courtesan Veronica Franco.

The plague struck Venice with regular frequency, including significant outbreaks in 1478, when the Scuola di San Rocco was instituted; again in 1527; and from 1575 to 1577, when one-third of Venice's population perished.[29] The constant anxiety of another plague outbreak was exacerbated with the late-fifteenth-century arrival of syphilis, the French disease (il mal francese), which further heightened the already entrenched fear of the female body. Pietro Rostinio in *Trattato del mal Francese* (1556, first edition) directly linked the contagion of the French disease to the female body, specifically to an unnamed "very beautiful prostitute" (una meretrice bellissima) who offered her services to the French troops as they lay siege to Naples during the Italian War of 1494 to 1498:

> Nel campo de Francesi del mille quattrocento era *una meretrice bellissima*, la quale nella bocca della matrice haveva una apostema putrefatta, et gli huomini che usavano con lei fregolando il collo della matrice, per la humidità & putredine del loco, nel membro virile cotrahevano una disposition, che ulcerava & per il membro qual'è mollissimo ascendeva una mala qualità fino alle vie enuntorie, et alle parti dell'inguini et la natura

> per scacciar fuori la mala qualità venenosa ivi faceva tumori, & ivi trasmetteva la materia. Poi quella mala qualità fino al figato ascendeva, & maculava il sangue (italics added).[30]

> (In the 15th century, in the camp of the French troops, there was *a very beautiful prostitute,* who had at the mouth of her uterus a putrid abscess, and the men who lay with her, rubbing against [it in] the neck of the uterus would contract an ulcerative condition, due to the humidity and putrefaction of that place. Through the very tender male member a harmful substance would then enter into the groin by way of the excretory pathways. The body [natura], in order to excrete the harmful venomous substance, would form pustules [tumori] into which it would transfer the harmful substance, which would then ascend all the way to the liver, where it would taint the blood.)

Rostinio, a few lines afterward, reemphasized the culpability of the "*meretrice bellissima,*" this time adding another adjective, *publica* (public):

> Et questo male cominciò a macular prima un'huomo, poscia due, et tre, & ceto, *perche quella era publica meretrice & bellissima* & si come la *natura humana* è appetitosa del coito, molte donne usando con questi huomini, *infettate* si trovavano di tal male. Et queste l'han participato con altri huomini, tal che il detto male si è sparso per tutta la Italia, Francia & per tutta l'Europa (italics added).[31]

> (Because she was a *very beautiful public prostitute,* this disease began to contaminate first one man, then two, and three, and so on. Since human nature is allured by coitus, the many women who would lie with these men found themselves infected with the disease. These women would then take up with other men, such that the disease spread all throughout Italy, France, and the whole of Europe.)

The "infected" (infettate) bodies of the prostitutes were paradoxically also the origin of their own infection, both mysterious *and* the source of the general contagion of the French disease, which was due precisely to the "public," communal and mobile nature of her body. The "humidity" and "putrefaction" of her "place" (la humidità e la putrudine del loco) rendered it hospitable to the incubation of the disease, facilitating its spread to other men, until the entire continent of Europe was infected. Surprisingly, given that the French soldiers were in fact "foreigners," there is no mention of the role of the male body in this contagion.[32] Men are merely implied but never mentioned as explicitly causing, provoking, or contributing to the contagion. The female prostitute is both the origin and vector of infection. In particular, the female body's "putrid abscess" (apostema putrefatta) is the disease's root cause, found deep inside of her womb (nella bocca della matrice) and thus hidden from the male gaze. The male gaze, naturally desirous of sex, is inspired by "a very beautiful prostitute" (meretrice bellissima), yet this natural desire Rostinio associated only with the male body as a constitutive element of masculinity, and thus it was not cited as a cause of disease or its propagation. In Rostinio's explanation, this desire was dismissed as nothing more than a natural condition of all humans—"human nature is allured by coitus" (si come la natura humana è appetitosa del coito)—and such a desire is evoked by the beauty of the prostitute. What is unnatural and diseased (putrefatta), however, is the female genitalia itself. The suggestion is that the characteristic putrefaction of syphilis is found within women themselves, particularly within beautiful and "public" women. And since Rostinio offered no theory of the origin of the putrefaction other than the conducive and humid environment of the womb itself, one is left to deduce that the genesis of the disease, as well as its contagion, are inherent to and constitutive of women themselves.

Just as the "public" female body was considered as a physically destructive contaminant of the "natural" male constitution, it was also harmful to the collective body of society at large. Syphilis contaminated a wide swath of society via sexual relations between prostitutes and men, particularly soldiers,[33] and this fear of the "putrefied" body of the prostitute infiltrating the male physical body was like the anxiety provoked by the entry of the body of the prostitute into the fabric of society at large, and therefore within its body politic. Guido Ruggiero established that this fear, generalized throughout the patriciate, related directly to potential for upward mobility via marriage of the courtesan into an ancient noble Venetian family. The potential for a prostitute to contaminate "the central institution of aristocratic society" was blamed on another "malady": witchcraft.[34] This disorder, unless contained and/or eliminated, was considered dangerous to society at large, not only to the particular family that was implicated.

Mythical Bodies

The family unit was the foundational institution of the Venetian republic. The upwardly mobile body of the courtesan, whose potential entry into the patriciate via marriage, or achievement of adjacent nobility because of her income, allowed the courtesan to get a little too close to the Venetian *buona vita*. Such an association between courtesan and nobility might taint not only the moral appearance of the Venetian patrician class, but perhaps more significantly its "purity" and closed status.[35] Domination and containment of the female was the basis for Venetian civic identity. This identity was founded on the "myth of Venice," through which Venice was allegorized as an "imperial virgin,"[36] which was then metaphorically dominated annually during the festivities on Ascension Day (Festa della Sensa) through the Marriage of the Sea (lo Sposalizio del Mare) ritual, during which the doge threw a golden wedding band into the sea, thus "depriv[ing it] of its frightening demeanor by [being ritualistically] feminized," as explained by Edward Muir. The sea's "marriage" to the doge, Muir argued, represented the unsteady female archetype's domination and containment: "The men who sailed abroad could most easily imagine the sea as a female archetype: unpredictable, fickle, sometimes violent, other times passive; but assuredly she could be mastered by the resolute male [. . .] in symbolizing sexual conquest the processional movement took full advantage of the female metaphor."[37]

Through the figurative domination via the Marriage of the Sea to the Venetian Republic, incarnated by the doge, the Venetian state thus imparted a pervasive message that the female was to be dominated, contained, and thereby remain pure, through the patriarchal institution of marriage. Venetian "virginity" was so ingrained in the collective psyche that even the most famous non-virgin of Renaissance Venice, Veronica Franco, also employed similar rhetoric to characterize her home city (and perhaps also identify herself similarly via association): "città veramente donzella immaculata ed inviolata, senza macchia d'ingiustizia, e on mai offesa in se stessa da forza nemica" (a truly maiden city, immaculate and never violated, free from the taint of injustice, never harmed by an enemy force).[38] The threat of military conquest and sexual metaphor collide in this characterization of Venice.

However, given the real threats to the Venetian Republic at this time, the portrayal of Venice as "intact"—immaculate (immaculata), unviolated (inviolata), and spotless (senza macchia)—can be interpreted instead as a compensatory measure to conceal vulnerability. In fact, the allegory reveals itself as quite fragile and vulnerable to complete collapse upon the return of the plague, a first "spot" (macchia) on the Venetian body politic. This public health crisis, interpreted as a punishment for immorality, licentiousness, and corruption, was unavoidably associated with the prostitute, even metaphorically.[39] As mentioned, an outbreak of plague in Venice, horrific and recurrent, was being referred to by anonymous poets as the deflowering of Venice: "Ah povera Venetia! . . . Za tempo intata e verzene . . . Adesso sporca Femena" (Oh poor Venice! . . . Intact and virginal for so long . . . but now a dirty woman).[40] Written during or shortly after the devastating plague outbreak of 1575, these verses in Venetian dialect from the anonymous poem "Sopra la peste" reveal how the metaphor of the virginal female allegory represents, in prosperity, Venice's glory; however, in adversity, it transforms into a tainted ("sporca") repository of all of Venice's sins.

In addition to the literal health crisis in Venice's body politic because of the plague, the Republic was also fragile economically, militarily, and politically. Venice was no longer in control of the Adriatic. By rounding the Cape of Good Hope in 1488 and discovering an eastern route to India, the Portuguese had found a way to circumvent the Venetian monopoly on trade in the Mediterranean, an economic loss that would consistently and increasingly weaken Venice. The Turks posed a constant threat and were chipping away at Venice's *stato da mar*. Venice sought to court France (previously an enemy), to establish an enduring alliance and keep the encroaching Hapsburg Empire at bay.

This complex climate made it challenging to articulate Venice's civic identity. Previously, Venice had resorted to the creation of elaborate and paradoxical imagery on which to base its mythical origins. The city's founding in 421 C.E. was on the day of the Annunciation of the Blessed Virgin Mary, and in 828 C.E. the translation of St. Mark's relics from Alexandria to Venice authorized Venice's claim to a sacred origin. This religious foundation was, however, tempered by its republican governmental structure, led by the doge, an elected head of state, and founded on the peace brokered between the pope and the emperor in 1177. As Jutta Sperling pointed out, in the sixteenth century "political discourse in Venice was governed by two mutually exclusive female body images. The virginal Mary expressed the closure and original perfection of the city, the republic and the patriciate [. . .] The sensual, inviting body of Venus, goddess of love, represented the city's beauty and riches gained through commerce."[41]

The *Apotheosis of Venice* (also *Pax Venetia*) (1585) by Paolo Veronese (see Figure 5.2), which adorns the ceiling of the Sala del Maggior Consiglio in the Palazzo Ducale, represents well the paradox of Venice: fragile and eternal, open and closed, chaste and lascivious, sacred and secular. This commission, a political statement evoking the myth of Venice—the harmonious balance of monarchy, aristocracy, and republicanism—features the female allegory of Venice inside

Figure 5.2. Paolo Veronese. *The Apotheosis of Venice* (1585). Ceiling panel, Sala del Maggior Consiglio, Palazzo Ducale, Venice. Photo courtesy of Peter Horree/Alamy Stock Photo.

the physical center of the government, and thus also at the center of the body politic. The allegory of Venice is depicted as a blonde, ostensibly virginal woman, floating on a cloud flanked by the towers of the Arsenale. The choice of the Arsenale, the architectonic representation of Venetian military might, is perfectly predictable and perhaps also ironic. The Arsenale's construction and the maintenance of the Venetian military were allegedly funded by taxation on prostitution,[42] a practice by a female body better represented by Venus instead of the virginal figuration of Venice. While this may be an oblique or unintentional indication of the significance of the prostitute to the Venetian body politic, it is not the only one found in Veronese's composition. At the center of the painting, just underneath the cloud, at a balcony stands a group of female figures wearing gowns of varying necklines. The central female figure, located directly below the allegory of Venice, displays her breasts almost completely, even perhaps revealing a nipple. This exposure, in contrast with the modesty of most of the figures surrounding her, especially that of the allegory of Venice herself, provokes questions regarding the status and intended identity of this figure. In clothing and bodily exposure, the figure contains compositional similarities to Veronese's depiction of Venus with bare breasts (see Figure 5.3) and Tintoretto's portrait of Veronica Franco (see Figure 5.4), in which she wears a dress with a low-cut neckline that allows for the exposure of a nipple. The similarly dressed figure in *Apotheosis* may not specifically or unequivocally imply a courtesan, but it is a curiously lascivious inclusion, perhaps alluding to Venice's female alter ego, Venus.

At the time Veronese painted *Apotheosis*, however, Venice's previous positive sensual association with Venus as the incarnation of beauty and the splendors of commerce had lost much of its appeal. As mentioned, in the period during and after the plague outbreak, the female figuration of Venice was transformed into the diseased body of the whore, "an urban body punished for having indulged in luxury and debauchery."[43] Veronese's composition was meant to restore pictorially the immaculateness and majesty of Venice through the allegory of Venice as an "imperial" virgin; thus the inclusion of a bare-chested figure is suggestive. Veronica Franco herself, in a letter on prostitution (discussed in greater detail later), associates an exposed chest with sex work—"col *petto spalancato* e ch'esce fuor dei panni [. . .] e con tutti quelli gl'altri abbellimenti che s'usano di fare perché la mercanzia trovi concorrenza nello spedersi" (with *bare breasts* spilling out of her dress [. . .] and every other embellishment people use to make their merchandise measure up to the competition; italics

Figure 5.3. Paolo Veronese. *Venus, Cupid and Mars* (ca. 1580). Oil on canvas, 165.20 × 126.50 cm. Accession Number NG 339. National Galleries of Scotland. Purchased by the Royal Institution in 1859, transferred to the National Gallery of Scotland in 1867. Photo courtesy of National Galleries of Scotland.

Figure 5.4. Jacopo Tintoretto (or follower). *Portrait of a Lady* (*Portrait of Veronica Franco*) (ca. 16th century, 1575–1594(?)). Oil on canvas, 61.4 × 47.1 cm. Worcester Art Museum, Worcester, Massachusetts, Austin S. Garver Fund and Sarah C. Garver Fund. Photo courtesy of Worcester Art Museum.

added)—while equating a covered chest with female honesty: "schitta d'abito [. . .] che conviene ad onesta donzella, co' veli chiusi dinanzi al petto" (simply clothed [. . .] suitable for a chaste girl, with veils covering her breasts).[44] The presence of this immodest figure in Veronese's composition, at the very least, contaminates the composition with doubt, for the figure offers a polar alternative to the eternally virginal figuration of the myth of Venice. At the point in history when Veronese painted the *Apotheosis,* the Serenissima's instability was pervasive, and it thus would have been essential for Venice to reiterate and reinforce its adherence to its foundational myths. The Apotheosis accomplishes a pictorial representation of the irreconcilability of the myth of Venice as virgin with the reality of its economic status as a capital of consumption, carnal or otherwise.

"Paradise of Venus": Carnal Commerce and the Venetian Body Politic

The consistent legal, ritual, and social attempts at restricting the body of the prostitute throughout Renaissance Venice are paradoxical when considered in light of the fact that at the same time "the Venetian state often sought to promote [the courtesan] for its own benefit."[45] On the one hand, domestically, the prostitute was disruptive to Venice's "purity" and "perfection"; yet on the other, with respect to offering hospitality, the courtesan served Venice as a cultural ambassador. The link between courtesanry and diplomacy is important for understanding the figure of Veronica Franco in Renaissance Venice. Diplomacy was the way in which Venice established its image and communicated it to the outside world, via the entertainment of foreign dignitaries. Elizabeth Horodowich likens the role of courtesan at court to that of the wife, since marriage and diplomatic relations were inextricably linked in the early modern world.[46] This is ironic considering the evidence presented previously, which demonstrated that courtesans were effectively barred from marrying into the patrician class, lest they be denounced as witches. Admitting the courtesan body as a stand-in for a Venetian *donna di palazzo* was authorized for pragmatic purposes, given that a patrician woman could not risk corrupting her honor "entertaining" at court; and it was deemed acceptable and advantageous for the body of the courtesan to be offered as a hospitable and carnal "gift" to foreign dignitaries.

The interstitial status of the courtesan—cultured, educated, glamorous, yet excluded from the patriciate—allowed her to be present in all her splendor, all the while not disrupting decorum or potentially sullying the *onestà* so essential to the maintenance of a Venetian patrician woman's status. The significant role of the courtesan in Renaissance Venetian diplomacy is discussed in more detail in the following analysis of Veronica Franco, but it is worth taking a closer look at the description Thomas Coryat gives of the "palaces" of some of Venice's most elite courtesans, which he refers to as the "Paradise of Venus":

> And indeede such is the variety of the delicious objects they minister to their lovers, that they want nothing tending to delight. For when you come into one of their *Palaces* (as indeed few of the principallest of them live in very magnificent and portly buildings fit for the entertainement of a great Prince) you seeme to enter into the *Paradise of Venus*. For their fairest roomes are most glorious and glittering to behold. The walles round being adorned with most sumptuous tapistry and gilt leather.[47]

This description of the courtesans' palatial dwellings, similar to the supreme sensuality evoked by Tasso's representation of Armida's island, implies that these palaces were designed for the purpose of stoking male desire and the fantasy of being "a great Prince." Princes did indeed visit the "palaces" of Venetian courtesans, as is discussed later regarding Veronica Franco's encounter with Henri III. However, given the small percentage of princes within the general male population, the ambience described by Coryat was intended to create and maintain the fantasy of being treated like a prince by a glamorous woman. The courtesans themselves were no less glamorous or gilded in appearance than the "sumptuous" palace in which they could be found:

> As for her selfe shee comes to thee decked like the Queene and Goddesse of love, in so much that thou wilt thinke she made a late transmigration from Paphos, Cnidos, or Cythera, the auncient habitation of Dame Venus. [. . .] For thou shalt see her decked with many chaines of gold and orient pearle like a second Cleopatra. [. . .] Her petticoate of red chamlet edged with rich gold fringe, stockings of carnasion silke, her breathe and her whole body, the more to enamour thee, most fragrantly perfumed.[48]

The mythological and regal persona is created by the courtesan's exquisite ornamentations: gold, silk, pearls, and perfume. These materials facilitate the assumption of a fictional persona by the courtesan, which, while necessary, also situates her outside the confines of society, into a realm of fantasy and within a temporal and material non-place in which she must sacrifice not only her body but her identity as well. Thus, while the courtesan could be considered elite and privileged in comparison to the lower categories of prostitutes in Renaissance society, this guise, along with the luxurious dwelling, the "Paradise of Venus," is but an elaborate fiction that responds to male sexual desire at the cost of the confinement and sacrifice of the body of the courtesan. In addition to a representation that caters to male sexual desire, the "Paradise of Venus" facilitated the fantasy of acting like the aristocracy, and thus the courtesan's palace was a place in which the patrons "could fashion themselves as a Renaissance elite."[49] This aristocratic fantasy, facilitated by the sale of the courtesan's body and other talents, was another way in which Venice could capitalize economically on the goods its consumption-based economy offered to foreigners and natives alike.[50] There were further indirect economic benefits provided by the visibility and the unique splendor of the courtesan. The writings of Thomas Coryat capitalized on depictions of the courtesan to attract readers, as did the Venetian writers, who looked to the courtesan to incarnate Venice's libertine culture, deriving the added benefit of generating publicity for their home city as a destination for luxurious and cultivated sexual tourism.[51]

It was not only Venice that benefited, of course. The courtesan received monetary compensation as well as other privileges regarding status and access to powerful men. It is, however, necessary to take note of the legal and economic factors that allowed for and encouraged this sex trade. First, as discussed, prostitution in Venice was legal in certain spaces.[52] In addition to the conflicting desires of controlling and tolerating prostitution, Venice projected fears related to its own vulnerability—fears associated with military threats and economic decline, as well as moral and social instability—onto the body of the prostitute. That body therefore became the locus of punishment for large-scale, insidious political and civic scapegoating. The economics of prostitution has been well documented by many social historians of the Renaissance.[53] In addition, Thomas Coryat, claimed to have gotten direct reports from Venetians that a reason for keeping prostitution legal was directly due to the economic benefits to the Republic: "The revenues which they [prostitutes] pay unto the Senate for their tolleration, doe maintaine a dozen of their galleys, (as many reported unto me in Venice) and so save them a great charge."[54] It remains ironic that it was the tax on courtesans, who were cast as an internal health and moral threat to society, that may have helped fund the Venetian military, including financing the *Arsenale*,[55] which would have aided them in national defense and foreign combat. The financial benefit to Venice from prostitution was not unique in Italy at the time. In Renaissance Ferrara, Diane Ghirardo found the same tension between the desire for the revenue generated by prostitution and the contradictory legal efforts aimed at controlling the sex trade.[56]

Beyond the significant economic benefits generated by a legalized and taxed sex trade, prostitution also yielded other advantages in terms of the "health" of the body politic via its allegedly salubrious effects on the fundamental institution of marriage. According to Coryat, Venetian men were particularly anxious and intolerant of the possibility of infidelity on the part of their wives: "For they thinke that the chastity of their wives would be the sooner assaulted, and so consequently they should be capricornified (which of all the indignities in the world the Venetian cannot patiently endure) were it not for these places of evacuation."[57] The violability of the body of the prostitute as a "place of evacuation" highlights the ambiguity of its confinement and prohibition from certain spaces. Their confinement to "these places of evacuation"—which may refer both to the prostitute's body and the brothel, just as the analogy of the carpenter referred both to the agent of production and the product—reassured Venetian men that their own wives would be safely distant from the "bad example" of prostitutes. Furthermore, the availability of the brothel provided other men with a "plac[e] of evacuation" so that their wives would remain inviolable to the sexual advances of other men. The maintenance of the sanctity of marriage, as well as that of both male and female honor, was ironically provided by "dishonorable" prostitutes, who also simultaneously provided the "service" of initiating the sexual practice of patrician men,[58] in other words, training younger men potentially to seduce the wives of older men.

Venetian Renaissance society made a space for the prostitute to be at once fundamental and feared. The figure of the prostitute thus became a convenient scapegoat onto which blame was openly laid and from which Venice quietly profited. This contradiction is portrayed by the increasingly stringent laws against prostitution, and the fact that the Renaissance courtesan was at the height of her fame and visibility.

Veronica Franco's *Lettere familiari*: A Courtesan's "Luoco Onesto" in the Body Politic

Lettere familiari a diversi (1580) by Veronica Franco (1546–1591) is the first published letterbook by a courtesan in Italy,[59] and only the third by a woman under her own name, after Vittoria Colonna's *Litere alla duchessa d'Amalfi* (1544) and Paola Antonia Negri's *Lettere spirituali* (1564), both of which are religious in orientation.[60] As Meredith Ray noted, Franco's epistolary was exceptional not only because its author was a woman, but indeed because she was "one of a small number of writers of either sex to write a 'true volume of "familiar" letters' in the later sixteenth century."[61] In this collection of fifty epistles, the range of topics include quotidian matters, such as a request for the loan of a wheelchair (XLIV) and an invitation to a dinner party (XIII). Other letters highlight Franco's many connections to members of the Venetian patriciate, and some are in regard to her editing a poetic anthology in honor of the military hero Estor Martinengo (XXXII and XL). In one of only a few letters whose recipient is named, Franco thanks the Venetian painter Tintoretto for his portrait of her (XXI). Others include allusions to poetry exchange and requests for advice regarding her own writing, likely to her mentor and protector, Domenico Venier (VI, XLI, XLIX). Additionally, in letters addressed to other unnamed patrician men, she assumed an authoritative voice that emphasized her intellectual inclination and moralist aspiration (XVII, XXI). Many of the letters serve to modify the stereotypical notion of the courtesan as greedy and exclusively sexual; yet, importantly, Franco did not distance herself from her roles as woman and mother. In a congratulatory letter to a new mother upon the birth of her baby son (XVI), Franco spoke as a woman experienced in the "pain and fatigue of childbirth" ("le fatiche e doglie del [. . .] parto"), and in another she referenced caring for her children sick with smallpox and how such a responsibility kept her from her correspondence and editing duties (XXXIX). In several letters she alluded to the reality of her profession, in which her livelihood and reputation are dependent on male public opinion, either slander or defense (XXXI, XLVII). Franco addressed most directly the harsh realities of sex work in the well-known letter in which she warned a mother against facilitating her own daughter's courtesanry (XXII).

In October 1580, the same year of the publication of *Lettere*, Franco was summoned to defend herself in front of the Inquisition courts of Venice against charges of her engagement in magical incantations—in short, witchcraft.[62] It would be revealed that her accuser was Ridolfo Vannitelli, her children's tutor, who Franco had suspected of having conspired with other servants in robbing her.[63] Furthermore, during Venice's devastating plague outbreak of 1575 to 1577, Franco was forced to flee Venice, resulting not only in the loss of income but additionally the looting of her home and possessions, which she explained in her

1577 petition to the Venetian council for the founding of the Casa del Soccorso.[64] Just two years after the publication of *Lettere*, in a tax declaration, Franco's residence was listed in the San Samuele district where the poorest prostitutes lived.[65]

These significant personal difficulties were met with what we can imagine as considerable obstacles to getting *Lettere* published. The Tridentine Council's chilling effects on the printing industry were worsened by the plague of 1575 to 1577.[66] The frontispiece to *Lettere* indicates neither the publisher nor place of publication, and the *privilegio*, or copyright, is also absent, all of which establish that the work was self-published; and Franco's demonstrated financial struggles at the time make it probable that she had to secure private subvention to fund the volume's publication.[67] Financial strain coupled with the Inquisition's damage to her reputation, her acquittal notwithstanding, suggest that Franco had quite a lot riding on the publication and success of *Lettere*. She reveals a desire to make her private experiences public, yet she did not write the salacious confessions of a courtesan. In fact, the frank sexuality found in her *Terze rime* (1575) is lacking in the "familiar" epistolary form, and she also eschews the popular publishing trend of love letter collections featuring lovelorn women.[68] In this collection, Franco exploits the "familiar" format by assuming a serious rhetorical stance to establish literary authority. Through her *Lettere*, Franco exits the enclosed space of the *ridotto* (salon) to address a wider public by assuming a traditionally male didactic role and displaying her mastery of an ancient literary genre dominated by men.[69] During the Renaissance the letter was often used as a vehicle for self-promotion, as is most obvious in the case of Pietro Aretino, and Franco certainly sought to promote herself with her letterbook. The format allows her to showcase her erudition and rhetorical skill as well as her extensive web of contacts among Venice's patriciate, whom she often addresses anonymously under the cloak of stern moral authority.

Franco's *Lettere*, I argue, also transcends strictly literary and self-promotional functions; her epistolary participation constitutes a politically significant act. The literary and moral authority Franco assumed through the guise of the intimacy of the "familiar" letter provided her with the necessary cover to express her concerns without implicating anyone in particular. The letters represent a public statement regarding gender and other issues of equality as they relate to political and power structures in Venice. As I emphasize in my analyses, Franco used the genre to insert herself into political affairs, confront politically unsavory topics, and take controversial positions, particularly in regard to gender inequity and perceived hypocrisy.[70] Franco's *Lettere* has garnered a considerable amount of critical attention in the last few decades,[71] and my hope with the following discussion is to add to the conversation by reframing Franco's epistolary collection in order to emphasize its political significance and undertones.

In Franco's letters she revealed a shrewd understanding of the political importance, and perhaps impertinence, of revealing her personal contact with political and consequential figures in a public forum. As Rosenthal argued, many of the letters to anonymous men include just enough information to make the intended recipient identifiable.[72] Franco thus maintained discretion while also reaping the cachet through her association with influential figures, such as Domenico Venier, Estor and Francesco Martinengo, and others. The most obvious example of Franco's political intent is found in the letters and accompanying sonnets dedicated to Henri III of Valois, future king of France (I, II). In July 1574, en route to Paris from Warsaw, where he had been crowned king of Poland in 1573, Henri enjoyed a protracted ten-day stay in Venice, during which Franco actively participated in his entertainment. Catherine de' Medici, Henri's mother, had insisted on his prompt return to Paris in order to seize the throne following the death of his older brother, Charles IX, the urgency of the matter being rooted in the fear that Henri's younger brother (and protestant sympathizer), François, duke of Alençon, would make a play for the crown.[73] His route avoided Protestant Northern Europe in lieu of the long, indirect journey back to Paris via Italy, yet there were still considerable dangers facing Henri along the way, which made every stop on his trip consequential for both the king[74] and the states that provided him safe passage and hospitality. Contemporary accounts indicate the unprecedented enthusiasm expressed by the Venetian Signoria at the prospect of the Henri's visit: "[La] Illustrissima Signoria di Venetia si rallegrò di questa venuta, piú che mai facesse, per la venuta di qual sia voglia altro Prencipe (The most Illustrious Signoria of Venice rejoiced in this visit as it never had before for the visit of any other prince).[75]

During Henri's lengthy stay in Venice, the Serenissima spared no expense. The festivals and events it arranged to honor the future Henri III were the most lavish ever seen in Venice until that time.[76] The triumphal entry of France's future king included a rush of entertainment by Venice's most renowned artists, including the "most pleasant surprise" (la più gradita sorpresa) of a performance by the renowned Gelosi troupe featuring Francesco and Isabella Andreini, who were called to Venice for the occasion to perform a tragedy composed by Cornelio Frangipani, with music set by Claudio Merulo.[77] Balls and banquets abounded. The grand finale, held at the Palazzo Ducale on the penultimate day of Henri's visit, presented an elaborate collation featuring over 1,260 confections, accompanied by hundreds of exquisite and artistically significant sugar sculptures made using molds of Venice's most renowned sculptors, Jacopo Sansovino and Danese Cattaneo.[78]

These sweet edibles reflect the overall sensual and eroticized display Venice offered the king, which included secluding him—as the only man—among a group of two hundred bejeweled noblewomen. Though the female bodies of these respectable noblewomen were not literally available to Henri, such a gesture, in the presence of the edible desserts, conveys Venice's overarching message regarding "the carnal availability of ladies, whose flesh could be tasted/kissed, like those desserts that they ate with the king."[79] This display, in the Palazzo Ducale, the home of Venice's body politic, emphasized that the civic identity of the Serenissima was built on its long association with Venus. Many of the details of this and all other official events of Henri's visit are detailed in Tommaso Porcacchi's *Le Attioni d'Arrigo Terzo Re di Francia, et Quarto di Polonia, descritte in dialogo* (1574), which predictably makes no mention of Henri's sexual encounter with Franco. This silence of the official record is what Franco's publication of her letter to Henri corrects.

Franco's letters and sonnets to Henri III align stylistically with the requisite highly laudatory style suitable to addressing a prince, which, to modern sensibilities, betrays insincerity and formulaic flattery.[80] For example, Franco is predictably (if exceedingly) self-deprecatory, insisting on her own unworthiness as well as that of the very letter she has set out to publish (and hopefully profit from), declaiming "for what can be born from me worthy of the supreme height of your heavenly soul and your fate?" (imperoché qual cosa può nascere da me che sia degna della suprema altezza dell'animo suo celeste e della sua beata fortuna?).[81] Insinuating one thing by declaring the opposite indicates Franco's familiarity with and mastery of the decorous, dissembling language of the court, and testifies to her political savvy and diplomatic adjacency.[82] Franco, however, did not speak of politics directly, evoking instead a strikingly personal tone that suggests intimacy and rapport within the letters. For example, in the first line of her first letter to Henri, Franco wrote: "to the immensely high favor that Your Majesty deigned to show me, coming to *my humble house*" (all'altissimo favor che la Vostra Maestà s'è degnata di farmi, venendo all'*umile abitazione mia*)."[83] What is remarkable is not what she says, but the fact that she says it at all in a public letter. In placing the future king of France in her "humble house," echoed twice in the accompanying sonnet to Henri—"umil tetto" (humble roof) and "mio povero ricetto" (my poor dwelling)—Franco is also claiming the importance of herself, her body, and its dwelling/space, to Venice's diplomatic, political, and cultural affairs. Refusing to be marginalized and silenced as a mere tourist attraction, Franco's publicizing of the event, and the insinuation of her sexual encounter with Henri, is necessarily political in its implications. In her writing, Franco's body substitutes for that of Venus, the feminized and eroticized allegory of Venice's body politic, and Henri, as soon-to-be regent, represents the French body politic. Their encounter is thus a symbolic meeting of the two states—a carnal diplomacy representing goodwill, affection, and allegiance.

In publicly associating herself with Henri, Franco revealed her covert service on behalf of Venice. No source before Franco's letter and sonnets reported their encounter.[84] Franco's activities with Henri III, however, must have been condoned and likely even facilitated by the Venetian government, which was nonetheless loath to recognize her "collaboration" officially.[85] Perhaps, as Margaret Rosenthal inferred, these letters to Henri were not written originally for inclusion in her own volume of *Lettere*, but were instead intended to be part of an edition honoring the future king and commemorating his visit to Venice.[86] In addition to the letter addressed to Henri occupying the first and most prominent position in the collection, it also functions as a second dedicatory letter. The letter's dedication to Henri, "All'Invittissimo e Cristianissimo Re Enrico III di Francia e I di Polonia," not only echoes the volume's official dedication to Cardinal Luigi d'Este, but it also essentially supplants it because of the superior stature of the king over Luigi d'Este, his crown cardinal. Furthermore, within the letter itself Franco refers to a book she intended to dedicate to the king: "Né posso con alcuna maniera di ringraziamento supplire in parte all'infinito merito delle sue benigne e graziose offerte fattemi nel proposito *del libro ch'io sono per dedicarle*" (Nor can I compensate even partly with any form of thanks for the infinite merit of the kindly and gracious offers you made to me on the subject of this book, which I am about to dedicate to you).[87] These amount to clues left behind by Franco to signal her thwarted intentions of publicly collaborating, in the company of Venice's prominent noblemen, on such an important project of cultural diplomacy.

This hypothesis allows for a more nuanced interpretation of the possible motivations behind Franco's publication of the letters and sonnets. One clear reason for publishing the texts for Henri was undoubtedly self-promotional. The validation and cultural capital Franco would have gained from being recognized as the courtesan selected by a king would have been too great to forgo. Given its similarity to the edition she was selected to curate in honor of deceased Venetian military hero Estor Martinengo,[88] the only edition of its kind in this period to have been curated by a woman,[89] it is reasonable to assume that Franco would have enthusiastically joined other poets in contributing to such a project.[90] It is also reasonable to presume that Franco's participation would have been excluded or concealed from this official, not to mention "distinguished and politically strategic edition,"[91] which would have rendered transparent the association between the courtesan and the same structures of power that discipline and controlled her. In this light, Franco's decision to publish the letters independently could very well have been a direct response to having been excluded from this endeavor, as well as an act of protest against the hypocrisy of such an exclusion. Her services as courtesan were likely requested as symbolic of Venetian hospitality, yet the sexual and illicit nature of those same services was precisely what precluded her from being part of the official story of the event; a true indication that the elite status of the courtesan was a fictional one. Her collaboration was permissible for the Martinengo edition, a text meant mostly for domestic consumption, but the international scope and diplomatic and political consequences of a courtesan's contribution to an edition honoring Henri's royal visit were likely too great. In France, in fact, rumors about Henri's Venetian dalliances proved problematic. The king's inability to produce an heir fueled rumors among his Protestant enemies that he had contracted syphilis while in Venice, resulting in sterility.[92]

Franco's probable exclusion from such a literary project serves to uncover the fictional status that she and all courtesans inhabited within Venetian culture and power structures. Her services were desired but repressed by the elite, which never officially admitted her to their ranks. Public and print references to Franco were limited to satire and invective. In fact, during her lifetime, there never appeared published praise of Franco by a Venetian patrician.[93] Not even Domenico Venier, her protector and advisor, ever acknowledged Franco in print, though he successfully vouched for her at her Inquisition trial. Franco's letters thus, in addition to their self-promotional function, could be seen as retaliation for the attempted erasure of her valuable diplomatic and cultural efforts. Just as the courtesan was banished from spaces of civic and religious importance by legal decree, this instance of probable literary (or cultural) exclusion is consistent with these other attempts by the Venetian power structures to contain the courtesan and her body. By self-publishing her letters, Franco reinstated herself, via literary production, into the political discourse as a significant political agent.

Franco's claiming of political agency through the letters, however, was not only tied to international heads of state and local noblemen. Quite different in tone and content, Veronica Franco's letter 22 addressed a much humbler subject, a mother who was considering facilitating her own daughter's prostitution. In the opening lines of Franco's letter to a mother who was considering enabling, or even possibly forcing, her daughter's entrance into prostitution, she characterized her response as an "*officio*" (a duty) done out of "*obligo all'umanità*" (an obligation to humanity).[94] This language emphasizes the seriousness and dignity of both her literary undertaking as well as of the subject of her letter: a (potential) prostitute. It is unsurprising that, unlike anti-prostitute satirical and invective texts, Franco never used the pejorative term *puttana* (whore), yet she also never employs *meretrice* (prostitute), resorting instead to circumlocution—"femina del mondo" (literally, "woman of the world," used to indicate a prostitute) and "donne di quest'essercizio" (women of this occupation)—to imply prostitution, but not state it explicitly.[95] This rhetorical evasion has the effect of humanizing the prostitute, identifying her first as a *donna* or *femina* who is part of the female community, rather than identifying her exclusively with her corporeal occupation.

Even the more neutral term *meretrice* echoes the punitive and restrictive legal and "scientific" documents, whose language removes the *meretrice* from any association with health and decency by inextricably linking sex workers with inferior, blameworthy, and immoral agents of disease and social destruction, rather than with human beings and members of society. We recall the physician Pietro Rostinio's striking juxtaposition of terms in his discussion of the origin of syphilis, located in the "meretrice bellissima" whose alluringly deceitful appearance hides her putrid and contagious reproductive system: "una meretrice bellissima, la quale nella bocca della matrice haveva una apostema putrefatta" (a very beautiful prostitute who had at the mouth of her uterus a putrid abscess).[96] The diseased body of the "meretrice" in Rostinio reflects the language of the Venetian statute barring prostitutes from churches, in which the allegation of moral indecency is also contagious: "Che *alcuna meretrice over Cortesana sia di che conditione esser si voglia* [. . .] *debbono star separate et lontane* da quelle acciò non diano scandalo alle altre persone da bene et di buona vita (*Any prostitute or courtesan, whatever her condition may be* [. . .] *must remain separate and distant* from churches so that they do not scandalize the other decent and respectable people; italics added).[97]

Through this letter Franco introduces the prostitute's body into discourse and thereby reclaims both voice and image. Publishing the letter achieves what the body of the prostitute could not: circulation among the "buona vita." This contact, facilitated by Franco's writing, confronted Venetian citizenry with the realities of prostitution, rather than using the practice as fodder for mockery and vituperation. In exposing the mechanisms of prostitution and portraying the prostitute as an innocent victim, Franco countered the literary subgenre that attacked and denigrated the figure of the courtesan. Franco's defense of the prostitute is humanist in orientation; refined linguistically and literarily as well as morally; and measured and serious in tone. In contrast, male-authored (most often in Venetian dialect) Renaissance literary and legal attacks on courtesans, abusive and pornographic in their vulgarity, can generally be considered attempts to reduce the courtesan to a purely bodily existence; in other words, these rhetorical and intellectual attacks sought to emphasize only the corporeal, nearly animalistic aspects of the prostitute.[98] Other such attempts in more formal venues, such as Inquisition hearings, were similar in this regard, claiming that a courtesan (though often educated and in the company of the socially elite) was a mere "pubblica meretrice."[99] This is essentially no different from Maffeo Venier's denigrating Veronica Franco in his poetic invective as "*ver unica puttana*" (veritably unique whore).[100]

Rather than "othering" the prostitute, Franco's letter centered on the suffering of the human body in sexual servitude. The prostitute, forced to exploit her own body for a living, was simultaneously forced to relinquish any sort of ownership over it, even at the most basic levels of health, clothing, basic survival, and sustenance. The paradox of prostitution lay in the exploitation of the body, which reduced women to a purely corporeal identity and yet also disowned her of that body, the only thing over which theoretically she could exert any control. In practice, the body of the prostitute was relinquished to "another" (altrui):[101]

> Troppo infelice cosa e troppo contraria al senso umano è l'obligar il corpo e l'industria di una tal servitú che spaventa solamente a pensarne. Darsi in preda di tanti, con rischio d'esser dispogliata, d'esser rubbata, d'esser uccisa, ch'un solo un dí ti toglia quanto con molti in molto tempo hai acquistato, con tant'altri pericoli d'ingiurie e di'infermità contagiose e spaventose; mangiar con l'*altrui* bocca, dormir con gli occhi *altrui*, muoversi secondo l'*altrui* desiderio, correndo in manifesto naufragio sempre

della facoltà e della vita: qual maggior miseria? quai ricchezze, quai commodità, quai delizie posson acquistar un tanto peso? (italics added)[102]

(It's a most wretched thing, contrary to human reason, to subject one's body and labor to a slavery terrifying even to think of. To make oneself prey to so many men, at the risk of being stripped, robbed, even killed, so that one man, one day, may snatch away everything you've acquired from many over such a long time, along with so many other dangers of injury and dreadful contagious diseases; to eat with *another's* mouth, sleep with *another's* eyes, move according to *another's* will, obviously rushing toward the shipwreck of your mind and your body: What greater misery? What wealth, what luxuries, what delights can outweigh all this?)

In this harsh description, Franco was clear to equate prostitution with servitude, leaving little room for an interpretation that allowed for the consideration of prostitution as an exercise of free will or a profession whose rewards warranted the inevitable sacrifices. The prostitute was the victim, the "prey," whose daily existence entailed running the risk of death, theft, and illnesses both contagious and horrific, among other sufferings. This description of prostitution was thus an inversion of the legal statutes and anti-prostitute texts discussed previously, which were precise in locating the threat of illness and other forces destructive to the body politic as *within* and inherent to the body of the prostitute. The body of the prostitute was the source, not the victim, of all contamination and societal ills. By refuting the animalistic attacks by male poets, here Franco aligned the prostitute with the most vulnerable animal of the hierarchy. In doing so, she revealed the inhumanity and savage tendencies of the prostitute's predators, both her male clients/abusers as well as the larger social structure that denied her refuge and profits from her exploitation.

Besides humanizing the prostitute by positioning her as victim rather than agent, Franco also rhetorically included the body of the prostitute within the fundamental unit of Venetian society: the family. Franco never labeled the prostitute as such, but instead referred to her as "vostra figliuola," a diminutive and therefore more intimate and affectionate form of *vostra figlia* (your daughter).[103] By addressing the letter to an anonymous mother, Franco addressed it to all of Venice and invited all the citizenry to consider the possibility that the anonymous "figliuola" could be their own. Franco also implicated the essential role

Venice, and its institutions, played in the care for its "figliuole" through the Casa delle Zitelle (spelled "Citelle" in Venetian dialect). Franco mentioned this institution as one of the only possible ways "to protect her virginity" (*aver cura della sua virginità*) from the insidious threats to unprotected women, "figliuola" and her mother alike: "'L mondo è così pericoloso e così fragile, e che le case delle povere madri non son punto sicure all'insidie amorose dell'appetitosa gioventú [. . .] m'offersi d'adoperarmi con ogni mezo possibile perch'ella fosse accettata nella Casa delle Citelle" (Since this world is so full of dangers and so uncertain, and the houses of poor mothers are never safe from the amorous maneuvers of lustful young men [. . .] I offered you all the help I could, to assure that she'd be accepted into the Casa delle Zitelle).[104]

The cause of prostitution is thus not the moral failing of the individual woman or her impoverished family, but instead a result of "this world [. . .] so full of dangers and so uncertain"—in other words, failures at the societal level. By naming the Casa delle Zitelle, Franco indicated that the issue of prostitution was systemic in Venice, pervasive enough to require the establishment of institutions to contain its reach and remedy its ills, and thus it could not be considered a problem limited to any one family or group. The two spaces mentioned in the letter are placed in contrast. The Casa delle Zitelle was an institution that protected young women from the dangerous city itself, whereas the private homes of poor mothers ("case delle povere madri") were vulnerable ("insicure"), like the preyed-on body of the prostitute. This amounted to an inversion of the type of legal and moralistic language that identified the prostitute as a threat to the health, moral and physical, of the city. On the contrary, Franco claimed that the dangerous and uncertain "world" ("mondo") is what threatened to violate the bodies and homes of Venice's vulnerable women.

Institutions such as the Casa delle Zitelle and the Casa delle Convertite suggest the fundamental role that Venice and its charitable arms played in the facilitation or avoidance of prostitution. The Venetian government was thus indirectly exhorted to assume responsibility for the care of its "figliuole," and ensure their virginity. Yet, Venice had a conflict of interest. While its institutions were the only bodies powerful enough to successfully safeguard vulnerable women from prostitution, Venice also profited from the sex trade, as discussed earlier. Like the mother to whom the letter was addressed, who would profit from the sale of her daughter's body, Venice, through its taxation of prostitution, enriched itself on the prostitutes' bodies.

Franco invited the reader to take a second look at the body of the prostitute, beyond the superficial vulgarity that facilitated its "sale" on the market: "con tutte quell'altre apparenze e con tutti quegl'altri abbellimenti che s'usando di fare perché *la mercanzia trovi concorrenza nello spedersi*" (with [. . .] every other embellishment people use to make their merchandise measure up to the competition).[105] Thus the body of the prostitute was not to be ostracized from human society as a mere product for sale ("mercanzia"). It had to be considered beyond its embellishments ("apparenze," "abbellimenti") and instead as a "figliuola," a member of the family unit as well as the body politic at large. The well-being, or lack thereof, of a "figiuola" could not be separated from the overall health and integrity of Venice.

Franco placed blame explicitly on the mother to whom she addressed her letter and did not implicate the Venetian state openly.

> E se ben primieramente si tratta l'interesse di vostra figliuola, io parlo della vostra persona, perché, s'ella diventasse femina del mondo, voi diventereste sua messaggiera col mondo e sareste da punir acerbamente, dove forse il fallo di lei sarebbe non del tutto incapace di scusa, fondata sopra le vostre colpe.[106]

> (Although it's mainly a question of your daughter's well-being, I'm talking about you as well, for her ruin cannot be separated from yours. And because you're her mother, if she should become a prostitute, you'd become her go-between and deserve the harshest punishment, whereas her error wouldn't perhaps be entirely inexcusable because it would have been caused by your wrongdoing).

She accuses the mother of acting as her own daughter's "messaggiera," procuress, and then likens her via metaphor to a butcher: "Non sostenete che non pur le carni della misera vostra figliuola si squarcino e si vendano, ma d'esserne voi stessa il macellaio" (Don't allow the flesh of your wretched daughter not only to be cut into pieces and sold but you yourself to become her butcher).[107] Franco inculpated the mother of a prospective prostitute by labeling her the "messaggiera," or "ruffiana," the figure who would also benefit monetarily from the prostitution. I suggest that, by logical extension, Franco implicated all bodies that profit from the sale of the "merchandise" ("mercanzia") of the female body, including Venice itself, a society whose economy was consumption and commerce.[108] By addressing one mother in a public letter, Franco spoke at once to all mothers and to collective civic bodies as well. This criticism was at once incisive and diplomatic. Franco urged the reader to look closer at the larger ecosystem, beyond questions of personal morality, to examine and recognize the hypocrisy of the entire society.

Through the metaphor of the virginal body of Venice, it is possible to read this letter as one written to Venice itself. The body of the mother acts as stand-in for the collective civic Venetian body, and just as the body of the mother is corrupted along with that of her daughter, so is that of Venice: "Io parlo della vostra persona, perché la rovina di lei non può esser separata dalla vostra" (I'm talking about you, as well, for her ruin cannot be separated from yours). The city of Venice was thus equated with the "messaggiera," the party that facilitated the exchange and the prostitution of Venice at the same time. Although it is unlikely that Franco was deliberately referring to a link between the figures of the "mezzana" and the "messaggiera"—in other words, an association between the pimp and the ambassador—her semantic choice indicates a point of confluence between the two figures. In employing the term "messaggiera," Franco suggested "mezzana," procuress. Just as Tasso linked the *messaggiero* ("ambassador") with the pimp ("ruffian"), here Franco substituted a term more exclusive to the sex trade (such as *mezzana* or *ruffiana*) with an otherwise bureaucratic one, "messaggiera."

Franco's "messaggiera" was not interested in the maintenance of the virginity of its "femine del mondo" precisely because she profited from the sale of her body. Instead, the role of the mother was to act as the opposite of the "messaggiera": "Voi sapete quante volte io v'abbia pregata ed ammonita ad aver cura della sua virginità; e poi il mondo è così pericoloso e così fragile" (You know how often I've begged and warned you to protect her virginity; and since this world is so full of dangers and so uncertain).[109] This is similar to the link between female virginity and the symbolic representation of Venice as a beautiful blonde virgin. Just as a mother ruined herself by allowing her daughter to become a "femina del mondo," a state that allowed and profited from the prostitution of its women and girls was thus guilty of prostituting itself as well. Or it could be considered guilty of exploiting its daughters while maintaining and reinforcing a pristine image.

Whereas legal statutes and spatial isolation focused on the body of the prostitute, Franco made clear that it was not the prostitute alone who actively chose to sell herself. There remained the necessity of a "messaggiera," who was but one part of a larger collective community that enabled, encouraged, and profited from prostitution. This was not, however, a misogynous implication of the mother figure alone, but any person or entity involved. In speaking about prostitution with the metaphor of literal carnal commerce, it is the *macellaio* (butcher) who kills, butchers, appropriates, and profits from the sale of the flesh of innocent animals. If there were no buyers, there would be no butchers. Franco implied a network of commerce that was at the root of the victimization and expropriation of the body of the prostitute.

I agree with Jutta Sperling[110] and Margaret Rosenthal,[111] whose interpretations of Franco's writings emphasize her self-representation as an "exception" to the horrors of prostitution, as well as her sense of responsibility to denounce both the miseries and realities of female subjugation via prostitution. In my reading, however, I argue additionally that implicit in Franco's commentary was a desire to extend her critique well beyond her own personal body and the "undignified servitude of the common prostitute's business."[112] In her letter, Franco implied that the prostitute could not be considered the focus of blame; like meat sold by a butcher, her body was part of a larger commercial network that implicated brokers ("messaggiere"), clients, and the state that authorized the trade. The abject poverty of some of Venice's citizens left women with few choices but to enter their body into carnal commerce. Gasparo Contarini, in his treatise *Della republica, e magistrati di Venezia* (1543), evoked the metaphor of the body politic in order to support his claim that "no class struggle divided rulers and citizens; as a pars pro toto, the functionally differentiated patrician government" led to a "harmonious integration of all components of society."[113] Thus, Franco strongly implied that this significant part of the body politic was not as integrated as a writer like Contarini would have liked to believe. The only way in which a courtesan could reintegrate herself within the body politic, gain sovereignty over her own body, and exercise this authority was via literature. In her letters, Franco reestablished the body of the prostitute and assumed its voice on behalf of all "femine del mondo." Rather than defining the body of the prostitute as a vector for the transmission of disease and the object that elicited destructive desire in men, Franco established it as a vulnerable locus of suffering and estrangement. In writing as a prostitute of this suffering and estrangement in a public and literary forum, Franco advocated for her political worth, and in doing so, reunited the corporeal with the intellectual, the body with the politic.

Notes

Introduction

1. Gasparo Bragaccia, *L'Ambasciatore. Opera divisa in libri sei. Nella quale si hanno avvertimenti Politici, & Morali per gli Ambasciatori, & intorno quelle cose, che sogliono accadere all'Ambasciarie. Utilissima alla Gioventù, così di Republica, come di Corte, che pretenda di salire per questa più breve via à gli honori, et principali dignità. Tratta dalla Pratica, confermata dalla Civile, e Morale, & coll'Historia illustrata* (Padua: Francesco Bolzetta, 1626), 61. All translations from this text are my own.

2. See *A Latin Dictionary*, comp. Charlton T. Lewis and Charles Short (Oxford: Clarendon Press, 1945), s.v. "ambactus."

3. Bragaccia, *L'Ambasciatore*, 61.

4. Bragaccia, *L'Ambasciatore*, 66, 61, 64–65.

5. Bragaccia, *L'Ambasciatore*, 68.

6. Bragaccia, *L'Ambasciatore*, 61.

7. In addition to Bragaccia, other authors of such texts include Ermolao Barbaro, Etiénne Dolet, Alberico Gentile, Jean Hotman, Hugo Grotius, and Juan Antonio de Vera y Zuñiga, to name only a few.

8. Patricia Fortini Brown, *Private Lives in Renaissance Venice* (New Haven, CT: Yale University Press, 2004), 163.

9. The term *cortigiana* appears as the female variant of *cortigiano* as a synonym for *femmina di mondo* (literally, "woman of the world," connoting "whore") in the second edition of *La Crusca* (1623): "E cortigiana diciamo a femmina di Mondo." See *Vocabolario degli Accademici della Crusca*, 5th ed., in *Lessicografia della Crusca in Rete* (Florence: Accademia della Crusca, 2000–2004), s.v. "cortegiano" §1, http://www.lessicografia.it/; and *Queen Anna's New World of Words, or, Dictionarie of the Italian and English Tongues, Collected and newly much augmented by Iohn Florio* (London, 1611), s.v. "Cortegiana: a curtezan, a strumpet."

10. Marin Sanudo, *I Diarii*, ed. Rinaldo Fulin, et al. (Venice: F. Visentini. 1879–1903), 19:138; and Sanudo, *Venice, Città Excelentissima: Selections from the Renaissance Diaries of Marin Sanudo*, eds. Patricia H. Labalme and Laura Sanguineti White, trans. Linda Carroll (Baltimore: Johns Hopkins University Press, 2008), 322.

11. For a discussion of the "irreducible ambiguity" and its effect on terminology referring to Renaissance prostitutes, see Elizabeth S. Cohen, "'Courtesans' and 'Whores': Words and Behavior in Roman Streets," *Women's Studies* 19 (1991): 201–208.

12. Brown, *Private Lives*, 170.

13. Timothy Hampton, *Fictions of Embassy: Literature and Diplomacy in Early Modern Europe* (Ithaca, NY: Cornell University Press, 2009), 9.

14. Elizabeth Horodowich, *Language and Statecraft in Early Modern Venice* (New York: Cambridge University Press, 2008), 200.

15. Although recent scholarship has focused on the cross-cultural and transhistorical phenomenon of courtesanship, the historical and geographical parameters of this study dictate that I limit my attention to the courtesan who flourished in Renaissance Italy. For an excellent collection of essays on the courtesan writ large, see Martha Feldman and Bonnie Gordon, eds., *The Courtesan's Arts: Cross-Cultural Perspectives* (Oxford: Oxford University Press, 2006).

16. Virginia Cox, *A Short History of the Italian Renaissance* (New York: I. B. Tauris, 2016), 191.

17. Feldman and Gordon, Introduction to *Courtesan's Arts*, 6.

18. This lexical link, "courtiers (*cortigiani*) are whores (*cortigiane*), whores are courtiers," is addressed by Paula Findlen in "Humanism, Politics and Pornography in Renaissance Italy," in *The Invention of Pornography: Obscenity and the Origins of Modernity, 1500–1800*, ed. Lynn Hunt (New York: Zone Books, 1993), 99.

19. See Courtney Quaintance, *Textual Masculinity and the Exchange of Women in Renaissance Venice* (Toronto: University of Toronto Press, 2015), 12–21; Paola Ugolini, *The Court and Its Critics: Anti-Court Sentiments in Early Modern Italy* (Toronto: University of Toronto Press, 2020), 75–76; and Guido Ruggiero, *The Renaissance in Italy* (Cambridge, UK: Cambridge University Press, 2015), 434–437.

20. See Ugolini, Introduction to *The Court and Its Critics*, 4.

21. Feldman and Gordon, Introduction to *Courtesan's Arts*, 6.

22. Feldman and Gordon, Introduction to *Courtesan's Arts*, 6.

23. Tessa Storey, "Courtesan Culture: Manhood, Honor, and Sociability," in *Erotic Cultures of Renaissance Italy*, ed. Sara F. Matthews-Grieco (Burlington, VT: Ashgate, 2010), 247.

24. See Garrett Mattingly, "The First Resident Embassies: Medieval Italian Origins of Modern Diplomacy," *Speculum* 2, no. 4 (October 1937): 423–439; and Mattingly, "The Renaissance Environment," in *Renaissance Diplomacy* (Boston: Houghton Mifflin, 1955), 47–54.

25. Douglas Biow, "Exemplary Work: Two Venetian Humanists Writing on the Resident Ambassador," in *Doctors, Ambassadors, Secretaries: Humanism and Professions in Renaissance Italy* (Chicago: University of Chicago Press, 2002), 102–104.

26. Mattingly, *Renaissance Diplomacy*, 44.

27. Biow, "Exemplary Work," 104. Though here Biow refers specifically to the Venetian context, this characterization can be applied more broadly to refer to the charge and expectations of Renaissance ambassadors.

28. See Biow, "Exemplary Work," 103. Biow discusses the work of Donald Queller in dispelling the myth of the Venetian patriciate's selflessness and patriotism. See also Queller, *The Venetian Patriciate: Reality versus Myth* (Champaign-Urbana: University of Illinois Press, 1986).

29. John Jeffries Martin, *Myths of Renaissance Individualism* (Basingstoke, UK: Palgrave Macmillan, 2004), ix.

30. Martin, *Myths of Renaissance Individualism*, x.

31. Jacob Burckhardt, *The Civilization of the Renaissance in Italy*, trans. S.G.C. Middlemore (1860; New York: Macmillan, 1921), 128. Burkhardt proceeds to claim that before the Renaissance, a person was denied individual identity and instead was "conscious [. . .] only as a member of a race, people, party, family, or corporation—only through some general category." More recent scholarship has demonstrated the invalidity of Burckhardt's determination that the birthplace of modern individualism occurred during the Italian Renaissance. Although the remarkable evidence of talent and creative production in Italy during the Renaissance can be construed as evidence that the makers and subjects of those works shared the impulse toward willful and autonomous self-expression, characteristics now ascribed to modern Western individualism, historians have since demonstrated that people in the Renaissance, despite evidence of their aspirations toward a demonstration of uniqueness, were still beholden to their collective identities and still derived their sense of self in a more relational way. See Martin, *Myths of Renaissance Individualism*; Martin, "The Myth of Renaissance Individualism," in *A Companion to the Worlds of the Renaissance*, ed. Guido Ruggiero (Oxford: Blackwell Publishing, 2002), 208–224; and Cox, *A Short History of the Italian Renaissance*, 110–131.

32. Steven Greenblatt, *Renaissance Self-Fashioning from More to Shakespeare* (1980; Chicago: University of Chicago Press, 2005), 256–257.

33. Cox, *Short History of the Italian Renaissance*, 124.

34. Martin, *Myths of Renaissance Individualism*, 8.

35. Timothy Hampton, "Baroque Diplomacy," in *The Oxford Handbook of the Baroque*, ed. John D. Lyons (Oxford: Oxford University Press, 2019), 734.

36. See Riccardo Fubini, "The Italian League and the Policy of the Balance of Power at the Accession of Lorenzo de' Medici," *Journal of Modern History* 67 (December 1995): S166–S199.

37. Giulio Andreotti, *"Presentazione" to L'Ambasciatore* (Rome: Vecchiarelli, 1989), vi.

38. Hampton, "Baroque Diplomacy," 735.

39. I borrow the term "invented" from a subheading, "The Invention of the Courtesan," found in Guido Ruggiero's "Discovery: Finding the Old in the New (c. 1450–c. 1560)," in *The Renaissance in Italy*, 434–437.

40. Maristella De P. Lorch, "The Epicurean in Lorenzo Valla's *On Pleasure*," in *Atoms, Pneuma, and Tranquillity: Epicurean and Stoic Themes in European Thought*, ed. Margaret J. Osler (Cambridge, UK: Cambridge University Press, 1991), 90.

41. Lorenzo Valla, *On Pleasure: De Voluptate (Of the True and the False Good)*, ed. Marstella Lorch, trans. A. Kent Hieatt and Maristella Lorch (New York: Albaris Books, 1977), 119.

42. Tessa Storey, "Courtesan Culture: Manhood, Honour, and Sociability," in *Erotic Cultures in Renaissance Italy*, ed. Sara F. Matthews-Grieco (Burlington, VT: Ashgate, 2010), 253.

43. Storey, "Courtesan Culture," 250.

44. Torquato Tasso, "Il Messaggiero," in *Opere*, ed. Bruno Maier (Milan: Rizzoli, 1964), 4:716.

45. Timothy Hampton, *Fictions of Embassy*, 198n8.

46. Martin, *Myths of Renaissance Individualism*, 14–15.

47. Hampton, *Fictions of Embassy*, 11.

48. Greenblatt, *Renaissance Self-Fashioning*, 21.

Chapter 1 From Mind to Body

1. Venetian legislation as far back as 1268 required that returning diplomats issue a written report of their mission and findings, which was then delivered orally. See Isabella Lazzarini, *Communication and Conflict: Italian Diplomacy in the Early Renaissance, 1350–1520* (Oxford: Oxford University Press), 55.

2. Donald Queller, "The Development of Ambassadorial *Relazioni*,"in *Renaissance Venice*, ed. John R. Hale (Totowa, NJ: Rowman & Littlefield, 1973), 176.

3. In addition to the first early modern treatises in the fifteenth century, diplomatic treatises flourished in the later sixteenth and seventeenth centuries, such as Étienne Dolet's *De officio legati* (1541); Ottaviano Maggio's *De legato* (1566); Alberico Gentili's *De legationibus libri tres* (1582) and *De iure belli* (1598); and Hugo Grotius's *De iure belli ac pacis* (1625). These texts were significant to the professionalization of the office of ambassador and the eventual triumph of diplomacy in the seventeenth century with the Peace of Westphalia, which was negotiated entirely by diplomats rather than a result of conquest by military combatants.

4. Betty Behrens, "Treatises on the Ambassador Written in the Fifteenth and Early Sixteenth Centuries," *English Historical Review* 51 (1936), 616–627.

5. Fubini, "Diplomacy and Government," 31.

6. Fubini, "Diplomacy and Government," 33; Behrens, "Treatises on the Ambassador," 622.

7. Fubini, "Diplomacy and Government," 30; Ermolao Barbaro, *De coelibatu, De officio legati*, ed. Vittore Branca (Florence: Leo S. Olschki, 1969), 159: "Finis legato idem est [. . .] ut ea faciant, dicant, consultant et cogitent, quae ad optimum suae civitatis status ed retinendum et amplificandum pertinere possent iudicent."

8. Fubini, "Diplomacy and Government," 33.

9. Fubini, "Diplomacy and Government," 33.

10. For an historical survey of the evolution of *ius gentium*, see Dante Fedele, "*Ius gentium*: The Metamorphosis of a Legal Concept (Ancient Rome to Early Modern Europe)," in *Empire and Legal Thought: Ideas and Institutions from Antiquity to Modernity*, ed. Edward Cavanagh (Leiden: Brill, 2020): 214–251.

11. Fedele, "*Ius gentium*: The Metamorphosis," 214.

12. For more exhaustive discussions of *ius gentium*, both in general and with respect to early modern law and culture, see Arthur Nussbaum, *A Concise History of the Law of Nations* (New York: MacMillan, 1947), especially 23–75; Christopher N. Warren, *Literature and the Law of Nations: 1580–1680* (Oxford: Oxford University Press, 2015); and Daniela Frigo, "Ambasciatori, ambasciata e immunità diplomatiche nella letteratura politica italiana

(secc. XVII–XVIII)," *Mélanges de l'École française de Rome: Italie et Méditerranée* 119, no. 1 (2007): 31–50.

13. The Aq Qoyunlu, known in English as the White Sheep Turkmen, was a confederation of Turkmen tribes that ruled an empire in what are today parts of Iran, Iraq, eastern Anatolia, Armenia, and Azerbaijan, from ca. 1340 to the Safavid conquest in 1508 by Ismail I, the grandson of Uzun Hasan. Barbaro and Contarini's travelogues generally refer to this area as "Persia" and its ruler, Uzun Hasan, as "King of Persia" (*Re di Persia*).

14. Giosafat Barbaro, "Viaggio di Iosafa Barbaro alla Tana e nella Persia," in *Giovanni Battista Ramusio: Navigazioni e Viaggi*, ed. Marica Milanesi (Turin: Einaudi, 1988), 3:518.

15. Barbaro, "Viaggio di Iosafa Barbaro," 3:517.

16. Vuillemin notes that Contarini was confident that his account did not contain sensitive state information at the time of publishing; however, Contarini's concern was to narrate his personal experience regardless of his duty to uphold diplomatic discretion. See Pascal Vuillemin, *Une itinérance prophétique. Le voyage en Perse d'Ambrogio Contarini (1474–1477)* (Paris: Classiques Garnier, 2016).

17. Ambrogio Contarini first wrote his travelogue in 1477, the same year he returned to Venice from his arduous embassy to Persia, and it was published for the first time ten years later in Venice: *Questo e el viazo de misier Ambrogio Contarin ambasador de la Illustrissima signoria de Venezia al signor Uxuncassan Re di Persia* (Venice: Annibale Fossio, 1487).

18. Giosafat Barbaro's text was first written in 1487, and there is archival evidence that it enjoyed robust manuscript circulation (see Andrea Canova, "Letteratura di viaggio e lessico esotico: musulmano in Giosafat Barbaro," *L'Ellisse* 15, no. 1 [2020]: 37–46). Barbaro's account was first published posthumously, along with Contarini's account, in Venice by Antonio Manuzio, son of Aldus, in 1543.

19. Giovanni Battista Ramusio, *Delle navigazioni et viaggi*, 3 vols. (Venice: Giunti, 1550–1559). Contarini and Barbaro's *viaggi* were published in volume 2 (1559). Quotations are taken from the modern edition of Ramusio, Giovanni Battista Ramusio, *Navigazioni e Viaggi*, ed. Marica Milanesi (Turin: Einaudi, 1988), despite any deviations and variations from the original Venetian language editions. An indication of any such variation or deviation, if found, is indicated in a note. All translations into English are my own unless otherwise noted.

20. Ambrogio Contarini, "Viaggio di Ambrosio Contarini, ambasciatore veneziano," in Ramusio, *Navigazioni e Viaggi*, 3:632. All translations of this text are my own.

21. In his account, Barbaro mentions Contarini's name only once as part of a list of other contemporary Venetian travel writers, but there is another more oblique sign of his reclaiming of narrative territory. In his preface (*esordio*), after stating that one of the reasons for his having written his account is to "please those who will enjoy reading of new things" (a consolazione di chi si diletterà di legger cose nuove), Barbaro then writes: "I will divide my account into two parts: in the first I will narrate my travels in Tana, and in the second those in Persia; however, *in neither the first account nor the second will I include a significant discussion of the hardships, the dangers and the discomforts* that happened to me." (Onde io dividerò il parlar mio i due parti: nella prima narrerò il viaggio mio della Tana,

nella seconda quello della Persia, *non mettendo però né nell'uno né nell'altro a una gran giunta le fatiche, li pericoli e disagi* i quali mi sono occorsi.) Barbaro, "Viaggio di Iosafa Barbaro," in Ramusio, *Navigazioni e Viaggi*, 3:486; italics added. This amounts to a discreet, if uncharitable, critique of Contarini's narrative, which seems to have appeared as a bit whiny even to his contemporaries, let alone some modern readers and critics.

22. Tana indicates a settlement at the mouth of the Don River delta on the Sea of Azov in what is today Southern Russia. Italian merchants had been present in Tana, located on a Silk Road route that departed northerly from Crimea and passed through the Gobi Desert on its way to Beijing, since the thirteenth century. Venetians reestablished a settlement there as a trading outpost in the fourteenth century, which was then taken over and administered by the Genoese until it was conquered by the Ottomans in 1471. Tana was the name Italian merchants in nearby Azak (now Azov, Ukraine) gave the settlement, in the general area of the ancient Greek colony of Tanais (modern-day Rostov-on-Don). See Lorenzo Pubblici, "Venezia e il Mar d'Azov: alcune considerazioni sulla Tana nel XIV secolo," *Archivio Storico Italiano* 163, no. 3 (2005): 435–483.

23. Daria Perocco, *Viaggiare e raccontare. Narrazione di viaggio ed esperienze di racconto tra Cinque e Seicento* (Alessandria, Italy: Edizioni dell'Orso, 1997), 8 and 8n3.

24. Ugo Tucci, "Mercanti, Viaggiatori, Pellegrini nel Quattrocento," in *Storia Della Cultura Veneta*, ed. Girolamo Arnaldi and Manlio Pastore Stocchi (Vicenza: Neri Pozza, 1976), 3:317–353.

25. Perocco, *Viaggiare e raccontare*, 7.

26. Queller, "The Development of Ambassadorial *Relazioni*," 175.

27. Queller, "The Development of Ambassadorial *Relazioni*," 179.

28. Kathryn Taylor, however, has recently argued that, over the course of the sixteenth century, Venetian *relazioni* increasingly included ethnographic reporting in addition to the requisite information regarding matters of state. See Taylor, "Matters Worthy of Men of State: Ethnography and Diplomatic Reporting in Sixteenth-Century Venice," *Sixteenth Century Journal* 51, no. 3 (Fall 2020): 741–762.

29. Queller, "The Development of Ambassadorial *Relazioni*," 184.

30. Isabella Lazzarini, *Communication and Conflict: Italian Diplomacy in the Early Renaissance, 1350–1520* (Oxford: Oxford University Press, 2015), 63; Hampton, *Fictions of Embassy*, 74.

31. Deborah Howard, "The Status of the Oriental Traveler in Renaissance Venice," in *Re-orienting the Renaissance: Cultural Exchanges with the East*, ed. Gerald M. MacLean (New York: Palgrave Macmillan, 2005), 33.

32. Tucci, "Mercanti, viaggiatori, Pellegrini," 329; see also Vuillemin, *Une itinerance prophétique*, 120–122. The modern Venetian language edition (Ambrogio Contarini, "Viaggio di Ambrogio Contarini," in *I Viaggi in Persia degli ambasciatori veneti Barbaro e Contarini*, ed. Lawrence Lockhart, Roberto Morozzo della Rocca, Maria Francesa Tiepolo [Rome: Istituto Poligrafico dello Stato, 1973], 175–234) was consulted and quoted if noteworthy deviations were found between it and the modern Ramusio edition. The modern Venetian edition is considered particularly reliable as it was based on the 1487 edition published in Contarini's lifetime, which is therefore assumed to have had his approval.

33. For an example of an anonymous merchant text, see Contarini, "Viaggio d'un mercante che fu nella Persia," in Ramusio, *Navigazioni e Viaggi*, 3:425–479.

34. Howard, "Status of the Oriental Traveler," 32–33.

35. Contarini, "Viaggio di Ambrosio Contarini," in Ramusio, *Navigazioni e Viaggi*, 3:632. The spirit of Ramusio's version is consistent with Contarini's original, but there are some lexical and syntactical variations that warrant reproducing the original here: "Di tutto quello ho dicto ho cercato dire el proprio de la verità non zonzando cosa alcuna" (Of all the things I said, I tried to tell the honest truth and not invent anything). Contarini, "Viaggio di Ambrogio Contarini," in *I Viaggi in Persia*, 232. Translation is my own.

36. "Ho provato e veduto molte cose che, per non esser usitate di qua, a quelli che l'udiranno, i quali, per modo di dire, non furono mai fuori di Venezia, forse parranno bugie. E questa è stata principalmente la cagione per la quale non m'ho mai troppo curato né di scriver quello che ho veduto, né eziando di parlarne troppo" (I experienced and saw many things that are not customary here, and since those who would hear of them have never, so to speak, been out of Venice, and for this main reason I was not particularly interested in writing down or even talking about what I had seen). Giosafat Barbaro, "Viaggio di Iosafa Barbaro," in *Navigazioni e Viaggi*, ed. Giovanni Baptista Ramusio and Marica Milanesi (Turin: Einaudi, 1988), 3:485.

37. In Stefano Jossa, "The Lies of the Poets: Literature as Fiction in the Italian Renaissance," in *Renaissance Studies in Honor of Joseph Connors*, ed. Machtelt Israëls and Louis A. Waldman (Cambridge, MA: Harvard University Press, 2013), 565–573, Jossa notes that Renaissance poets were the first to "question poetry's truthfulness within poetry itself" (565). For more on the emergence in literary discourse of deceit as a vehicle for truer truth, see Jossa, "The Lies of the Poets"; and Jossa, "Da Ariosto a Tasso: la verità della storia e le bugie della poesia," *Studi rinascimentali* 1, no. 2 (2004): 79–92.

38. Ambrogio Contarini, *Viazo de misier Ambrogio Contarin ambasador de la illustrissima Signoria de Venesia al signor Uxuncassan re di Persia* (Venice: Annibale Fosio, 1487).

39. For example, see Elizabeth Hordowich, "Armchair Travelers and the Venetian Discovery of the New World," *The Sixteenth Century Journal* 36, no. 4 (Winter 2005): 1039–1062; Deborah Howard, *Venice and the East: The Impact of the Islamic World on Venetian Architecture 1100–1500* (New Haven, CT: Yale University Press, 2000), 44–48; and Howard, "Status of the Oriental Traveler," 35.

40. "La relazione, redatta in prima persona, del viaggio del Contarini in Persia *non è da annoverarsi tra le migliori dell'epoca: la persona del protagonista, le sue vicissitudini e i suoi disagi ne occupano infatti una parte troppo importante*. Essa possiede tuttavia un grande valore documentario: le capacità di osservazione del C[ontarini] sono di alto livello—caratteristica comune agli ambasciatori veneti—e si applicano ad ambienti e a personaggi degni di studio" (Contarini's first-person account of his travels in Persia *cannot be counted as one of the best of the period: the figure of the protagonist, his vicissitudes and his hardships, indeed, make up too important of a part*. It nevertheless possesses great documentary value: Contarini's observational capacity are of a high level—a common characteristic among Venetian ambassadors—and are applied to environments and to people worthy of study). Marica Milanesi, "Ambrogio Contarini," in *Dizionario Biografico degli Italiani*, vol. 28 (Rome: Istituto della Enciclopedia Italiana, 1983), https://www.treccani.it/enciclopedia

/ambrogio-contarini_%28Dizionario-Biografico%29/. Translation is my own; italics added. Milanesi, incidentally, is the editor of the only modern edition still in print in Italy of Ramusio's *Navigazioni e viaggi*, 4 vols. (Turin: Einaudi, 1978–1983).

41. Contarini, "Viaggio di Ambrosio Contarini," in Ramusio, *Navigazioni e Viaggi*, 3:582.

42. Contarini, "Viaggio di Ambrosio Contarini," in Ramusio, *Navigazioni e Viaggi*, 3:582.

43. Contarini, "Viaggio di Ambrosio Contarini," in Ramusio, *Navigazioni e Viaggi*, 3:582.

44. Tucci, "Mercanti, viaggiatori, Pellegrini," 326.

45. Contarini, "Viaggio di Ambrosio Contarini," in Ramusio, *Navigazioni e Viaggi*, 3:581–582.

46. Contarini, "Viaggio di Ambrosio Contarini," in Ramusio, *Navigazioni e Viaggi*, 3:582–583.

47. Contarini, "Viaggio di Ambrosio Contarini," in Ramusio, *Navigazioni e Viaggi*, 3:582–583.

48. Contarini, "Viaggio di Ambrosio Contarini," in Ramusio, *Navigazioni e Viaggi*, 3:583.

49. Contarini, "Viaggio di Ambrosio Contarini," in Ramusio, *Navigazioni e Viaggi*, 3:583.

50. Contarini, "Viaggio di Ambrosio Contarini," in Ramusio, *Navigazioni e Viaggi*, 3:584.

51. Contarini, "Viaggio di Ambrosio Contarini," in Ramusio, *Navigazioni e Viaggi*, 3:584.

52. Contarini, "Viaggio di Ambrosio Contarini," in Ramusio, *Navigazioni e Viaggi*, 3:586.

53. Contarini, "Viaggio di Ambrosio Contarini," in Ramusio, *Navigazioni e Viaggi*, 3:586.

54. Contarini refers to Kyiv by two names, "Chio" and "Magraman," the latter being a transliteration of the Turkic name for the city Menkermen. See Donald Ostrowski, "City Names of the Western Steppe at the Time of the Mongol Invasion," *Bulletin of the School of Oriental and African Studies* 61, no. 3 (1998): 465.

55. Being "treated like a king" could, however, be problematic in diplomacy. The body of the king was *not* inviolable, even rhetorically. Rulers therefore were understandably wary of negotiating in person, which is why they sent a representative in their place, who should theoretically and rhetorically be treated as the ruler, but with one significant difference: He was supposedly protected with immunity and safe conduct, two courtesies not necessarily extended to the ruler. See Linda S. Frey and Marsha L. Frey, *History of Diplomatic Immunity* (Columbus: Ohio State University Press, 1999), 131.

56. Ambrogio Contarini, "The Travels of the Magnificent M. Ambrosio Contarini, Ambassador of the Illustrious Signory of Venice to the Great Lord UssunCassan, King of Persia in the Year 1473," in *Travels to Tana and Persia by Josafa Barbaro and Ambrogio Contarini*, trans. William Thomas and S. A. Roy, ed. Lord Stanley of Alderley (London: The Hakluyt Society,1873), 167

57. In the original edition in Venetian dialect, the phrase is "aferar la man," which even more emphatically and less equivocally indicates the "grasp[ing]" of hands than "pigliar mano" (hold the hand), the phrase found in the Ramusio edition. See Contarini, "Viaggio di Ambrogio Contarini," in *I Viaggi in Persia*, 182.

58. Contarini, "Viaggio di Ambrosio Contarini," in Ramusio, *Navigazioni e Viaggi*, 3:586. I thank the anonymous reviewer of this manuscript for suggesting that this phrase may be read as perhaps "[carrying] some sense of menace."

59. "Preposizione, che denota sito di luogo superiore, contrario di sotto. Latin. *super, supra*"; "Fare, e ordinare uno sopra qualche ufficio, cioè darnegli il governo, e farnelo sopracciò. Lat. *praeficere*." See "sopra," *Vocabolario degli accademici della crusca*, 2013.

60. Contarini, "The Travels of the Magnificent M. Ambrosio Contarini," in *Travels to Tana and Persia*, trans. Thomas and Roy, 112–113.

61. Contarini, "Viaggio di Ambrosio Contarini," in Ramusio, *Navigazioni e Viaggi*, 3:586.

62. On the importance and symbolism of the horse as a gift, see Anthony Cutler, "Significant Gifts: Patterns of Exchange in Late Antique, Byzantine, and Early Islamic Diplomacy," *Journal of Medieval and Early Modern Studies* 38, no. 1 (2008): 79–101.

63. Contarini, "Viaggio di Ambrosio Contarini," in Ramusio, *Navigazioni e Viaggi*, 3:586n4.

64. Contarini, "Viaggio di Ambrosio Contarini," in Ramusio, *Navigazioni e Viaggi*, 3:586.

65. Contarini, "Viaggio di Ambrosio Contarini," in Ramusio, *Navigazioni e Viaggi*, 3:587.

66. Contarini, "Viaggio di Ambrosio Contarini," in Ramusio, *Navigazioni e Viaggi*, 3:587.

67. Contarini, "Viaggio di Ambrosio Contarini," in Ramusio, *Navigazioni e Viaggi*, 3:587.

68. Contarini, "Viaggio di Ambrosio Contarini," in Ramusio, *Navigazioni e Viaggi*, 3:587.

69. Contarini, "Viaggio di Ambrosio Contarini," in Ramusio, *Navigazioni e Viaggi*, 3:587.

70. Contarini, "Viaggio di Ambrosio Contarini," in Ramusio, *Navigazioni e Viaggi*, 3:580.

71. In Ramusio's edition, an entire sentence is added that has the effect of diminishing Contarini's religious framing, perhaps to better align the narrative with the target reader's appetite for marvel and virtual geography: "E parendomi che 'l dar notizia di un tanto e sí lungo viaggio *possa esser dilettevole e utile a' nostri discendenti*" (And seeming to me that giving news of such a very long journey *could be delightful and beneficial to our descendants*; italics added). Contarini, "Viaggio di Ambrosio Contarini," in Ramusio, *Navigazioni e Viaggi*, 3:580. Contarini's original, however, is limited to expressing his duty to record "such a very long" mission: "Et parendomi mio debito de un tanto e sì longo viazo *farni memoria*" (And seeming to me that it is my duty *to commit* such a very long journey *to memory*; italics added). Contarini, "Viaggio di Ambrogio Contarini," in *I Viaggi in Persia*, 3:177.

72. Laura Benedetti and Enrico Musacchio, *Da Venezia al Cairo: Il viaggio di Zaccaria Pagani nel primo Cinquecento* (Padua: Il Poligrafo, 2021).

73. For a study of the relationship between masculinity, fashion, adornment, beauty, and political power at the Renaissance court, see Timothy McCall, *Brilliant Bodies: Fashioning Courtly Men in Early Renaissance Italy* (University Park: Pennsylvania State University Press, 2022). See also Marcello Fantoni, *Italian Courts and European Culture* (Amsterdam: Amsterdam University Press, 2022), 237–248; and Fantoni, "Le corti e i "modi" di vestire," in *Storia d'Italia*, Annali 19, *La moda*, ed. Marco Belfanti and Fiorella Giusberti (Turin: Einaudi, 2003), 737–765. For discussions of the making of subjects and identities through clothing in the Renaissance, see Ann Rosalind Jones and Peter Stallybrass, *Renaissance and the Materials of Memory* (Cambridge, UK: Cambridge University Press, 2000).

74. Zaccaria Pagani, *Viagio del Magnifico et Preclarissimo Cavalier et Procurator di San Marco Domino Dominicho Trivisano*, in MS Paris, Bibliothèque Nationale de France, Archives et Manuscripts, Italien 2111.

75. For discussion of Venice's considerable dedication to maintaining diplomatic relations with the Ottomans during this trying period of its history, see Eric Dursteler, "The Bailo in Constantinople: Crisis and Career in Venice's Early Modern Diplomatic Corps," *Mediterranean Historical Review* 16, no. 2 (December 2001): 1–30, https://doi.org/10.1080/714004583.

76. In 1508, Pietro Zen arrived as Venetian consul in Damascus, where he was almost immediately approached secretly by envoys of Ismail I (1487–1524), "Il Sofi," founder of the Safavid dynasty and establisher of Shia Islam as the official religion in his newly established Persian Empire. The consequences of Ismail's recent conquest of Baghdad were being felt in nearby Aleppo, where the rulers and other prominent Sunni Aq Quoyunlu ("White Sheep Turkmen") were in exile. The Mamluks were understandably wary of Ismail's intentions, which prompted Zen to convene secretly with Ismail's messengers, who sought artillery technology and training from the Serenissima, and then arrange for their inconspicuous departure for Venice via Beirut, to avoid Mamluk suspicion. The issue came to a head in the summer of 1510, when Venetian merchants arrested by the Mamluks were found to be carrying incriminating letters, including those from Ismail to the Doge as well as to Zen himself, which implicated Venice in aiding and conspiring with the Persians against both the Ottomans and the Mamluks. A subsequent attack on Mamluk ships by Rhodian corsairs fueled the sultan's suspicions, leading to a blockade of European commerce, an interdict on pilgrimage sites in the Holy Land, and the arrest orders for Zen and the Venetian consul at Alexandria, Tommaso Contarini. For a detailed account of the affair, see Francesca Lucchetta, "L''affare Zen' in Levante nel primo cinquecento," *Studi veneziani* 10 (1968): 109–219.

77. For further information, Sergio Zamperetti, "De Franceschi, Andrea," in *Dizionario biografico degli Italiani*, vol. 36 (Rome: Istituto dell'Enciclopedia Italiana, 1986), https://www.treccani.it/enciclopedia/andrea-de-franceschi_%28Dizionario-Biografico%29/.

78. For a more detailed account of the manuscript's history before it became part of the collection of the Bibliothèque Nationale de France, in addition to information regarding its French translation and publication, see Laura Benedetti, "From Venice to Cairo: Notes

from an Early 16th-Century Voyage across the Mediterranean," *Mediterranea* 7 (2022): 514–516; and Benedetti and Musacchio, *Da Venezia al Cairo*, 38–44.

79. Zaccaria Pagani, *Viaggio di Domenico Trevisan: ambasciatore veneto al gran sultano del Cairo nell'anno 1512*, ed. Niccolò Barozzi (Venice: Antonelli, 1875). I cite from this edition despite Barozzi's aggressive "Italianization" of the original *veneziano*, as Benedetti and Musacchio note, because its standardized Italian allows for a wider readership and a more direct engagement with a text close to the original. For more discussion of Barozzi's edition, see Benedetti and Musacchio, *Da Venezia al Cairo*, 40.

80. Giuseppe Gullino, "Trevisan, Domenico," in *Dizionario biografico degli Italiani*, vol. 96 (Rome: Istituto dell'Enciclopedia Italiana, 2019),

81. Lucchetta, "L'"affare Zen,'" 171–172.

82. Lucchetta, "L'"affare Zen,'" 163, 166.

83. Archivio di Stato di Venezia, Deliberazioni del Senato (Segreta), reg. 44 cc. 75v–76r, in Lucchetta, "L'"affare Zen,'" 171.

84. See John Wansbrough, "A Mamluk Ambassador to Venice in 913/1507," *Bulletin of the School of Oriental and African Affairs, University of London* 26, no. 3 (1963): 503–530.

85. Lucchetta, "L'"affare Zen,'" 168.

86. This letter is copied in Marino Sanudo, *I diarii*, ed. Niccolò Barozzi, vol. 12 (Venice: F. Visentini, 1886), 239. The translation is my own. The year of the date of the letter indicated by Sanudo (1510) is incorrect and should instead read 1511, see Lucchetta, "L'"affare Zen,'" 167n222.

87. Pagani, *Viaggio di Domenico Trevisan*, 12. All translations of this text are my own.

88. See Maaike van Berkel, "The People of the Pen: Self-Perceptions of Status and Role in the Administration of Empires and Polities," in *Prince, Pen, and Sword: Eurasian Perspectives*, ed. Maaike van Berkel and Jeroen Duindam (Leiden: Brill, 2018), 442–443, 443n215.

89. Pagani, *Viaggio di Domenico Trevisan*, 13.

90. Pagani, *Viaggio di Domenico Trevisan*, 13.

91. Cesare Vecellio, *De gli habiti antichi et moderni di diversi parti del mondo* (Venice: Zenaro, 1590). The text was recently published in English edition and translation, *The Clothing of the Renaissance World: Europe, Asia, Africa, the Americas*, ed. and trans. Ann Rosalind Jones and Margaret F. Rosenthal (London: Thames & Hudson, 2008).

92. In the text that accompanies the depiction of the Mamluk sultan, Al-Ashraf Qansuh al-Ghuri, Vecellio directly credits Pagani as his source; see Benedetti, "From Venice to Cairo," 515.

93. Pagani, *Viaggio di Domenico Trevisan*, 22.

94. Pagani, *Viaggio di Domenico Trevisan*, 21.

95. s.v. "restagno," https://www.gdli.it/sala-lettura/vol/15?seq=894.

96. Pagani, *Viaggio di Domenico Trevisan*, 23.

97. Pagani, *Viaggio di Domenico Trevisan*, 22–23.

98. Benedetti and Musacchio verify that a letter to Domenico Trevisan indicating his diplomatic orders from the Doge, Leonardo Loredan, was found with Pagani's manuscript in Paris (MS Paris, Bibliothèque Nationale de France, Archives et Manuscripts, Italien 2110) and is transcribed and included as an appendix to their edition. See "Appendice 2: Lettera di

istruzioni a Domenico Trevisan da parte del Doge Leonardo Loredan 31 Dicembre 1511," in Benedetti and Musacchio, *Da Venezia al Cairo*, 103–108.

99. Pagani, *Viaggio di Domenico Trevisan*, 24–25, 28–29. For context on these types of gift exchanges and the dignitaries involved, see Jesse J. Hysell, "Interpreting the Veneto-Mamluk Gift Exchanges of 894–5/1489–90," in *Culture matérielle et contacts diplomatiques entre l'Occident latin, Byzance et l'Orient islamique (XIe–XVIe siècle)*, ed. Frédéric Bauden (Leiden: Brill, 2021); and Beatrice Saletti, "Gift Exchanges and Traces of Material Life in Mamluk Diplomacy: First Notes on Embassies from Egypt to Italy and Italian Missions to Cairo (1421–1512)," in *Culture matérielle et contacts diplomatiques entre l'Occident latin, Byzance et l'Orient islamique (XIe–XVIe siècle)*, ed. Frédéric Bauden (Leiden: Brill, 2021), 273–287, and 203–273, respectively.

100. Pagani, *Viaggio di Domenico Trevisan*, 30.

101. Pagani, *Viaggio di Domenico Trevisan*, 31.

102. Pagani's version of the sultan's opinion of Zen's conduct is overly generous in comparison with other accounts. In fact, Trevisan's son, the future Doge Marco Antonio, who accompanied his father on the mission, writes in a letter that the furious sultan called Zen a "dog" who intended to betray his state, and nearly caused a rupture in relations between the states ("sto can ha voluto tradir el mio stado; per lui quasi che non sono venuto a le rote con Signoria" [this dog wanted to betray my state; it was because of him that I was almost forced to end relations with the Signoria]) as well as one of the "thieves" (*ladri*) and "[his] enemies" (*mii nimici*). See "Appendice 6: Lettera di Marco Antonio Trevisan al fratello Piero Luglio 1512," in Benedetti and Musacchio, *Da Venezia al Cairo*, 125.

103. Pagani, *Viaggio di Domenico Trevisan*, 31.

Chapter 2 Ambassadors in "Utopia"

1. Stephen Greenblatt, *Renaissance Self-Fashioning: From More to Shakespeare* (Chicago: University of Chicago Press,1980), 21.

2. Critical attention on all aspects of early modern diplomacy has been significantly increasing. Since the early 2000s a number of important works have expanded the seminal work of Donald Queller, *The Office of Ambassador in the Middle Ages* (Princeton, NJ: Princeton University Press, 1967), and Garrett Mattingly *Renaissance Diplomacy* (Boston: Houghton Mifflin,1955), which were beholden to a teleological narrative of modern state formation and focused on bureaucracy and foreign policy. For some examples of recent studies, see Douglas Biow, *Doctors, Ambassadors, Secretaries: Humanism and Professions in Renaissance Italy* (Chicago: University of Chicago Press, 2002); Catherine Fletcher, *Diplomacy in Renaissance Rome: The Rise of the Resident Ambassador* (Cambridge, UK: Cambridge University Press, 2015); Isabella Lazzarini, *Communication and Conflict: Italian Diplomacy in the Early Renaissance, 1350–1520* (Oxford: Oxford University Press, 2015); Diego Pirillo, *The Refugee-Diplomat: Venice, England, and the Reformation* (Ithaca, NY: Cornell University Press, 2018); John Watkins, *After Lavinia: A Literary History of Premodern Marriage Diplomacy* (Ithaca, NY: Cornell University Press, 2017); and Ellen Welch, *A Theater of Diplomacy: International Relations and the Performing Arts in Early Modern France* (Philadelphia: University of Pennsylvania Press, 2017).

3. Timothy Hampton, *Fictions of Embassy: Literature and Diplomacy in Early Modern Europe* (Ithaca, NY: Cornell University Press, 2009), 37.

4. Henry Wotton, *Reliquiae Wottonianae. Or, A Collection of Lives, Letters, Poems; With Characters of Sundry Personages: And other Incomparable Pieces of Language and Art. By the Curious Pensil of the Ever Memorable Sr Henry Wotton Kt, Late Provost of Eton College*, ed. Edward H. Clarendon (London: Maxey, 1651).

5. Melanie Ord, "Returning from Venice to England: Sir Henry Wotton as Diplomat, Pedagogue, and Italian Cultural Connoisseur," in *Borders and Travelers in Early Modern Europe*, ed. Thomas Betteridge (Burlington, VT: Ashgate, 2007), 147, 147n2.

6. Francesco Guicciardini, *Ricordi*, ed. Giorgio Masi (Milan: Mursia, 1994); and Guicciardini, *Maxims and Reflections of a Renaissance Statesman (Ricordi)*, trans. Mario Domandi, intro. Nicolai Rubinstein (New York: Harper & Row, 1965), 84.

7. John Berger, *Ways of Seeing* (London: BBC/Penguin, 1972), 90–91.

8. "Before Hervey's identifications, the painting showed two anonymous men; the objects, by contrast, were carefully inscribed in ways that make them specifically identifiable" (Ann Rosalind Jones and Peter Stallybrass, *Renaissance and the Materials of Memory* [Cambridge, UK: Cambridge University Press, 2000], 46).

9. Mary F. S. Hervey, *Holbein's "Ambassadors": The Picture and the Men; An Historical Study* (London: George Bell and Sons, 1900), 1; Hagi Kenaan, "The 'Unusual' Character of Holbein's *Ambassadors*," *Artibus et Historiae* 23, no. 46 (2002): 61–75.

10. Kenaan, "The 'Unusual' Character," 68.

11. Kenaan, "The 'Unusual' Character," 72. Jodi Cranston notes the prevalence of portraits commemorating friendship by identifying many significant examples of contemporary double portraits of two men. To note only a few examples: Raphael's portrait of *Andrea Navagero and Agostino Beazzano* (1516) and *Raphael and His Fencing Master* (1518), as well as Pontormo's *Double Portrait* (1522), in addition to earlier examples by Mantegna. Cranston also discusses the "affections" that such portraits seek to memorialize: "The association between portraits and friendship, defined by the ideal of a shared identity among friends, extends the traditional conception of a portrait as an image that is devoted to commemorate an individual or individuals within a group to one that potentially commemorates the affections." Jodi Cranston, *The Poetics of Portraiture in the Italian Renaissance* (Cambridge, UK: Cambridge University Press, 2000), 66. Kenaan acknowledges the trend of Italian Mannerist "friendship portraits," yet dismisses the possibility that *The Ambassadors* can be considered as part of this genre by speculating that the painting somehow "blurs the nature of the relationship between its two subjects" (Kenaan, "The 'Unusual' Character," 75n18).

12. Kenaan, "The 'Unusual' Character," 71.

13. Hervey, *Holbein's "Ambassadors."*

14. The historical identity and genealogy of Julius are clearly depicted by the finials of the pope's throne, which are in the shape of acorns and thus clearly representative of the Della Rovere family. Julius's notoriety aside, there has never been any historical debate regarding the sitter, nor has he ever been misidentified as merely "a pope"; it has always been obvious that the figure represented is Pope Julius II, and this disambiguation was

undoubtedly the intention of Raphael. Although Holbein, in his portrait of Henry VIII, accentuates certain qualities while deemphasizing or omitting less desirable aspects of Henry's physical presence, it would still be impossible to mistake him for any other sitter, and this rendering has become the most recognizable image of the Tudor king, even though the Holbein original has been lost.

15. In her landmark study, Hervey notes that the "traditional title" was *Two Ambassadors*, information perhaps found in a catalog of the painting's eighteenth-century owner, Jean- Baptiste-Pierre Le Brun. See Hervey, *Holbein's "Ambassadors,"* 7–8.

16. Lisa Jardine, *Worldly Goods: A New History of the Renaissance* (New York: W. W. Norton, 1998), 255.

17. Select Venetian ambassadors, upon return to Venice, were obliged to don an honorary sash of gold during state ceremonies, an accessory that signified induction into the Ordine della Stola d'Oro. Entry into this chivalric order was not hereditary and was limited to patricians who previously "served as ambassadors at foreign courts and had been granted knighthood by foreign sovereigns for their service." Though clearly meant as an honor, it still marks an obscuring of the diplomats' personal identities and alludes to possession of the body of the ambassador by the state apparatus. Patricia Fortini Brown, *Private Lives in Renaissance Venice* (New Haven, CT: Yale University Press, 2004), 21.

18. Hervey transcribes a note from the catalog of the 1787 sale of the estate of M. Nicola Beaujon, a French millionaire who owned *The Ambassadors*, which specifies that Dinteville (misidentified as a certain "d'Avaux") was wearing clothing typical of the Northern countries to which he was sent: "Il représente deux ambassadeurs, MM. de Selve e d'Avaux, l'un Ambassaduer à Venise, et l'autre dans les pays du Nord, avec le costume des nations chez lequelle ils ètoient envoyés" (It [the painting] represents two ambassadors, Monsieurs de Selve and d'Avaux, one an ambassador to Venice, and the other to the Northern countries, wearing clothing typical of the countries to which they were sent) (Hervey, *Holbein's "Ambassadors,"* 10; translation is my own). The notes do not specify Tudor-style clothing, indicating only a general geographic ("northern") style of clothing. As mentioned previously, the similarities between the clothing Holbein represents Henry VIII wearing in his portrait and Dinteville's garments allow for the more specific designation of the clothing as Tudor style.

19. Stephen Greenblatt, *Renaissance Self-Fashioning*, 20–21.

20. Greenblatt, *Renaissance Self-Fashioning*, 19.

21. Norbert Elias, *The Court Society* (Oxford: Basil Blackwell, 1983), 55. On Elias and the early modern court, see Jeroen Duindam, *Myths of Power: Norbert Elias and the Early Modern European Court* (Amsterdam: Amsterdam University Press, 1995); and Jon Snyder, *Dissimulation and the Culture of Secrecy in Early Modern Europe* (Berkeley: University of California Press, 2009), 68–95.

22. On the court as a place of machinations, see Paola Ugolini, *The Court and Its Critics: Anti-Court Sentiments in Early Modern Italy* (Toronto: University of Toronto Press, 2020). On the early modern court generally, see Ronald G. Asch and Adolf M. Birke, ed., *Princes, Patronage, and the Nobility: The Court at the Beginning of the Modern Age, ca. 1450–1650* (London: German Historical Institute, London, 1991); Marcello Fantoni, *Italian Courts and European Culture* (Amsterdam: Amsterdam University Press, 2022); Marcello Fantoni,

ed., *The Court in Europe* (Rome: Bulzoni, 2012); and Stephen Kolsky, *Courts and Courtiers in Renaissance Northern Italy* (Burlington, VT: Ashgate/Variorum, 2003).

23. For more on this quotation, see note 19 above.

24. Hervey, *Holbein's "Ambassadors,"* 90. The catalog that accompanied the painting's exhibit at the National Gallery includes discussion of Dinteville's letters; see Susan Foister, Ashok Roy, and Martin Wyld, *Making and Meaning in Holbein's "Ambassadors"* (London: National Gallery of London, 1998), 14–19.

25. Lisa Jardine and Jerry Britton, *Global Interests: Renaissance Art Between East and West* (London: Reaktion, 2000), 50–51. The original French text is taken from Hervey, *Holbein's "Ambassadors,"* 80.

26. Hervey, *Holbein's "Ambassadors,"* 90. For the text of the entire letter, see Nicolas Camusat, *Meslanges historiques* (Troyes, France: Noel Moreau, 1619), 131. Translation is my own.

27. Jardine and Britton, *Global Interests*, 51, 195n86.

28. Ambassador as gift is discussed in chapter 1. There is also a literary topos of the unattractive ambassador likened to an offensively inadequate gift from one sovereign to another. At least eight of Franco Sacchetti's novellas treat the ambassador. The appearance and physical dignity of the diplomat is the focus of novella 74, *Messer Beltrando da Imola manda un notaio per ambasciadore a messer Bernabò, il quale, veggendolo piccolino e giallo, il tratta come merita* (Sir Beltrando of Imola sends a notary as his ambassador to Sir Bernabò, who, upon seeing the puny and yellowish man before him, treats him as he deserves to be treated).

29. Jardine and Britton, *Global Interests*, 49.

30. Jardine and Britton, *Global Interests*, 194n82.

31. Jardine and Britton, *Global Interests*, 50, 194n83.

32. Greenblatt, *Renaissance Self-Fashioning*, 17.

33. See Hampton, *Fictions of Embassy*, 35; and Edoardo Rossetti, "Meraviglia, Giovanni Alberto," in *Dizionario Biografico degli Italiani*, vol. 73 (Rome: Istituto della Enciclopedia Italiana, 2009), https://www.treccani.it/enciclopedia/giovanni-alberto-meraviglia_(Dizionario-Biografico).

34. Andrea Alciati, *Emblematum liber* (Augsburg: Heinrich Steyner,1531).

35. Hervey, *Holbein's "Ambassadors,"* 228.

36. Attilio Portioli, "Altre notizie sulla morte di Alberto Maraviglia," *Archivio storico Lombardo* 2 (December 1875), 33. This descriptive quotation from a letter from the ambassador of the duke of Mantua, Federico Gonzaga, is reproduced in the article.

37. Portioli, "Altre notizie sulla morte di Alberto Maraviglia," 30–50.

38. The annexation of Milan into the Holy Roman Empire upon the death of Francesco Maria posthumously legitimized his sense of insecurity.

39. In addition to Portioli, "Altre notizie sulla morte di Alberto Maraviglia," see Carlo Romussi, "La morte di Alberto Maraviglia (1533)," *Archivio Storico Lombardo* 1 (1874): 249–274.

40. Martin Du Bellay and Guillaume Du Bellay, *Mémoires de Martin et Guillaume Du Bellay*, 7 vols. (Paris: Prault, 1753) 2:292–293, 294. All translations of this text are my own.

41. Du Bellay and Du Bellay, *Mémoires*, 2:293.

42. Du Bellay and Du Bellay, *Mémoires*, 2:292.

43. Du Bellay and Du Bellay, *Mémoires*, 2:292–293.

44. René Girard, *The Scapegoat*, trans. Yvonne Freccero (Baltimore: Johns Hopkins University Press, 1986).

45. Linda S. Frey and Marsha L. Frey, *History of Diplomatic Immunity* (Columbus: Ohio State University Press, 1999), 131–133.

46. See Michel Foucault, *Discipline and Punish: The Birth of the Prison*, trans. Alan Sheridan (New York: Vintage Books, 1995), especially 3–72.

47. Hampton, *Fictions of Embassy*, 35–39.

48. Frey and Frey, *History of Diplomatic Immunity*, 132.

49. See Romussi, "La morte di Alberto Maraviglia," 258.

50. Portioli reproduces excerpts from Maraviglia's will, which contained a list of debtors and specified that Sforza owed Maraviglia money. See Portioli, "Altre notizie sulla morte di Alberto Maraviglia," 36–38.

51. Hampton, *Fictions of Embassy*, 35–39.

52. Montaigne, "Des menteurs," in *Essais de messire Michel de Montaigne* (Bordeaux: S. Millanges, 1580).

53. Alberico Gentili, *De Legationibus libri tres*, 2 vols., ed. James Brown Scott, trans. Gordon J. Laing (Oxford: Oxford University Press, 1924).

54. Jean Hotman, *De la charge et la dignité d'ambassadeur* (Dusseldorf: Buys, 1613; originally published in 1603).

55. The ceremonies that accompany the arrival of a foreign ambassador are discussed in chapter 1. The ambassadorial body, much like gifts exchanged between heads of states, is a richly symbolic entity, deprived of agency but of essential importance to both giver and receiver. See also Edward Muir, *Civic Ritual in Renaissance Venice* (Princeton, NJ: Princeton University Press, 1981), 233.

56. Gentili does not discuss the specific contingencies that rendered Maraviglia's affair unique, if not excusable. While Sforza was technically the duke of Milan, Francis I still coveted his loss of the duchy as stipulated by the Treaties of Madrid and Cambrai. Charles V, the de facto ruler of the duchy, remained suspicious of Francis and his persistent designs on Milan. This situation thus made diplomatic ties between France and Milan necessarily secretive and dangerous.

57. Alberico Gentili, *De legationibus libri tres*, 1:112.

58. Gentili, *De legationibus*, 2:123.

59. Hampton, *Fictions of Embassy*, 38.

60. See *Oxford English Dictionary Online*, s.v. "person, *n*," https://www.oed.com/dictionary/person_n, accessed March 1, 2023.

61. Charlton T. Lewis, *An Elementary Latin Dictionary*, s.v. "gerō."

62. See Hervey, *Holbein's "Ambassadors,"* 90–93. These pages address the horror Jean de Dinteville, patron and subject of Holbein's *The Ambassadors* and Francis's ambassador to Henry VIII, must have felt in direct relation to the Maraviglia assassination. Holbein's painting and Maraviglia's death were contemporaneous (1533). See also Portioli, "Altre notizie sulla morte di Alberto Maraviglia," 43. Portioli mentions the little-discussed fact

that the Sforza's own ambassador at Francis's court (not Taverna, who was an extraordinary ambassador sent specifically to handle the death of Maraviglia) abandoned his post and fled France with neither Francis's nor Sforza's permission. This is testament to the widespread tension this episode provoked in courts all over Europe, and the danger the ambassadors themselves must have felt to consider violating their duty by abandoning post.

63. Camusat, *Meslanges historiques*, 135. The full text of the two letters dated July 16 and August 12, 1533, from Francis to Dinteville ("Bailley de Troyes mon Ambassadeur"), are found in Camusat, *Meslanges historiques*, 133–136. Translation is my own.

64. Michel de Montaigne, "Des Menteurs," in *Les Essais de Michel de Montaigne*, ed. Pierre Villey and Verdun Louis Saulnier (Paris: Presses Universitaires de France, 1965), 37; and Michel de Montaigne, "Of Liars," in *The Complete Essays of Montaigne*, trans. Donald M. Frame (Stanford, CA: Stanford University Press, 1958), 24.

65. Montaigne, "Des Menteurs," 38; Montaigne, "Of Liars," 25.

66. Montaigne, "Des Menteurs," 37; Montaigne, "Of Liars," 159.

67. John Jeffries Martin, *Myths of Renaissance Individualism* (Basingstoke, UK: Palgrave Macmillan, 2004), 13–17, and 30–40.

68. "Francesco Sforza threatened his envoys with death, perpetual banishment, and confiscation of their possessions if they did not obey his orders" (Frey and Frey, *History of Diplomatic Immunity*, 132–133).

69. Frey and Frey, *History of Diplomatic Immunity*, 140.

70. Frey and Frey, *History of Diplomatic Immunity*, 123. This was not unheard of; even diplomatic theorists and former diplomats urged rulers to dismiss resident diplomats, whom they regarded as little more than spies.

71. In a late nineteenth-century article, Portioli mentions the little-discussed fact that the Sforza's own ambassador at Francis's court abandoned his post and fled France because of the escalating tension caused by Maraviglia's assassination and the potential that more violence could be exacted on diplomats in retaliation. This is testament to the widespread tension this episode provoked in courts all over Europe, and the danger the ambassadors themselves must have felt to consider violating their duty by abandoning post. Portioli, "Altre notizie sulla morte di Alberto Maraviglia," 31.

72. Portioli, "Altre notizie sulla morte di Alberto Maraviglia," 43.

73. "Francesco Sforza threatened his envoys with death, perpetual banishment, and confiscation of their possessions if they did not obey his orders" (Frey and Frey, *History of Diplomatic Immunity*, 140).

74. Frey and Frey, 130–131.

75. Greenblatt, *Renaissance Self-Fashioning*, 27.

76. This is the converse of Thomas More's treatment by Henry VIII, who instead disguised a personal matter as a state affair in order to execute More as a traitor.

77. Izaak Walton, *The Lives of Dr. John Donne, Sir Henry Wotton, Mr. Richard Hooker, Mr. George Herbert* (London: Thomas Newcomb for Richard Marriot, 1670).

78. Wotton originally penned the infamous quote in Latin: "*Legatus est vir bonus, peregrè missus ad mentiendum Reipublicae causâ*," in which he bluntly equates deceit (*mentiendum*) with the office of the ambassador (*legatus*). The Latin expression lacks the ambiguity

of the English verb "to lie," which connotes both "to reside temporarily (to lodge)" in addition to "to tell untruths with deceitful intention." Wotton's use of literary Latin, a foreign tongue, may have facilitated his honesty, relieving him of the necessity to disguise himself and his true intentions via dissimulation.

79. Ord, "Returning from Venice," 150–154.

80. Walton, *Lives*, 28.

81. Walton, *Lives*, 24.

82. Walton, *Lives*, 24.

83. Walton, *Lives*, 25.

84. Walton, *Lives*, 27.

85. Ord, "Returning from Venice," 148.

86. Henry Wotton, "Letter to Marcus Welser," in *Reliquiae Wottonianae*, ed. Izaak Walton (London: Roycroft, 1672), e6v–f2r.

87. See Jon Snyder, *Dissimulation and the Culture of Secrecy*; and Jean-Pierre Cavaillé, "Pour une histoire de la dis/simulation—Per una storia della dis/simulazione," *Les dossiers GRIHL (Groupe de Recherches Interdisiplinaires sur l'Histoire du Littéraire)* 3, no. 2 (February 2009), https://doi.org/10.4000/dossiersgrihl.3666.

88. Cavaillé, "Per una storia della dis/simulazione," 31.

89. Cavaillé, "Per una storia della dis/simulazione," 27.

90. See Logan Persall Smith, *The Life and Letters of Sir Henry Wotton* (Oxford: Clarendon Press, 1907), 126–127.

91. Henry Wotton, "Letter to Marcus Welser," e6v–f2r.

92. Schoppe took advantage of the complex political and religious atmosphere during James's reign, including conflict between the Church of England and Puritans intolerant of any vestiges of Catholicism, as well as the general English Reformation polemics against the Catholic Church. James, considered moderate toward Catholics at the beginning, quickly alienated those English Catholics who had been hopeful they would suffer less persecution during his reign than during that of Elizabeth I. This disappointment led to Catholic conspiracies against James, culminating in the failed assassination attempt by Catholic dissidents, the Gunpowder Treason Plot of 1605, resulting in harsher anti-Catholic measures and the instatement of the Oath of Allegiance of the king's authority over that of the pope.

93. Vera Keller, "Painted Friends: Political Interest and the Transformation of International Learned Sociability," in *Friendship in the Middle Ages and Early Modern Age: Explorations of a Fundamental Ethical Discourse*, ed. Albrecht Classen and Marilyn Sandidge (Berlin: De Gruyter, 2010), 682.

94. Keller, "Painted Friends," 683.

95. Walton, *Lives*, 55.

Chapter 3 Tasso's Messengers

1. See Dante Fedele, "Uno scritto sull'ambasciatore del secondo Cinquecento: 'Il Messaggiero' di Torquato Tasso," *Il pensiero politico* 51, no. 1 (2018): 113–114.

2. Torquato Tasso, "Il Messaggiero," in *Opere*, ed. Bruno Maier (Milan: Rizzoli, 1964), 4:728. All translations of this text are my own.

3. Torquato Tasso, *Gerusalemme Liberata* (*GL*), ed. Lanfranco Caretti (Turin: Einaudi, 1993), 1.3. All citations of this text are to this edition. All translations are from Torquato Tasso, *Jerusalem Delivered: An English Prose Version*, ed. and trans. Ralph Nash (Detroit: Wayne State University Press, 1987). In-text citations indicate the numbers for the book and octaves from which the citations come.

4. In "Discorsi dell'arte poetica," Tasso made this explicit: "Dovendo il poeta con la sembianza de la verità ingannare i lettori, e non solo persuader loro che le cose da lui trattate sian vere, ma sottoporle in guisa a i lor sensi, che credano non di leggerle, ma di esser presenti, e di vederle, e di udirle, è necessitato di guadagnarsi ne l'animo loro questa opinion di verità" (In order to earn the reader's opinion of truth, the poet has to deceive readers with the semblance of truth, not only persuade them; [the poet] must present the things he crafts to the readers' senses in such a way that they believe not that they are reading them, but that they are present, seeing them and hearing them). Torquato Tasso, "Discorsi dell'arte poetica," in *Le prose diverse di Torquato Tasso*, ed. Cesare Guasti (Florence: Successori Le Monnier, 1875), 1:11. Translation is my own.

5. On the court and anti-court sentiment pervasive in the period, including a contextualization of Tasso's view, see Paola Ugolini, *The Court and Its Critics: Anti-Court Sentiments in Early Modern Italy* (Toronto: University of Toronto Press, 2020), 13–49.

6. See Amedeo Quondam, "'Nato ed allevato in Corte': Torquato Tasso," *LibrosdelaCorte.es* 22 (2021): 399–423, https://doi.org/10.15366/ldc2021.13.22.015.

7. Virginia Cox, "Tasso's *Malpiglio overo de la corte: The Courtier* Revisited," *The Modern Language Review* 90, no. 4 (October 1995): 902.

8. Tasso, "Il Messaggiero," 4:712.

9. Tasso, "Il Messaggiero," 4:726.

10. Tasso here also alluded to Castiglione, whose seminal text, *Il libro del Cortegiana*, attempted to "formare con parole un perfetto cortegiano" (form with words the perfect courtier, I.XII; translation is mine). Castiglione's words, in turn, quoted Cicero's *De oratore*, I, XXVI.118: "Sed quia de oratore quaerimus, fingendus est nobis oratione nostra detractis omnibus vitiis orator atque omni laude cumulatus" (But since it is "The Orator" we are seeking, we have to picture to ourselves in our discourse an orator from whom every blemish has been taking away, and one who moreover is rich in every merit). Cicero, *On the Orator: Books 1–2*, trans. E. W. Sutton and H. Rackham (Cambridge, MA: Harvard University Press, 1942), 83. This intertextual palimpsest is of further interest since Tasso in the very same treatise discussed both the semantic lineage as well as the historical link between the "orator," Cicero's subject, which evolved into the early modern "messaggiero," or "ambasciatore," Tasso's subject. Castiglione's courtier thus provides the link between ancient and modern diplomatic practice, an undertaking Castiglione himself knew well as the *nunzio papale* to the Hapsburg court of Charles V.

11. Tasso, "Il Messaggiero," 4:728.

12. Tasso, "Il Messaggiero," 4:728.

13. Dante Fedele noted that in his letters Tasso expressed diplomatic and ecclesiastical ambitions. See Fedele, "Uno scritto sull'ambasciatore," 113–114.

14. Christopher Besoldus, German jurist, mentioned Tasso's *Il Messaggiero*, and Juan Antonio de Vera y Zuñiga, writer of *El Enbajador* (Seville, 1620) and future

ambassador to Phillip IV, considered Tasso's dialogue to be an inspiration for his own ambassadorial treatise and even cited from it directly. See Fedele, "Uno scritto sull'ambasciatore," 114.

15. Tasso, "Il Messaggiero," 4:711.

16. Tasso's optimistic view of the purpose of embassy was peace, and thus the idea that all ambassadors aim toward that end was refuted by contemporary jurist Alberico Gentili (1552–1608), who, among other accomplishments, is credited as one of the founders of the field of international law. See Diego Pirillo, "Tasso at the French Embassy: Epic, Diplomacy, and the Law of Nations," in *Authority and Diplomacy from Dante to Shakespeare*, ed. Jason Powell and William T. Rossiter (Farnham, UK: Ashgate, 2013): 135–153.

17. Timothy Hampton, *Fictions of Embassy: Literature and Diplomacy in Early Modern Europe* (Ithaca, NY: Cornell University Press, 2009), 52.

18. Tasso, "Il Messaggiero," 4:729.

19. Tasso, "Il Messaggiero," 4:715.

20. Tasso, "Il Messaggiero," 4:731.

21. Tasso, "Il Messaggiero," 4:715.

22. Robert F. Sutton, "The Invention of the Female Nude: Zeuxis, Vase-Painting, and the Kneeling Bather," in *Athenian Potters and Painters II*, ed. John H. Oakley and Olga Palagia (Oxford: Oxbow Books, 2009), 275.

23. A bit later in the dialogue, Tasso further connected erotics and politics through a comparison between the messenger and the pimp: "Non men convenevole di quello mi par che si possa fare tra l'arte de l'ambasciatore e quella del ruffiano" (It seems to me no less useful [a comparison] than that which one could make between the art of the ambassador and that of the pimp). This same link comes to the fore in *Liberata* through the figure of Armida, discussed in the next chapter (Tasso, "Il Messaggiero," 4:715–716). Translation is the author's.

24. Tasso, "Il Messaggiero," 4:716.

25. Tasso, "Il Messaggiero," 4:730.

26. Walter Stephens, "St. Paul Among the Amazons: Gender and Authority in *Gerusalemme Liberata*," in *Discourses of Authority in Medieval and Renaissance Literature*, ed. Kevin Brownlee and Walter Stephens (Hanover, NH: Dartmouth College by University Press of New England, 1989), 192.

27. See *Vocabolario degli Accademici della Crusca*, 5th ed., in *Lessicografia della Crusca in Rete* (Florence: Accademia della Crusca, 2000–2004), s.v. "cingere," http://www.lessicografia.it/.

28. "[E] chi nissuna cosa *fingesse*, chi in somma s'obligasse a que' particolari ch'ivi son contenuti, poeta non sarebbe, ma istorico"; "la *licenza di fingere*, la quale è necessarissima a i poeti" ([A]nd he who *invents* nothing, who limits himself to the details contained within history, would not be a poet, but an historian"; "the *freedom [license] to invent* is something most necessary to poets). Torquato Tasso, "Discorso primo," in *I discorsi dell'arte poetica, Il padre di famiglia, e L'Aminta*, ed. Angelo Solerti (Turin: G. B. Paravia, 1901), 14–15. Translation is mine; italics added.

29. The term *messaggio* and its derivative *messo* have been employed as a synonym for *messaggiero* going back as far as the *stilnovisti* poets. As I argue above, Tasso's employment of *messaggio* as opposed to *messaggiero* is intriguing in light of his attention to the physical appearance of the ambassadors, which also implies a conflation between the message and the messenger.

30. Hampton, *Fictions of Embassy*, 84.

31. Tasso, "Il Messaggiero," 4:729.

32. Alete and Argante arrive with an entourage, display diplomatic manners, and are dressed in foreign garb, clear symbols of an ambassadorial atmosphere. Though they act in a wholly peaceful manner ("ogni lor atto . . . pacifico"), they are still looked at with suspicion; here are murmurs of suspicion in the Christian camp at the end of Alete's long discourse of persuasion and rhetorical seduction: "Qui tacque Alete, e 'l suo parlar seguiro/con *basso mormorar que' forti eroi;/e ben ne gli atti disdegnosi apriro/quanto ciascun quella proposta annoi*" (Here Aletes fell silent. And those brave heroes followed his speech with a low murmuring, and in their scornful gestures clearly displayed how much that proposition annoys each one, Tasso, "Il Messaggiero," 2.80).

33. Tasso, "Il Messaggiero," 4:729.

34. *Fabro*, translated by Ralph Nash as "fabricator," was, of course, the same term employed by Dante in *Purgatorio* 26 in reverence of the Provençal poet Arnaut Daniel, "miglior fabbro," which Robert and Jean Hollander translate as "a better craftsman" (*Purgatorio*, XXVI.117 [New York: Doubleday/Anchor, 2003], 581). Tasso's inclusion of this lexical link thus subtly reinforces his equation of poetry and diplomacy with the centrality of deception to both practices.

35. There is another "mediatory" figure, Vafrino, whom Tasso invested with certain powers of narration. Walter Stephens noted that, just as in the case of Alete, whose name means "without simulation," Vafrino's name alludes to verbal prowess: "Vafrino's very name embodies Tasso's challenge to Homer, for it declares him the quintessential trickster: it is the diminutive of *vafro*, the Italianized form of Latin *vafer*, which denotes the subtlety, craftiness, and cunning of the trickster." Stephens, "Trickster, Textor, Architect, Thief: Craft and Comedy in *Gerusalemme Liberata*," in *Renaissance Transactions: Ariosto and Tasso*, ed. Valeria Finucci (Durham, NC: Duke University Press, 1999), 147. For Tasso's discussion of rhetorical license, see his *Discorso primo*.

36. Torquato Tasso, *Jerusalem Delivered*, trans. Anthony M. Esolen (Baltimore: Johns Hopkins University Press, 2000), 422.

37. See Sergio Zatti, "Dalla parte di Satana: sull'imperialismo cristiano nella *Gerusalemme Liberata*," in *La Rappresentazione dell'altro nei testi del Rinascimento*, ed. Sergio Zatti (Lucca, Italy: M. Pacini Fazzi, 1998), 146–182.

38. Tasso, "Il Messaggiero," 4:718–719.

39. This verse echoes (in reverse), "di nemica ella divenne amante" (and from his enemy she became his lover, 14.67), which describes the pivotal moment in which the tender sight of a sleeping and vulnerable Rinaldo softens Armida toward him, causing her to abandon inimical plans for vendetta and instead to fall in love with him. Moreover, beyond signaling Armida's transformation and the beginning of her romance with Rinaldo,

this verse links lexically politics and erotics, diplomacy and seduction, love and war, and therefore epic and romance. For an in-depth discussion of the enemy in Tasso and the Renaissance epic in general, see Andrea Moudarres, *The Enemy in Italian Renaissance Epic: Images of Hostility from Dante to Tasso* (Newark, NJ: University of Delaware Press, 2019).

40. Timothy Hampton observed that "Tasso shows the rhetorical culture of Renaissance humanism under pressure from the newly militant Church of the Counter-Reformation and ends up offering a rejection of diplomatic rhetoric" (Hampton, *Fictions of Embassy*, 114).

41. I interrogate only here this instance of Rinaldo's expression of and reputation for irascibility. For a discussion of Rinaldo's (often excessive) anger throughout the poem, see Bitül Dilmac, "Epic Anger in *La Gerusalemme Liberata*: Rinaldo's Irascibility and Tasso's *Allegoria della Gerusalemme*," in *Discourses of Anger in the Early Modern Period*, ed. Karl A. E. Enenkel and Anita Traninger (Boston: Brill, 2015), 288–311.

42. Torquato Tasso, "Allegoria del poema," in *Le prose diverse di Torquato Tasso*, ed. Cesare Guasti (Florence: Successori Le Monnier, 1875), 303.

43. I thank one of the anonymous reviewers for pointing out that this verse is echoed in the poem's final canto by Rinaldo, now a victorious warrior, when he declares himself Armida's "campione e servo" (20.134).

44. Tasso, "Allegoria del poema," 306; Tasso, *Jerusalem Delivered*, trans. and ed. Ralph Nash, 473.

45. "Tasso shows the rhetorical culture of Renaissance humanism under pressure from the newly militant Church of the Counter-Reformation" (Hampton, *Fictions of Embassy*, 114).

46. Francesco Erspamer clarifies Goffredo's moral certainty in this way: "La forza di Goffredo, che fa di lui prima il capitano supremo e poi il vincitore (e infine il protagonista del poema), è proprio la dogmaticità. Chi è carico di un pubblico potere, chi le scelte è obbligato a compiere anche per gli altri, e avverte su di sé il peso dell'investimento emotivo di un gruppo, non può ascoltare né le ragioni del cuore né quelle della mente, entrambe fonti di errore e di esitazione. Goffredo sacrifica la curiosità alla coerenza, e forse per questo è un personaggio così freddo, statico; non ha nulla di cercare, perché il presupposto di ogni ricerca è il dubbio, e Goffredo non può dubitare" (The power of Goffredo, which makes him the supreme captain, then victor [and eventually the protagonist of the poem] is precisely his dogmatism. He who is charged with public power is obliged to make choices also on behalf of others and to take upon himself the weight of a group's emotional investment, and cannot listen to reasons of the heart or the mind, both of which are sources of error and hesitation. Goffredo sacrifices curiosity to coherence, and perhaps this is why he is such a cold and static character; he has nothing to seek, because the prerequisite of any search is doubt, and Goffredo cannot doubt). Francesco Erspamer, "Il 'pensiero debole' di Torquato Tasso," *La Menzogna*, ed. Franco Cardini (Florence: Ponte alle Grazie, 1989), 131. Translation is mine.

47. Erspamer, "Il 'pensiero debole,'" 134. On doubt in early modernity, see Marco Faini, *Standing at the Crossroads: Stories of Doubt in Renaissance Italy* (Cambridge, UK: Legenda, 2023).

Chapter 4 Armida's Mission

1. Adriana Cavarero, *Corpo in figure: Filosofia e Politica Della Corporeita* (Milan: Feltrinelli, 1995); Cavarero, *Stately Bodies: Literature, Philosophy, and the Question of Gender*, trans. Robert de Lucca and Deanna Shemek (Ann Arbor: University of Michigan Press, 2002), 97. Citations are from this English translation.

2. Cavarero, *Stately Bodies*, 16.

3. Cavarero, *Stately Bodies*, 103.

4. Armida is the character from the *Liberata* that perhaps most inspired artists and composers as well as scholars. Some important recent studies include Laura Benedetti, "*La sconfitta di Diana. Note per una rilettura della Gerusalemme Liberata*," *MLN* 108, no. 1 (January 1993): 31–58; Jo Ann Cavallo, "Tasso's Armida and the Victory of Romance," in *Renaissance Transactions: Ariosto and Tasso*, ed. Valeria Finucci (Durham, NC: Duke University Press, 1999), 77–111; Luisa Del Giudice, "Armida: *Virgo Fingens* (The Broken Mirror)," in *Western Gerusalem: University of California Studies on Tasso*, ed. Luisa Del Giudice (New York: Out of London Press, 1984), 29–53; Melinda Gough, "Tasso's Enchantress, Tasso's Captive Woman," *Renaissance Quarterly* 54, no. 1 (2001): 523–552; Marilyn Migiel, "Secrets of a Sorceress: Tasso's Armida," *Quaderni d'Italianistica* 8, no. 2 (1987): 149–166; and Marilyn Migiel, *Gender and Genealogy in Tasso's* Gerusalemme Liberata (Lewiston, ME: Edwin Mellen Press, 1993).

5. Robert Durling, "The Epic Ideal," in *The Old World: Discovery and Rebirth*, eds. David Daiches and Anthony Thorlby (London: Aldus Books, 1974), 122. As Durling argues, Tasso's poem represents Renaissance neoclassicism in its adherence to formal aspects of classical epic, a genre that celebrates empire, which in turn reflect the European political climate in the sixteenth and seventeenth centuries, a period that witnessed imperial ambitions among ruling European families, such as the Este family of Ferrara, Tasso's patrons.

6. All citations are from Torquato Tasso, *Gerusalemme Liberata* (*GL*), ed. Lanfranco Caretti (Turin: Einaudi, 1993); all translations are from Torquato Tasso, *Jerusalem Delivered: An English Prose Version*, ed. and trans. Ralph Nash (Detroit: Wayne State University Press, 1987).

7. Torquato Tasso, "Allegoria del poema," in *Le prose diverse di Torquato Tasso*, ed. Cesare Guasti (Florence: Successori Le Monnier, 1875), 1:307.

8. Timothy Hampton, *Fictions of Embassy: Literature and Diplomacy in Early Modern Europe* (Ithaca, NY: Cornell University Press, 2009), 81.

9. Douglas Biow, *Doctors, Ambassadors, Secretaries: Humanism and Professions in Renaissance Italy* (Chicago: University of Chicago Press, 2002), 185.

10. For a discussion of how Tasso incorporated Petrach's lyrical language into the epic, see Ayesha Ramachandran, "Tasso's Petrarch: The Lyric Means to Epic Ends," *MLN* 122, no. 1 (2007): 186–208. Ramachandran's analyses are helpful to see how Tasso's efforts to introduce corporeality and erotics necessitated a detour into lyrical poetry.

11. For a discussion of the parallels between Armida and the courtesan, see Paola Ugolini, *The Court and Its Critics: Anti-Court Sentiments in Early Modern Italy* (Toronto: University of Toronto Press, 2020), 50–83.

12. These phrases are taken from the Venetian statute from the *Esecutori contra la Bestemmia* (regulation of speech and crimes of speech; examined more closely in chapter 5), which sought to keep prostitutes, particularly courtesans, from "offending" respectable society either by physical actions or words. See Capitolare Primo, *Provveditori alla Sanità*, 1485–1574, carta 157 in Giovanni Battista de Lorenzi, *Leggi e memorie venete sulla prostituzione* (Venice: Marco Visentini, 1870–1872), 119. See also Elizabeth Horodowich, "The Language of Courtesans," *Language and Statecraft in Early Modern Venice* (Cambridge, UK: Cambridge University Press, 2008), 165–206.

13. Virgil, *Eclogues; Georgics; Aeneid: Books 1–6*, ed. George P. Goold, trans. H. Rushton Fairclough (Cambridge, MA: Harvard University Press, 1999), 1.1. All citations and translations of this text are from this edition.

14. See Crescenzo Formicula, "Dark Visibility: Lavinia in the *Aeneid*," *Vergilius* 52 (2006): 76–95.

15. The marginality and silence of Virgil's Lavinia inspired Ursula K. Le Guin's 2008 fantasy novel *Lavinia*, in which the author imagines Lavinia's life and the love Virgil never recounts.

16. Elina Pyy, *Women and War in Roman Epic* (Leiden: Brill, 2021), 32.

17. Lavinia's famous blush at the opening of book 12 is characterized as "the sole depiction of Lavinia as an individual, as a human being in her own right." Ruth W. Todd, "Lavinia Blushed," *Vergilius* 26 (1980): 27–33.

18. For a discussion of the continuation and development of this trope, see Katharine Ann Jensen, *Writing Love: Letters, Women, and the Novel in France, 1605–1776* (Carbondale: Southern Illinois University Press, 1995).

19. Virgil's reference to the cruelty of the Hyrcanian tigress became "proverbial" after the *Aeneid*. See Ronald Syme, "The Casdusii in History and in Fiction," *Journal of Hellenic Studies* 108 (1988): 145. In antiquity, the tiger was thought to be a species composed exclusively of females. The tigress was evoked to symbolize cruelty and inhumanity, a characterization that continued into the medieval and early modern literary tradition, particularly when referencing love, with the tiger's diamond-hard heart symbolizing resistance to love and mercy.

20. Tasso, "Allegoria del poema," 1:304.

21. Interestingly, Dido's fate proved moving to many male authors. Ovid, St. Augustine, and Dante are but three towering figures who expressed great sympathy for Dido in their own texts. Ovid ventriloquized Dido in a dying letter/monologue to Aeneas (*Heroides*); St. Augustine, in his *Confessions*, recalled how he wept more for Dido's fate than for his own; in the *Divine Comedy* Dante considered Dido's greater sin to be uncontrolled desire for Aeneas, rather than desperate suicide. Dido, instead of being placed in the wood of suicides, is found among the lustful whose sins are of incontinence. We come to understand that Dido and her wanton companions in canto 5 of *Inferno* evoke profound empathy and serve as a mirror for Dante of the character's own desires, even when Dante the author condemned her for being unfaithful to the ashes of her dead husband. Dante, like other male authors mentioned, tended to reduce Dido's suffering to purely emotional devastation. Dido's suicide, according to Dante, was not the sin for which she was punished, because her suicide was not committed out of "despair," but was due to her "uncontrolled

desire for Aeneas." Dido's suicide, for Dante, is rather an act meant "to give expression to her need for her lover," as John Hollander puts it. See *Inferno,* trans. Robert and Jean Hollander (New York: Doubleday/Anchor, 2000), 105n61.

22. "Virgil intended to show that Dido was a woman of the highest moral character by making her feel that this requirement was a moral and religious duty." Richard Heinze, *Virgil's Epic Technique* (Berkeley: University of California Press, 1994), 126.

23. "O mia sprezzata forma, a te s'aspetta/(ché tua l'ingiuria fu) l'alta *vendetta*" (O my despised beauty, since yours was the injury, the noble deed of *vengeance* waits on you, *GL* 16.65:7–8; italics added); "Io che sarò d'ampie ricchezze erede,/d'*una vendetta* in guiderdon son presta" (I (who will be the heiress of ample riches) stand ready to be the reward of a single *vendetta, GL* 16.66:5–6; italics added); "sol fa la speme/de la dolce *vendetta* ancor ch'io viva" (Only the hope of sweet *revenge* makes me still live on, *GL* 16.67; italics added). Armida repeats her call for vengeance (*vendetta*) in canto 17. In fact, thirteen of the forty-five times (nearly 30%) the term "vendetta" is employed in the *Liberata* it is spoken by or made in reference to Armida, who additionally uses the plural of *vendetta, vendette* (vengeances), as well as etymologically related terms, including *vendicata* (avenged) and *invendicata* (unavenged).

24. Walter Stephens, "Saint Paul Among the Amazons: Gender and Authority in *Gerusalemme Liberata,*" in *Discourses of Authority in Medieval and Renaissance Literature,* eds. Kevin Brownlee and Walter Stephens (Hanover, NH: Dartmouth College by University Press of New England, 1989), 169–200.

25. Torquato Tasso, "Il Messaggiero," in *Opere,* ed. Bruno Maier (Milan: Rizzoli, 1964), 4:711. All translations from this text are my own.

26. Tasso, "Il Messaggiero," 4:715–716.

27. Tasso, "Il Messaggiero," 4:716.

28. Tasso, "Allegoria del poema," 1:307.

29. The following works exemplify the visual semantics of the Renaissance courtesan: Titian, *Venus with a Mirror* (1555), National Gallery of Art, Washington D.C.; Tintoretto (or follower), *Portrait of a Lady (Portrait of Veronica Franco)* (1575?), Worcester Art Museum, Worcester, MA; and Giambattista Tiepolo, *Rinaldo e Armida* (1760), Berlin, Staatliche Museen.

30. Just as Armida transgresses battle lines, her body—particularly the exhibition of her breasts—also refuses containment, similar to Mikhail Bakhtin's "grotesque body," which "is not separated from the rest of the world. It is not a closed, completed unit; it is unfinished, outgrows itself, transgresses its own limits. The stress is laid on those parts of the body that are open to the outside world, that is, the parts through which the world enters the body or emerges from it, or through which the body itself goes out to meet the world. This means that the emphasis is on the apertures or the convexities, or on various ramifications and outshoots: the open mouth, the genital organs, the breasts, the phallus, the potbelly, the nose. The body discloses its essence as a principle of growth that exceeds its own limits only in copulation, pregnancy, childbirth, the throes of death, eating, drinking, or defecation. This is the ever unfinished, ever creating body, the link in the chain of genetic development, or more correctly speaking, two links shown at the point where they enter into each other." M. M. Bahktin, *Rabelais and His World,* trans. Hélène Iswolsky (Bloomington: Indiana University Press, 1984), 26.

31. "La ragione per cui Goffredo non crede ad Armida è del tutto irrazionale e decisamente faziosa; l'incontro con Argante gli ha insegnato che anche un pagano può essere incrollabilmente sincero" (The reason that Goffredo does not believe Armida is completely irrational and decidedly biased; the encounter with Aragante taught him that even a pagan can be steadfastly sincere). Francesco Erspamer, "Il 'pensier debole' di Torquato Tasso," in *La menzogna*, ed. Franco Cardini (Firenze: Ponte alle Grazie, 1989), 130.

32. Armida is referred to, or treated, as an envoy in the following octaves: "Mentre, sospesa alquanto, *alcuna guida*/che la conduca al capitan richiede" (While somewhat hesitant, she is requesting some guide who can lead her to the captain, *GL* 4.33; italics added); "che da te *si ricerca?* ed *onde viensi?*/qual tua ventura o nostra or qui *ti mena?*/Fa' che sappia chi sei; fa' ch'io non erri" (*what are you seeking?* and *whence do you come?* What fate of yours, or ours, now leads you here? Let me know who you are; let me make no mistake in honoring you, *GL* 4.35; italics added); "È ben ragion ch'a l'un germane/l'altro *ti guidi*, e *intercessor ti sia*" (It makes good sense that one brother guide you to the other and be your intercessor, *GL* 4.37; italics added).

33. Walter Stephens, "Trickster, Textor, Architect, Thief: Craft and Comedy in *Gerusalemme Liberata*," in *Renaissance Transactions*, ed. Valeria Finucci (Durham, NC: Duke University Press, 1999), 157.

34. Armida is referred to as "bella peregrine" (beautiful pilgrim, *GL* 4.28) by the narrator, who represents the thoughts of the Crusaders. Additionally, Armida describes herself as "vergine peregrina" (wandering maiden, 4.36). The other "peregrine" characters are Erminia (6.69; 19.113), Arsete (12.33), Vafrino (19.57), and Rinaldo's soul, which leaves his body and makes a "pilgrimage" to Armida (16.19).

35. As the much-cited verse "magnanima menzogna" (noble lie, *GL* 2.22), in reference to Sofronia's attempted martyrdom attests, "menzogna" (lie) is not categorically immoral in the *Liberata*, but its morality is instead subject to the intentions of the speaker.

36. The term *essecutrice* (feminine variant of *esecutore*, "agent or executor") was uncommon in this period. The rare use of the feminine variant of the noun *es[s]ecutor* in the period demonstrates the new type of female character offered by Tasso's fiction. The term first appears in the fourth edition of *Vocabolario degli Accademici della Crusca* (1729–1738), half a century after the *Liberata*'s publication; moreover, the only two cited examples of the word's use are by Tasso and he employs the term only two times in the *Liberata*. See *Vocabolario degli Accademici della Crusca*, 4th ed., in *Lessicografia della Crusca in Rete* (Florence: Accademia della Crusca, 2000–2004), s.v. "esecutrice," http://www.lessicografia.it/.

One cited example is in reference to Sofronia, a Christian counter-figure to Armida, "sol consigliera, e sola essecutrice" (*GL* 2.23), and the other is the same example I cite, by Idraote in his instructions to Armida: "Tessi la tesa ch'io ti dimostro ordita/di cauto vecchio, *essecutrice* ardita" (4.24). The male form, *essecutor*, is also used in the text, but significantly, only in reference to Rinaldo as Goffredo's *essecutor*. There is, however one instance of the plural form, *essecutori* (18.42), in reference to those who build wooden war machines under the command of Guglielmo.

Nonetheless, this lexical link between Rinaldo and Armida is significant insofar as it demonstrates that both figures were agents under a master, thus both "secondary," that is, under another's command. In the case of Armida, she begins her journey in the text as "essecutrice ardita" (bold-hearted agent, 4.24) of her uncle Idraote, whose goal it is to deprive the Christian camp of their most important warriors and thereby force them to relinquish their fight to recapture Jerusalem. Armida in this instance is sent to act as the agent of her uncle. However, as the poem progresses, as argued in this chapter, she gains autonomy and thus acts as her own "agent" and advocate.

The process is similar in Rinaldo's character as well. He starts as a figure clearly subordinate to Goffredo, the leader "chosen" (*eletto*) by God to unite the Christian cavaliers and inspire them to overcome their obstacles, both intrinsic and extrinsic, to liberate Jerusalem and re-Christianize the Holy Land. Rinaldo, however, after the poem ends will gain autonomy by marrying Armida and founding the Estense dynasty, thus assuming the role as "head" of his own political entity.

37. Armida as ambassador embodies the delicate and problematic nature of Renaissance diplomacy, the risks for the envoy, and both the states sending as well as receiving the envoy. Armida's risk lies in acting as an unofficial envoy and was received with suspicion by the enemy camp, rendering her thus vulnerable and without the protections of the customary *ius gentium* laws of diplomacy. The state that sent her also risked her being "turned" and the recipient state also risked allowing a spy/dangerous element into its ranks. Armida's case, except for gender and sexuality, was a type of incognito diplomacy, or even espionage, which was practiced in Renaissance Europe. In chapter 2, I analyze a well-known diplomatic case that ended in death by dismemberment of the (potentially) unofficial envoy, as well as an international scandal involving the most powerful nation-states in Europe, France, and Habsburg Spain as well as the ill-fated duchy of Milan, which would soon be subsumed by Spain.

38. Tasso's "Allegoria," as Jane Tylus notes, "has a singularly complicated relationship to the poem itself; Tasso's letters from the period suggest that it was largely a creation to appease the Roman Inquistor Silvio Antoniani, who needed to approve the poem before it could be published." Tylus, "Tasso's Trees: Epic and Local Culture," in *Epics in the Contemporary World: The Poetics of Community*, eds. Margaret Beissinger, Jane Tylus, and Susanne Wofford (Berkeley: University of California Press, 1999), 120n26. In fact, in one such letter to Luca Scalabrino, Tasso himself separates the two texts into the different intellectual spheres of poetry (*Liberata*) and philosophy (*Allegoria*), the same distinction Plato makes when declaring the "quarrel" between the two disciplines in *Republic* (607b5–6): "Stanco di poetare, mi son volto a filosofare, ed ho disteso minutissimamente l'Allegoria non d'una parte ma di tutto il poema [. . .] Non so se quel che sia per parerne al Signore e al signor Flaminio ed a cotesti altri dotti romani; chè non per altro, a dirvi il vero, l'ho fatto, se non per dare pasto al mondo. Farò il collo torto, e mostrerò ch'io non ho avuto altro fine che di servire il politico; e con questo scudo cercherò d'assicurare ben bene gli amori e gli'incanti" (Tired of writing poetry, I turned to philosophizing and composed the Allegory in the most minute way, not only of one part, but of the entire poem [. . .] I do not know how it will be received by Your Lordship, by Signor Flaminio, or by these other Roman clerics. Because, to tell the truth, I did so for no other reason than to quell those who dissent. I will bow my head and make it known that I had no other aim than to serve the political; and with this shield I will attempt to safeguard the loves and the enchantments very well). Letter 76 to Luca Scalabrino, 1576, in *Lettere di Torquato Tasso*, ed. Cesare Guasti (Florence: Successori Le Monnier, 1852), 1:185. Translation is my own.

39. See Ralph Nash, *Jerusalem Delivered: An English Prose Version* (Detroit: Wayne State University Press, 1987), 74n3.

40. Cicero, *De officiis*. From the lat. *Officium, officiis,* which indicates the political and ethical connotations of "ufficio."

41. Scholars have identified Tasso's allusions to Judith in his character of Armida. The evidence linking Armida and Judith is convincing, yet Tasso likely modeled Armida on Salome as well. The two female figures were often conflated in the early modern pictorial tradition, however, because the iconography of the severed head could indicate either Judith or Salome. Titian's *Salome with the Head of John the Baptist* (ca. 1515, Palazzo Doria Pamhilij, Rome) is one such example of this iconographical confusion. Nevertheless, Tasso demonstrates awareness of both their similarities as well as their distinctions. Similar to Tasso's composition of Armida from different women of the poetic tradition (Dido, Circes, Laura, et al.), he overlays Salome and Judith to increase the complexity and changeability of Armida's character.

This strategy of character composition, as we have seen, coincides with Tasso's own theory of artistic creation developed in his treatise *Il Messaggiero*. In this episode, Armida explicitly performs seduction, echoed by her revealingly short skirt and the abandonment of the veil she wore when she first approached the Crusaders in canto 4. Such a frank demonstration of sexuality is at odds with the association between Judith and enduring widowly chastity and piety despite her strategic and God-ordained seduction (and assassination) of Holofernes to save her besieged city of Bethulia.

For studies linking Judith and Armida, see Eugenio Refini, "Giuditta, Armida e il velo della seduzione," *Italian Studies* 68, no. 1 (2013): 78–98; and Paola Cosentino, "Sulle orme del Tasso: L'epopea eroica di Giuditta nel '600," in *Le donne della Bibbia, la Bibbia delle donne: Teatro, letteratura e vita,* ed. Rossana Gorris Camos (Fasano, Italy: Schena Editore, 2012), 371–390. On the rich iconography and ideology of Judith, see Elena Ciletti, "Patriarchal Ideology in the Renaissance Iconography of Judith," in *Refiguring Women: Perspectives on Gender and the Italian Renaissance,* eds. Marilyn Migiel and Juliana Schiesari (Ithaca, NY: Cornell University Press, 1991), 35–70.

42. Vulgate and King James Version.

43. In *The Enemy in Italian Renaissance Epic: Images of Hostility from Dante to Tasso* (Newark, NJ: University of Delaware Press, 2019), Andrea Moudarres places Armida's narrative within a geopolitical reading in which he discusses how her dubious conversion to Christianity undermines imperialist ideology of the *Gerusalemme Liberata*. See chapter 4, "The Geography of the Enemy: Christian and Islamic Empires from the Fall of Constantinople to Tasso's *Gerusalemme Liberata,*" particularly 117–127.

44. Jo Ann Cavallo, "Tasso's Armida and the Victory of Romance," in *Renaissance Transactions: Ariosto and Tasso,* ed. Valeria Finucci (Durham, NC: Duke University Press, 1999), 97.

45. In her important article "Tasso's enchantress, Tasso's Captive Woman," *Renaissance Quarterly* 54, no. 2 (Summer 2001): 523–552, Melinda Gough links Armida's incomplete conversion to Christianity to Tasso's own ambivalence to submit fully his poetics to the moral dictates of a Christian epic.

46. Stephens, "Saint Paul Among the Amazons," 194.

47. Marilyn Migiel, "Secrets of a Sorceress: Tasso's Armida," *Quaderni d'Italianistica* 8, no. 2 (1987): 149, 156, 161.

48. Migiel, "Secrets of a Sorceress," 159.

49. Robert Durling, "The Epic Ideal," in *The Old World: Discovery and Rebirth*, eds. David Daiches and Anthony Thorlby (London: Aldus Books, 1974), 125.

50. Cavarero, *Stately Bodies*, 16, 97.

51. David Quint, "Political Allegory in the *Gerusalemme Liberata*," *Renaissance Quarterly* 43, no. 1 (Spring 1990): 1–29.

52. Quint, "Political Allegory," 14n19.

53. Quint, "Political Allegory," 13.

54. For more on the effects of the Counter-Reformation on Italian poetry, see Jennifer Helm, *Poetry and Censorship in Counter-Reformation Italy* (Leiden: Brill, 2015); and Ugo Rozzo, *La letteratura italiana negli indici del Cinquecento* (Urbino, Italy: Forum, 2006).

55. "Farò il collo torto, e mostrerò ch'io non ho avuto altro fine che di servire il politico; e con questo scudo cercherò d'assicurare ben bene gli amori e gli'incanti" (I will bow my head and make it known that I had no other aim than to serve the political; and with this shield I will attempt to safeguard very well the love affairs and the enchantments). Letter 76 to Luca Scalabrino, 1576, in *Lettere di Torquato Tasso*, 1:185.

56. Letter 76 to Luca Scalabrino, 1576, in *Lettere di Torquato Tasso*, 1:185.

57. Letter 76 to Luca Scalabrino, 1576, in *Lettere di Torquato Tasso*, 1:185.

58. Francesco Erspamer, "Il 'pensiero debole' di Torquato Tasso," in *La Menzogna*, ed. Franco Cardini (Florence: Ponte alle Grazie, 1989), 134.

59. For a different take, see this recent reevaluation of Goffredo as a more complex and "less perfect" figure, see Andrea Moudarres, "A Less Perfect Captain: Reconsidering Goffredo in the *Gerusalemme Liberata*," *Forum Italicum* 55, no. 1 (2021): 3–20.

60. Through a Virgilian allusion spoken by the character of Pietro l'Eremita, Tasso confirms that from Rinaldo the Estense dynasty will arise: "ben di lui nasceran degni i figli/De' figli i figli, e chi verrà da quelli/quinci avran chiari e memorandi essempi; [. . .] così verrà che vóle/l'aquila estense oltra le vie del sole" (and sons well worthy of him will be born. Sons from those sons, and they who will come from them will have from him famous and memorable examples [. . .] So it will come that the Eagle of the Este flies beyond the roadways of the sun, *GL* 10.75–76). The fact that those "sons well worthy" do not emerge exclusively from Rinaldo, but from the body of Armida, is silenced here, just as Virgil suggests that Aeneas's progeny are produced by him alone without Lavinia's participation. Despite this silence, it is Armida's fertility that poetically solves the sterility of the Estense line, and it is her character who most lives on and "reproduces" beyond the confines of the poem. Armida's irresistible ambiguity inspired innumerable paintings, ballets, and operas, including those by Monteverdi, Lully, Handel, Vivaldi, Haydn, Rossini, and Dvořák.

61. Cavarero, *Stately Bodies*, 13–97.

62. Torquato Tasso's father, Bernardo, frequented Ca' Venier, the salon (*ridotto*) of Domenico Venier, Franco's protector and advisor, and the two men exchanged sonnets and letters (*Rime di Domenico Veniero, senatore viniziano*, ed. Pierantonio Serassi [Bergamo, Italy: Pietro Lancellotto, 1751], 79, 105). Torquato does not seem to have been a regular

visitor at Ca' Venier; however, he consulted Venier regarding literary advice on at least two occasions. While a student at Padua, Tasso sought Venier's counsel about his *Rinaldo*, in recognition of which Tasso mentions Venier in the poem (9.30); additionally, Tasso contacted Venier again in 1575 about his *Gerusalemme Liberata* (Tasso, *Rime di Domenico Veniero*, xviii. See also Margaret Rosenthal, *The Honest Courtesan: Veronica Franco, Citizen and Writer in Sixteenth-Century Venice* (Chicago: University of Chicago Press, 1992), 178, 213. The dedicatee of Veronica Franco's *Lettere familiari a diversi* (discussed in detail in chapter 5), Cardinal Luigi d'Este, was an early patron of Tasso, and Angelo Ingegneri, editor of the first complete edition of *Gerusalemme Liberata*, was well acquainted with Maffio Venier, Domenico's nephew and writer of invective poetry against Veronica Franco. Courtney Quaintance, *Textual Masculinity and the Exchange of Women in Renaissance Venice* (Toronto: University of Toronto Press, 2015), 128, 155.

63. Diana Robin, "Courtesans Celebrity and Print Culture in Renaissance Venice," in *Italian Women and the City: Essays*, eds. Janet Levarie Smarr and Daria Valentini (Madison, WI: Fairleigh Dickinson University Press, 2003), 47.

64. Guido Ruggiero, *Binding Passions: Tales of Magic, Marriage, and Power at the End of the Renaissance* (Oxford: Oxford University Press, 1993), 38.

65. Horodowich, *Language and Statecraft*, 166.

Chapter 5 Controlling Her Corpus

1. Margaret Rosenthal, *The Honest Courtesan: Veronica Franco, Citizen and Writer in Sixteenth-Century Venice* (Chicago: University of Chicago Press, 1992), 131.

2. See Saundra Weddle, "Mobility and Prostitution in Early Modern Venice," *Early Modern Women* 14, no. 1 (Fall 2019): 95–108; for historical sources that examine prostitution in other parts of Italy, see note 54 below.

3. Thomas Coryate, *Coryat's Crudities*, ed. James Maclehose (1611; reprint, Glasgow: University of Glasgow Press, 1905), vol. 1.

4. For more general legislative trends of prostitution in Europe, see Leah Lydia Otis, *Prostitution in Medieval Society: The History of an Urban Institution in Languedoc* (Chicago: University of Chicago Press, 1985), 9–39, 100–110.

5. Guido Ruggiero, *Binding Passions: Tales of Magic, Marriage, and Power at the End of the Renaissance* (Oxford: Oxford University Press, 1993), 48–49; see also Paula C. Clarke, "The Business of Prostitution in Early Renaissance Venice," *Renaissance Quarterly* 68, no. 2, (Summer 2015): 419–464.

6. Giovanni Battista de Lorenzi. *Leggi e memorie*, 120—"Registro 30, *Comuni Consiglio de' Dieci*, 1571–1572, carta 101 verso.

7. Marin Sanudo, *I diarii di Marino Sanuto*, ed. Niccolò Barozzi (Venice: Visentini, 1882), vol. 8, col. 414.

8. Coryate, *Coryat's Crudities*, 402.

9. On Venice's *Convertite*, see Laura Jane McGough, "'Raised from the Devil's Jaws': A Convent for Repentant Prostitutes in Venice, 1530–1670" (PhD diss., Northwestern University, 1997). For a discussion of the *Convertite* in a broader Italian and historical context relating to dishonored women more generally, see Brian Pullan, *Tolerance, Regulation and Rescue: Dishonoured Women and Abandoned Children in Italy, 1300–1800* (Manchester:

Manchester University Press, 2016). For perspective on the development of social institutions serving women, see Sherrill Cohen, *The Evolution of Women's Asylums since 1500: From Refuges for Ex-Prostitutes to Shelters for Battered Women* (New York: Oxford University Press, 1992).

10. "Young women and girls 'at risk' on account of their beauty—were accepted into the *Zitelle*. New entrants had to be at least twelve years old but not older than eighteen, healthy, and beautiful; the governors should be particularly attentive to cases of impoverished, very beautiful girls, whose own parents or guardians might be tempted to let the girl be led astray in order to alleviate the family's extreme poverty." See Laura Jane McGough, "Quarantining Beauty in Early Modern Venice," in *Sins of the Flesh: Responding to Sexual Disease in Early Modern Europe*, ed. Kevin Patrick Siena (Toronto: Centre for Reformation and Renaissance Studies, 2005), 229. On the Zitelle in Venice, see Barbara Boccazzi Mazza, "Governare i 'luoghi pii': La casa delle Zitelle," *Studi veneziani* 49 (2005): 293–300, esp. 298, regarding the bequests of Venetian noblewomen to the Zitelle. See also Cecilia Cristellon, "Ritratto di una cortigiana del Cinquecento: Caterina de Medici da Verona e le sue vicende (1518–1582)," in *Ritratti. La dimendione individuale nella storia (secoli XV–XX): Studi in onore di Anne Jacobson Schutte*, ed. Robert A. Pierce and Silvana Seidel Menchi (Rome: Edizioni di storia e letteratura, 2009), 147–176. Monica Chojnacka, "Women, Charity and Community in Early Modern Venice: The Casa delle Zitelle," *Renaissance Quarterly* 51, no. 1 (1998): 68–91, considers the founding of these institutions to be evidence "of a new spirit of activism inspired by religious conviction."

11. Guido Ruggiero speaks to the complicated social use of prostitution in relation to normative sexual and marriage practices: "It [prostitution] educated young men through nonmarital sexuality and sustained many married men in extramarital sexuality. Thus, while legal in itself, it undermined legitimate sexuality, which was theoretically marriage-centered with an eye toward continuing the family line." Ruggiero, *The Boundaries of Eros: Sex Crime and Sexuality in Renaissance Venice* (New York: Oxford University Press, 1985), 11.

12. Elizabeth S. Cohen, "'Courtesans' and 'Whores': Words and Behavior in Roman Streets," *Women's Studies* 19 (1991). Cohen commented further on the excessive attention paid to the creation and maintenance of a hierarchy of early modern prostitutes, an exercise she sees as an attempt "to leave observers comfortable, because it permits them to overlook the fundamental predicament of doubleness common to all prostitutes, high and low" (201–202).

13. Capitolare Primo, *Provveditori alla Sanità*, 1485–1574, carta 157 in Giovanni Battista de Lorenzi, *Leggi e memorie venete sulla prostituzione* (Venice: Marco Visentini, 1870–1872), 119. Phrases like "any prostitute or courtesan, whatever her condition may be" (Che alcuna meretrice over Cortesana di che conditione esser si voglia) are first found in Venetian laws or ordinances (at least in those reproduced in *Leggi e memorie*), starting at least as early as 1539 (101–102). This period reflects the flourishing of the courtesan and the entrance of the term "courtesan" (*cortesana* is the Venetian spelling) into the lexicon, a word perhaps first documented in a 1514 entry in Marin Sanudo's *I Diarii*. Starting with the Middle Ages, laws condemning prostitution consistently sought to lump prostitutes of all economic means into one ostracized group with the term *meretrice*, which sprang from a need to

specify that the economic condition of courtesans did not distinguish them from the prostitute class.

14. Pietro Aretino, *Ragionamento e Dialogo*, ed. Giorgio Bàrberi Squarotti (Milan: Rizzoli, 1988), 136; and Aretino, *Aretino's Dialogues*, ed. Margaret Rosenthal, trans. Raymond Rosenthal (Toronto: University of Toronto Press, 2018), 127.

15. Elizabeth Horodowich, in *Language and Statecraft in Early Modern Venice* (Cambridge, UK: Cambridge University Press, 2008), 194, noted: "In many ways, courtesans disrupted the categories of masculine and feminine and sometimes even represented a third sex, both in terms of their behavior and depictions of it."

16. Cesare Vecellio, *De gli habiti antichi et moderni di diversi parti del mondo* (Venice: Zenaro, 1590).

17. Vecellio, *De gli habiti antichi e moderni*, 144.

18. Cesare Vecellio, *The Clothing of the Renaissance World*, eds. and trans. Ann Rosalind Jones and Margaret F. Rosenthal (London: Thames and Hudson, 2008), 199.

19. Coryate, *Coryat's Crudities*, 400.

20. Ruggiero, *Binding Passions*, 49. For more on the sumptuary laws, and their ineffectiveness as they relate more broadly in Venetian society, see Patricia Fortini Brown, "Vain Legislation Against vana ostentazione: Sumptuary Laws in the Venetian Dominion," *Artibus et Historiae* 38, no. 76 (2017): 53–76.

21. Coryate, *Coryat's Crudities*, 407.

22. McGough, "Quarantining Beauty," 231.

23. Ian Frederick Moulton, *Before Pornography: Erotic Writing in Early Modern England* (Oxford: Oxford University Press, 2000), 149.

24. Moulton, *Before Pornography*, 148.

25. "La narration d'una gaglioffa rancia/C'ha fatto più con la potta ch'Orlando/Non fece colla spada e con la Lancia" (The story of a rotten scoundrel/who did more with her cunt than Orlando/did with his sword and his lance). Lorenzo Veniero, *La Puttana errante* (Paris: Isidore Liseux Éditeur, 1883), 12. Translation is my own.

26. Veniero, *Puttana errante*, 10.

27. Ruggiero, *Binding Passions*, 50.

28. McGough, "Quarantining Beauty," 229, 230–231.

29. Deborah Howard, *The Architectural History of Venice* (New Haven, CT: Yale University Press, 1980), 156; Mary Lindemann, *Medicine and Society in Early Modern Europe* (Cambridge, UK: Cambridge University Press, 1999), 41.

30. Pietro Rostinio, *Trattato del mal Francese* (Venice: Lodovico Avanzi, 1559), 20–21.

31. Rostinio, *Trattato del mal Francese*, 21.

32. Deanna Shemek similarly notes that the (anonymous, likely male) author of *Lamento di una cortigiana ferrarese* denies any culpability for the scourge's contagion to the male clients of prostitution. Instead, they, like the male readers of satirical and invective literature targeting the courtesan, are represented as "innocent victims of women." See Shemek, "'Mi mostrano a dito tutti quanti': Disease, Deixis, and Disfiguration in the *Lamento di una cortigiana ferrarese*," in *Medusa's Gaze: Essays on Gender, Literature, and Aesthetics in the Italian Renaissance in Honor of Robert J. Rodini*, ed., Paul A. Ferrara, Eugenio Giusti, and Jane Tylus (Boca Raton, FL: Bordighera Press, 2004), 54–58.

33. McGough, "Quarantining Beauty," 223–224.

34. Ruggiero, *Binding Passions*, 32.

35. See Jutta Sperling, "Marvelous Venice: A Virgin City and Its Noble Body Politic," in *Convents and the Body Politic in Late Renaissance Venice* (Chicago: The University of Chicago Press, 1991), 72–114.

36. Ann Rosalind Jones and Margaret F. Rosenthal, "Introduction: The Honored Courtesan," in *Veronica Franco: Poems and Selected Letters*, eds. and trans. Ann Rosalind Jones and Margaret F. Rosenthal (Chicago: The University of Chicago Press, 1998), 11.

37. Edward Muir, *Civic Ritual in Renaissance Venice* (Princeton, NJ: Princeton University Press, 1981), 133.

38. Veronica Franco, *Lettere*, ed. Stefano Bianchi (Rome: Salerno Editrice, 1998), 37; Franco, *Veronica Franco*, 29.

39. Sperling, *Convents and the Body Politic*, 89–90.

40. Antonio Pilot, "Di alcuni versi inediti sulla peste del 1575," *Ateneo Veneto* 26 (1903): 355, in Sperling, *Convents and the Body Politic*, 308n61.

41. Sperling, *Convents and the Body Politic*, 83.

42. Rosenthal, *The Honest Courtesan*, 268n44. Marin Sanudo, in his *Diarii* entry of October 25, 1514, alleges that a taxation on prostitutes was proposed and accepted for the explicit purpose of funding the construction of the Arsenale (*I Diarii di Marino Sanuto*, ed. Niccolò Barozzi [Venice: Visentini, 1882] vol. 19, col. 165–166). Paula C. Clarke notes, however, that there does not seem to be any documentary evidence to substantiate that such a proposal was enacted (Clarke, "The Business of Prostitution," 423, 423n12). Elizabeth Horodowich states that, although Venice did tax prostitutes, the stigma of sex work makes it difficult for historians to determine with precision the earnings of prostitutes and the amount of revenue Venice gained from sex work, forcing us to "only speculate on the symbolic significance of such taxation" (*Language and Statecraft*, 196–197, 197n82).

43. Sperling, *Convents and the Body Politic*, 97.

44. Franco, *Lettere*, 72; and Rosalind and Rosenthal, *Franco: Poems and Selected Letters*, 38.

45. Horodowich, *Language and Statecraft*: "Courtesans may have been despised for their sexual nature, but were empowered by the fact that they were economic agents: a figure that, like the Jews, the Venetian state often sought to promote for its own benefit" (198).

46. Horodowich, *Language and Statecraft*, 200.

47. Coryate, *Coryat's Crudities*, 403.

48. Coryate, *Coryat's Crudities*, 403–405.

49. Guido Ruggiero, *Binding Passions*, 38.

50. Horodowich, *Language and Statecraft*: "Venice was among the premier cities whose economy was driven by consumption" (198).

51. Horodowich, *Language and Statecraft*: "Courtesans clearly commercialized language: a business that was both culturally associated with the city and contributed significantly to its economy. This is especially evident in the way that writers exploited courtesans and their eloquence as a tourist attraction [. . .] the sale of sex and [. . .] conversation came

to be closely associated with the lagoon city and defined it in the minds of both locals and foreigners as a mark of Venetian culture" (197–198).

52. Ruggiero, Guido. *Binding Passions*, 26.

53. In addition to Horodowich, *Language and Statecraft*, 197, see Tessa Storey, *Carnal Commerce in Counter-Reformation Rome* (Cambridge, UK: Cambridge University Press, 2008), 63–65; and Diane Yvonne Ghirardo, "The Topography of Prostitution in Renaissance Ferrara," *Journal of the Society of Architectural Historians* 60, no. 4 (December 2001): 406.

54. Coryate, *Coryat's Crudities*, 403.

55. Horodowich, *Language and Statecraft*, 197.

56. Ghirardo, "Topography of Prostitution," 406.

57. Coryate, *Coryat's Crudities*, 402–403.

58. Horodowich, *Language and Statecraft*, 197. It has been well demonstrated by historians that courtesans served nonmarital and extramarital sexual services for noble men (see note 11).

59. The scope of this study limits discussion to Veronica Franco, but there is at least one other remarkable writer who published at the same time and under similar circumstances to Franco: Tullia d'Aragona (1510–1556), the Roman courtesan and poet who published *Rime* (1547), an innovative philosophical dialogue on the nature of love; *Dialogo dell'infinità d'amore* (1547), as well as an epic poem, *Il Meschino altramente detto il Guerrino* (1560). For more on the courtesan poet in the wider context of women's writing in early modern Italy, see Virginia Cox, *Women's Writing in Italy, 1400–1650* (Baltimore: Johns Hopkins University Press, 2008); and Cox, *The Prodigious Muse* (Baltimore: Johns Hopkins University Press, 2011). On d'Aragona, see Julia L. Hairston, "Tullia d'Aragona," in *Oxford Bibliographies in Renaissance and Reformation*, ed. Margaret L. King (Oxford: Oxford University Press, 2016) and Hairston, "'*Di sangue illustre & pellegrino*': The Eclipse of the Body in the Lyric of Tullia d'Aragona," in *The Body in Early Modern Italy*, ed. Julia L. Hairston and Walter Stephens (Baltimore: Johns Hopkins University Press, 2010), 158–175; Ann Rosalind Jones, "New Songs for the Swallow: Ovid's Philomela in Tullia d'Aragona and Gaspara Stampa," in *Refiguring Woman: Perspectives on Gender and the Italian Renaissance*, ed. Marilyn Migiel and Juliana Schiesari (Ithaca, NY: Cornell University Press, 1991), 263–277; Ann Rosalind Jones, "The Poetics of Group Identity: Self-Commemoration through Dialogue in Pernette du Guillet and Tullia d'Aragona," in *The Currency of Eros: Women's Love Lyric in Europe, 1540–1620* (Bloomington: Indiana University Press, 1990), 79–117; and Rinaldina Russell, "Introduction," in *Dialogue on the Infinity of Love* (Chicago: University of Chicago Press, 1997), 21–42.

60. Maria Luisa Doglio, "Scrittura e "offizio di parole" nelle *Lettere familiari* di Veronica Franco," in *Lettera e donna. Scrittura epistolare tra Quattro e Cinquecento* (Rome: Bulzoni, 1993), 34. I follow Doglio in excluding the *Lettere amorose* (1562) di Celia Romana from the list of letterbooks published by women. This collection of love letters enjoyed considerable popularity and numerous editions, yet there are doubts about the (female) identity and/or existence of "Celia."

61. Meredith Ray, "The Courtesan's Voice: Veronica Franco's *Lettere familiari*," in *Writing Gender in Women's Letter Collections of the Italian Renaissance* (Toronto: Univer-

sity of Toronto Press, 2009), 125–126. For an excellent discussion of women's letter writing in early modern Italy, see the introductory chapter of the same monograph, "Women's Vernacular Letters in Context," 19–42.

62. For a full account of Franco's Inquisition trial, see Rosenthal, "Denouncing the Courtesan: Franco's Inquisition Trial and Poetic Debate," in *Honest Courtesan*, 153–203.

63. Rosenthal, *Honest Courtesan*, 156.

64. Rosenthal, *Honest Courtesan*, 132.

65. Jones and Rosenthal, "Introduction: The Honored Courtesan," to *Veronica Franco*, 4. For a transcription of the tax declaration, see Rosenthal, *Honest Courtesan*, 115. Paula C. Clarke also establishes that San Samuele was a district well known for its resident prostitutes; see Clarke, "The Business of Prostitution," 427n33, 429n38, 460n164.

66. Diana Robin, "Courtesans, Celebrity, and Print Culture in Renaissance Venice," in *Italian Women and the City: essays*, ed. Janet Levarie Smarr and Daria Valentini (Madison, WI: Fairleigh Dickinson University Press, 2003), 35–59.

67. Rosenthal, *Honest Courtesan*, 117–118.

68. In addition to Celia Romana's *Lettere amorose di Madonna Celia, gentildonna Romana* (ten editions, 1562 to 1628), other love letter (*lettere amorose*) collections popular at the time include Andrea Calmo, *I piacevoli et ingeniosi discorsi in più lettere* (four books, all with numerous editions from 1547 to 1610); Alvise Pasqualigo, *Lettere amorose* (ten editions, from 1563 to 1607); Girolamo Parabosco, *Delle lettere amorose* (four books, all with numerous editions from 1545 to 1617); and Matteo Aldrovandi, *Lettere amorose* (two editions, 1568 and 1600). See Amedeo Quondam, *Le "Carte messaggiere": Retorica e modelli di comunicazione epistolare. Per un indice dei libri di lettere del Cinquecento* (Rome: Bulzoni, 1981), 279–316.

69. Maria Luisa Doglio, "Letter Writing, 1350–1650," in *A History of Women's Writing in Italy*, ed. Letizia Panizza and Sharon Wood (Cambridge, UK: Cambridge University Press, 2000), 21–22; For a broader discussion on women writers and didactic authority, see Virginia Cox, "Authorizing Women: The Problem of Docere," in *The Prodigious Muse* (Baltimore: Johns Hopkins University Press, 2011), 219–226.

70. Rosenthal, *The Honest Courtesan*, 152.

71. Recent criticism on Franco includes Fiora A. Bassanese, "Private Lives and Public Lies: Texts by Courtesans of the Italian Renaissance," *Texas Studies in Literaure and Language* 30, no. 3 (1987): 295–319, and Bassanese, "Selling the Self; or, the Epistolary Production of Renaissance Courtesans," in *Italian Women Writers from the Renaissance to the Present: Revising the Canon*, ed. Maria Ornella Marotti (University Park: Penn State University Press, 1996), 69–82; Maria Luisa Doglio, "Scrittura e "offizio di parole" nelle *Lettere familiari* di Veronica Franco," in *Lettera e donna. Scrittura epistolare tra Quattro e Cinquecento* (Rome: Bulzoni, 1993), 33–48; Elvira Favretti, "Rime e Lettere di Veronica Franco," *Giornale storico della letteratura italiana* 163 (1986): 344–382; Ann Rosalind Jones, "City Women and Their Audiences: Louise Labé and Veronica Franco," in *Rewriting the Renaissance: The Discourses of Sexual Difference in Early Modern Europe*, ed. Margaret W. Ferguson, Maureen Quilligan, and Nancy J. Vickers (Chicago: University of Chicago Press, 1986), 299–314; Marilyn Migiel, *Veronica Franco in Dialogue* (Toronto: University of

Toronto Press, 2022); Gabriel Niccoli, "Autobiography and Fiction in Veronica Franco's Epistolary Narrative," *Canadian Journal of Italian Studies* 16, no. 47 (1993): 129–142; Jones and Rosenthal, "Introduction: The Honored Courtesan," in *Veronica Franco*, 1–22 (English of selected letters can be found in this same volume); Ray, "The Courtesan's Voice," 123–155; Rosenthal, *The Honest Courtesan*, 116–152, and Rosenthal, "Veronica Franco's Terze Rime: The Venetian Courtesan's Defense," *Renaissance Quarterly* 42, no. 2 (1989): 227–257; and Dolora Wojciehowski [now Hannah] Chapelle, "Veronica Franco vs. Maffio Venier: Sex, Death, and Poetry in Cinquecento Venice," *Italica* 83, nos. 3–4 (2006): 367–390.

72. Rosenthal, *The Honest Courtesan*, 125.

73. Laurie Stras, "'Onde havrà 'l mond'esempio et vera historia': Musical Echoes of Henri III's Progress through Italy," *Acta Musicologica* 72, no. 1 (2000): 8.

74. Henri's reputation as Protestant vanquisher made him a target. A letter from Catherine de' Medici indicates her concern for Henri's safety in northern Europe (see Stras, "Musical Echoes," 8, 8n4), which was warranted since Henri III would have been particularly valuable as ransom given the vacuum on the French throne at the time and the raging Wars of Religion. The fear of capture was not theoretical, as Henri's own father, Henri II, as a child was held as a political captive for four years, to secure the release of Francis I, who was captured by Spanish Imperial forces at the Battle of Pavia (1525).

75. Pietro Buccio, *Le coronationi di Polonia e di Francia del Christianissimo Re Henrico III* (Padua: Lorenzo Pasquati, 1576), 176.

76. Rosenthal, *Honest Courtesan*, 102, 302n92; Ewa Kociszewska, "Displays of Sugar Sculpture and the Collection of Antiquities in Late Renaissance Venice," *Renaissance Quarterly* 73 (2020): 442.

77. Pierre De Nolhac and Angelo Solerti, *Il viaggio in Italia di Enrico III Re di Francia e le feste a Venezia, Ferrara, Mantova, Torino* (Turin: L. Roux, 1890), 110–112, 33.

78. Kociszewska, "Displays of Sugar Sculpture," 444.

79. Kociszewska, "Displays of Sugar Sculpture," 457. For a more extended discussion of the event and its sensual imagery, 452–457.

80. Ray emphasizes Franco's diligent adherence to rhetorical protocol found in epistolary manuals, such as Francesco Sansovino's *Del secretario* (Venice: n.p., 1573) and Girolamo Ruscelli's *Lettere di principi*. Ray, "The Courtesan's Voice," 136.

81. Veronica Franco, *Lettere*, ed. Stefano Bianchi (Rome: Salerno Editrice, 1998), 30; and Jones and Rosenthal, *Franco: Poems and Selected Letters*, 24.

82. For a discussion of the convergence of diplomacy and seduction in Venice, see Horodowich, *Language and Statecraft*, 202–206.

83. Franco, *Lettere*, 30; Jones and Rosenthal, *Franco: Poems and Selected Letters*, 24.

84. Ray, "The Courtesan's Voice," 128–129.

85. Henri was joined in Venice by his cousin, Alfonso II d'Este, Duke of Ferrara, who can be considered to have been a semiofficial guide to Venice. More directly, the Venetian signoria elected a group of nobles to serve the king during his stay ("elezione dei nobili destinati a servire il re"), which even wore uniforms honoring Henri's mourning of his brother, Charles IX. See De Nolhac and Solerti, *Il viaggio in Italia*, 58–59. For additional

discussion of the theories about the arrangement of the encounter between Henri and Franco, see Rosenthal, *The Honest Courtesan*, 104, 203n96.

86. Rosenthal, *The Honest Courtesan*, 105. Stefano Bianchi also notes that Franco's name is not associated with the edited volume that was published in commemoration of Henri's triumphal entry in Venice, and verifies there are no documents attesting to her collaboration. See Franco, *Lettere*, 119n4. The volume in honor of Henri's visit is entitled *Compositioni volgari e latine fatte da diversi nella venuta in Venetia di Henrico III Re di Francia e di Polonia* (Venice: Farri, 1574).

87. Franco, *Lettere*, 30; Franco, *Poems and Selected Letters*, 24.

88. Veronica Franco, ed. *Rime di diversi eccellentissimi auttori nella morte dell'illustre sign. Estor Martinengo conte di Malpaga. Raccolte et mandate all'illustre et valoroso colonnello il s. Francesco, suo fratello, conte di Malpaga dalla signora Veronica Franca* (Venice: n.p., 1575?).

89. Courtney Quaintance, *Textual Masculinity and the Exchange of Women in Renaissance Venice* (Toronto: University of Toronto Press, 2015), 157.

90. Franco also contributed to other commemorative editions. See Rosenthal, *The Honest Courtesan*, 99–102.

91. Rosenthal, *The Honest Courtesan*, 105.

92. Guy Poirier, "A Contagion at the Source of Discourse on Sexualities: Syphilis during the French Renaissance," in *Imagining Contagion in Early Modern Europe*, ed. Claire L. Carlin (Basingstoke, UK: Palgrave Macmillan, 2005), 170–171.

93. Muzio Manfredi published a letter dated October 30, 1591, three months after Franco's death, in his epistolary collection, *Lettere brevissime* (Venice: Meglietti, 1606), in which he thanks her for the sonnet she wrote in admiration of his tragedy *Semiramis* (Bergamo: Comin Ventura, 1593) and praises the "rarity" and "divinity" of Franco's talent (la sua rarità, la divinità dell'ingegno). See Rosenthal, *The Honest Courtesan*, 152; and Stefano Bianchi's introduction to Franco, *Lettere*, 7–8, 20n4. Quaintance notes that a poem commending Franco by a certain Giovanni Scrittore (possibly a pseudonym) appeared in the commemorative volume honoring Estor Martinengo, edited by Franco, see *Textual Masculinity*, 139–140.

94. Franco, *Lettere*, 71; Jones and Rosenthal translate "all'obligo all'umanità" as "a humane obligation." Franco, *Poems and Selected Letters*, 38.

95. Franco uses the term *cortigiane* once. See *Lettere*, 73.

96. Rostinio, *Trattato del mal Francese*, 21.

97. See note 13.

98. See Quaintance, *Textual Masculinity*, and Courtney Quaintance, "Defaming the Courtesan: Satire and Invective in Sixteenth-Century Italy," in *The Courtesan' Arts: Cross-Cultural Perspectives*, ed. Bonnie Gordon and Martha Feldman (Oxford: Oxford University Press, 2006), 199–208.

99. From the "charge" (denuncia) against Franco by Ri[e]dolfo Vannitelli, her employee, to the Holy Office of the Inquisition of Venice: "Io Redolfo Vannitelli per discarico della mia coscienza, et non per altro effetto do' in notitia al Santissimo Offitio dell'Inquisitione come una Veronica Franca *pubblica meretrice*" (I, Redolfo Vannitelli, wishing to unburden my conscience and for no other reason, hereby inform the Most Holy

Office of the Inquisition that Veronica Franca, a *public prostitute . . .* ; italics added). ASV, Sant'Uffizio, Processi, 1580 in Margaret Rosenthal, *The Honest Courtesan*, 153.

100. Rosenthal, *The Honest Courtesan*, 153.

101. Jones and Rosenthal indicate that this passage echoes a part of a conversation between Nanna, a prostitute, and her daughter Pippa in Aretino's *Dialoghi*. See *Veronica Franco*, 13; and Rosenthal, *The Honest Courtesan*, 128. Ray further established another allusion to discusses to Sperone Speroni's dialogue "Della cura famigliare," a wifely conduct manual. Ray, "The Courtesan's Voice," 152.

102. Franco, *Lettere*, 74; Jones and Rosenthal, *Franco: Poems and Selected Letters*, 39.

103. See *Grande Dizionario della Lingua Italiana*, Prototipo edizione digitale (Turin: UTET Grandi Opere; Florence: Accademia della Crusca, 2018), s.v. "Figliòla," https://www.gdli.it/sala-lettura/vol/5?seq=972.

104. Franco, *Lettere*, 71; and Franco, *Poems and Selected Letters*, 38.

105. Franco, *Lettere*, 72; and Franco, *Poems and Selected Letters*, 38.

106. Franco, *Lettere*, 71; and Franco, *Poems and Selected Letters*, 38.

107. Franco, *Lettere*, 75; and Franco, *Poems and Selected Letters*, 39.

108. "Implicit, however, in Franco's condemnation of the mother's conduct is her own painful awareness of the hypocrisy at the heart of Venetian social practices: owning to poverty and to the absence of a male protector, women end up being forced to do precisely those things they would otherwise choose to avoid" (Rosenthal, *The Honest Courtesan*, 129).

109. Franco, *Lettere*, 71; Jones and Rosenthal, *Franco: Poems and Selected Letters*, 38.

110. "In portraying herself as an admirable exception, Veronica Franco seemed to agree with contemporary polemics against the deceitfulness and undignified servitude of a common prostitute's business. In her writings, Franco was preoccupied with protecting her personal dignity, but she also portrayed the abuse and humiliations a prostitute typically had to endure" (Sperling, *Convents and the Body Politic*, 99).

111. "Critics have repeatedly interpreted Franco's letter 22 as proof of her desire to denounce the horrors of her profession and her need to announce her conversion to a life of repentance. Rather, I would argue, this epistle questions the ideological assumptions that have forced an innocent young woman and her mother into a morally compromising situation. What Franco condemns in the letter is the impossibility of freely choosing one's future—a situation in which she too must have found herself as a child. Franco paints a cruel and violent picture of female subjugation, inequality, and suffering. Her message is not repentance, I believe, but profound indignation. [. . .] she argues that not all Venetian citizens are free, nor do they share equally in the prosperity touted by the Venetian state" (Rosenthal, *The Honest Courtesan*, 127).

112. Sperling, *Convents and the Body Politic*, 99.

113. Sperling, *Convents and the Body Politic*, 75.

Bibliography

Manuscripts

Bibliothèque Nationale de France, Paris

Pagani, Zaccaria. *Viagio del Magnifico et Preclarissimo Cavalier et Procurator di San Marco Domino Dominicho Trivisano*. In MS Paris, Archives et Manuscrits, Italien 2111.

Primary Sources

Alciati, Andrea. *Emblematum liber*. Augsburg: Heinrich Steyner, 1531.

Alighieri, Dante. *Inferno*. Edited by Robert Hollander, translated by Robert and Jean Hollander. New York: Doubleday/Anchor, 2000.

———. *Purgatorio*. Edited by Robert Hollander, translated by Robert and Jean Hollander. New York: Doubleday/Anchor, 2003.

Aretino, Pietro. *Aretino's Dialogues*. Edited by Margaret Rosenthal, translated by Raymond Rosenthal. Toronto: University of Toronto Press, 2018.

———. *Ragionamenti e Dialoghi*. Edited by Giorgio Barberi Squarotti. Milan: Rizzoli, 1988.

Barbaro, Ermolao. *De Coelibatu; De Officio Legati*. Edited by Vittore Branca. Firenze: L. S. Olschki, 1969.

Barbaro, Giosafat. "Viaggio di Iosafa Barbaro alla Tana e nella Persia." In *Navigazioni e Viaggi*, vol. 3, edited by Giovanni Baptista Ramusio and Marica Milanesi. Turin: Einaudi, 1988.

Barbaro Giosafat, and Ambrogio Contarini. *I Viaggi in Persia Degli Ambasciatori Veneti Barbaro E Contarini*. Edited by Laurence Lockhart, Raimondo Morozzo Della Rocca, and Maria Francesca Tiepolo. Roma: Istituto Poligrafico dello Stato, 1973.

Bragaccia, Gasparo. *L'Ambasciatore*. Padua: Francesco Bolzetta, 1627.

Camusat, Nicolas. *Meslanges historiques*. Troyes: Noel Moreau, 1619.

Capellanus, Andreas. *The Art of Courtly Love*. Translated by John Jay Parry. New York: Columbia University Press, 1990.

Castiglione, Baldassarre. *Il libro del Cortegiano*. Edited by Walter Barberis. Turin: Einaudi, 1998.

Cicero. *On the Orator: Books 1–2*. Translated by E. W. Sutton and H. Rackham. Cambridge, MA: Harvard University Press, 1942.

Contarini, Ambrogio. *Questo e el viazo de misier Ambrogio Contarin ambasador de la Illustrissima signoria de Venezia al signor Uxuncassan Re di Persia*. Venice: Annibale Fossio, 1487.

———. "Viaggio di Ambrosio Contarini, ambasciatore veneziano." In *Navigazioni e Viaggi*, 6 vols., vol. 3. Edited by Marica Milanesi. Turin: Einaudi, 1988.

———. "Viaggio d'un mercante che fu nella Persia." In Giovanni Battista Ramusio, *Navigazioni e Viaggi*, 6 vols., vol. 3. Edited by Marica Milanesi. Turin: Einaudi, 1988.

Contarini, Ambrogio, and Giosafat Barbaro. *Travels to Tana and Persia by Josafa Barbaro and Ambrogio Contarini*. Translated by William Thomas and S. A. Roy, edited by Lord Stanley of Alderley. London: Hakluyt Society, 1873.

Coryate, Thomas. *Coryat's Crudities; Hastily Gobled up in Five Moneths Travells in France, Savoy, Italy, Rhetia Commonly Called the Grisons Country, Helvetia Alias Switzerland, Some Parts of High Germany and the Netherlands; Newly Digested in the Hungry Aire of Odcombe in the County of Somerset, and Now Dispersed to the Nourishment of the Travelling Members of This Kingdome*. Compiled by George Coryate. Glasgow: J. MacLehose, 1905.

d'Aragona, Tullia. *Dialogo della signora Tullia d'Aragona della infinità di amore*. Venice: Gabriel Giolito de Ferrari, 1547.

———. *Il Meschino, altramente detto il Guerrino, fatto in ottaua rima dalla signora Tullia D'Aragona*. Venezia: Giovan Battista, et Melchior Sessa fratelli, 1560.

———. *Rime della signora Tullia di Aragona, et di diversi a lei*. Venice: Gabriel Giolito de Ferrari, 1547.

De Nolhac, Pierre, and Angelo Solerti. *Il viaggio in Italia di Enrico III Re di Francia e le feste a Venezia, Ferrara, Mantova, Torino*. Turin: L. Roux, 1890.

Dolet, Étienne. *De officio legati*. Lyons: Dolet, 1541.

Du Bellay, Martin, and Guillaume Du Bellay. *Mémoires de Martin et Guillaume Du Bellay*. 7 vols. Paris: Prault, 1753.

Franco, Veronica. *Lettere*. Edited by Stefano Bianchi. Rome: Salerno, 1998.

Franco, Veronica, ed. *Rime di diversi eccellentissimi auttori nella morte dell'illustre sign. Estor Martinengo conte di Malpaga. Raccolte et mandate all'illustre et valoroso colonnello il s. Francesco Martinengo, suo fratello, conte di Malpaga dalla signora Veronica Franca*. Venice: n.p., [1575?].

Gentili, Alberico. *Des legationibus libri tres*. 2 vols. Edited by James Brown Scott, translated by Gordon J. Laing. Oxford: Oxford University Press, 1924.

Grotius, Hugo. *De iure belli ac pacis*. Paris: Nicolas Buon, 1625.

Guicciardini, Francesco. *Maxims and Reflections of a Renaissance Statesman (Ricordi)*. Translated by Mario Domandi, introduction by Nicolai Rubinstein. New York: Harper & Row, 1965.

———. *Ricordi*. Edited by Giorgio Masi. Milan: Mursia, 1994.

Hotman, Jean. *De la charge et la dignité d'ambassadeur*. Dusseldorf: Buys, 1613; originally published in 1603.

de Lorenzi, Giovanni Battista, ed. *Leggi e memorie venete sulla prostituzione*. Venice: Marco Visentini, 1870–1872.

Maggi, Ottaviano. *De legato libri duo*. Venice: Lodovico Avanzi, 1566.

Manfredi, Muzio. *Lettere brevissime*. Venice: Meglietti, 1606.

———. *Semiramis*. Bergamo: Comin Ventura, 1593.

Montaigne, Michel de. "Des menteurs." In *Essais de messire Michel de Montaigne*. Bordeaux: S. Millanges, 1580.

———. *Les Essais de Michel de Montaigne*. Edited by Pierre Villey and Verdun Louis Saulnier. Paris: Presses Universitaires de France, 1965.

———. "Of Liars." In *The Complete Essays of Montaigne*. Translated by Donald M. Frame. Stanford, CA: Stanford University Press, 1958.

Pagani, Zaccaria. *Viaggio di Domenico Trevisan: ambasciatore veneto al gran sultano del Cairo nell'anno 1512*. Edited by Niccolò Barozzi. Venice: Antonelli, 1875.

Petrarca, Francesco. *Canzoniere*. Edited by Marco Santagata. Milan: A. Mondadori, 1996.

———. *Trionfi e Rime*. Edited by Vincio Pacca and Laura Paolino. Milan: Mondadori, 1996.

Ramusio, Giovanni Battista. *Delle navigazioni et viaggi*. 3 vols. Venice: Giunti, 1550–1559.

———. *Navigazioni e Viaggi*. 6 vols. Edited by Marica Milanesi. Turin: Einaudi, 1985.

Rostinio, Pietro. *Trattato del mal francese*. Venice: Lodovico Avanzi, 1559.

Ruscelli, Girolamo. *Lettere di principi*. Venice: Giordano Ziletti, 1577.

Sansovino, Francesco. *Delle cose notabili della città di Venetia Libri II: Ne I quali contengono usanze antiche*. Venice: Valgrisio, 1587.

———. *Del Secretario*. Venice: n.p., 1573.

Sanudo, Marino. *I diarii di Marino Sanuto*. Vol. 12. Edited by Niccolò Barozzi. Venice: F. Visentini, 1886.

Tasso, Torquato. "Allegoria del poema." In *Le prose diverse di Torquato Tasso*. Edited by Cesare Guasti. Florence: Successori Le Monnier, 1875.

———. "Discorsi dell'arte poetica." In *Le prose diverse di Torquato Tasso*. Edited by Cesare Guasti. Florence: Successori Le Monnier, 1875.

———. "Discorso primo." *I discorsi dell'arte poetica, Il padre di famiglia, e L'Aminta*. Edited by Angelo Solerti. Turin: G. B. Paravia, 1901.

———. *Gerusalemme Liberata: Torquato Tasso*. Edited by Lanfranco Caretti. Turin: Einaudi, 1993.

———. "Il Messaggiero." In *Opere*. 5 vols. Edited by Bruno Maier. Milan: Rizzoli, 1964. First published Venice: Bernardo Giunti, 1582.

———. *Jerusalem Delivered (Gerusalemme Liberata)*. Translated by Anthony M. Esolen. Baltimore: Johns Hopkins University Press, 2000.

———. *Torquato Tasso; Jerusalem Delivered: An English Prose Version*. Edited and translated by Ralph Nash. Detroit: Wayne State University Press, 1987.

Valla, Lorenzo. *On Pleasure: De Voluptate (Of the True and the False Good)*. Edited by Maristella Lorch, translated by A. Kent Hieatt and Maristella Lorch. New York: Albaris Books, 1977.

Vecellio, Cesare. *The Clothing of the Renaissance World: Europe, Asia, Africa, the Americas: Cesare Vecellio's Habiti Antichi Et Moderni*. Edited and translated by Ann Rosalind Jones and Margaret F. Rosenthal. London: Thames & Hudson, 2008.

———. *De gli habiti antichi et moderni di diversi parti del mondo*. Venice: Zenaro, 1590.

Veniero, Lorenzo. *La Puttana Errante*. Paris: Isidore Liseux Editeur, 1883.

Wotton, Henry. "Letter to Marcus Welser." In *Reliquiae Wottonianae*. Edited by Izaak Walton. London: Roycroft, 1672.

———. *Reliquiæ Wottonianæ: Or, a Collection of Lives, Letters, Poems; With Characters of Sundry Personages: And Other Incomparable Pieces of Language and Art, By the Curious Pensil of the Ever Memorable Sr Henry Wotton Kt, Late Provost of Eton College*. Edited by Edward H. Clarendon. London: Maxey, 1651.

Secondary Sources

Andreotti, Giulio. *"Presentazione" to L'Ambasciatore*. Rome: Vecchiarelli, 1989.

Asch, Ronald G., and Adolf M. Birke, eds. *Princes, Patronage, and the Nobility: The Court at the Beginning of the Modern Age, c. 1450–1650*. London: German Historical Institute, 1991.

Bahktin, M. M. *Rabelais and His World*. Translated by Hélène Iswolsky. Bloomington: Indiana University Press, 1984.

Bassanese, Fiora A. "Private Lives and Public Lies: Texts by Courtesans of the Italian Renaissance." *Texas Studies in Literature and Language* 30, no. 3 (1987): 295–319.

———. "Selling the Self; or, the Epistolary Production of Renaissance Courtesans." In *Italian Women Writers from the Renaissance to the Present: Revising the Canon*. Edited by Maria Ornella Marotti. University Park: Penn State University Press, 1996.

Behrens, Betty. "Treatises on the Ambassador Written in the Fifteenth and Early Sixteenth Centuries." *English Historical Review* 51 (1936): 616–627.

Benedetti, Laura. "From Venice to Cairo: Notes from an Early 16th-Century Voyage across the Mediterranean." *Mediterranea* 7 (2022): 503–517.

———. "La sconfitta di Diana. Note per una rilettura della Gerusalemme Liberata." *MLN* 108, no. 1 (January 1993): 31–58.

Benedetti, Laura, and Enrico Musacchio. *Da Venezia al Cairo. Il viaggio di Zaccaria Pagani nel primo Cinquecento*. Padua: Il Poligrafo, 2021.

Berger, John. *Ways of Seeing*. London: BBC/Penguin, 1972.

Biow, Douglas. *Doctors, Ambassadors, Secretaries: Humanism and Professions in Renaissance Italy*. Chicago: University of Chicago Press, 2002.

Boccazzi Mazza, Barbara. "Governare i 'luoghi pii': La casa delle Zitelle." *Studi veneziani* 49 (2005): 293–300.

Brown, Patricia Fortini. *Private Lives in Renaissance Venice: Art, Architecture, and the Family*. New Haven, CT: Yale University Press, 2004.

———. "Vain Legislation Against vana ostentazione: Sumptuary Laws in the Venetian Dominion." *Artibus et Historiae* 38, no. 76 (2017): 53–76.

Buccio, Pietro. *Le coronationi di Polonia e di Francia del Christianissimo Re Henrico III*. Padua: Lorenzo Pasquati, 1576.

Burckhardt, Jacob. *The Civilization of the Renaissance in Italy*. Translated by S.G.C. Middlemore. New York: Macmillan, 1860; rev. ed. 1921.

Canova, Andrea. "Letteratura di viaggio e lessico esotico: musulmano in Giosafat Barbaro." *L'Ellisse* 15, no. 1 (2020): 37–46.

Cartwright, Julia Mary. *Baldassare Castiglione: The Perfect Courtier.* New York: E. P. Dutton, 1908.

Cavaillé, Jean Pierre. "Per una storia della dissimulazione." *Les dossiers GRIHL (Groupe de Recherches Interdisiplinaires sur l'Histoire du Littéraire).* February 2009. https://doi.org/10.4000/dossiersgrihl.3666.

Cavallo, Jo Ann. "Tasso's Armida and the Victory of Romance." In *Renaissance Transactions: Ariosto and Tasso,* edited by Valeria Finucci. Durham, NC: Duke University Press, 1999.

Cavarero, Adriana. *Corpo in Figure: Filosofia e Politica Della Corporeita.* Milan: Feltrinelli, 1995.

———. *Stately Bodies: Literature, Philosophy, and the Question of Gender.* Translated by Robert De Lucca and Deanna Shemek. Ann Arbor: University of Michigan, 2002.

Chojnacka, Monica. "Women, Charity and Community in Early Modern Venice: The Casa delle Zitelle." *Renaissance Quarterly* 51, no. 1 (1998): 68–91.

Ciletti, Elena. "Patriarchal Ideology in the Renaissance Iconography of Judith." In *Refiguring Women: Perspectives on Gender and the Italian Renaissance,* edited by Marilyn Migiel and Juliana Schiesari. Ithaca, NY: Cornell University Press, 1991.

Clarke, Paula C. "The Business of Prostitution in Early Renaissance Venice." *Renaissance Quarterly* 68, no. 2 (Summer 2015): 419–464.

Cohen, Elizabeth S. "'Courtesans' and 'Whores': Words and Behavior in Roman Streets." *Women's Studies* 19, no. 2 (1991): 201–208.

Cohen, Sherrill. *The Evolution of Women's Asylums since 1500: From Refuges for Ex-Prostitutes to Shelters for Battered Women.* New York: Oxford University Press, 1992.

Cosentino, Paola. "Sulle orme del Tasso: L'epopea eroica di Giuditta nel '600." In *Le donne della Bibbia, la Bibbia delle donne: Teatro, letteratura e vita,* edited by Rossana Gorris Camos. Fasano, Italy: Schena Editore, 2012.

Cox, Virginia. "Authorizing Women: The Problem of Docere." In *The Prodigious Muse.* Baltimore: Johns Hopkins University Press, 2011.

———. *The Prodigious Muse.* Baltimore: Johns Hopkins University Press, 2011.

———. *A Short History of the Italian Renaissance.* New York: I. B. Tauris, 2016.

———. "Tasso's *Malpiglio overo de la corte: The Courtier* Revisited." *Modern Language Review* 90, no. 4 (October 1995): 897–918.

———. *Women's Writing in Italy, 1400–1650.* Baltimore: Johns Hopkins University Press, 2008.

Cranston, Jodi. *The Poetics of Portraiture in the Italian Renaissance.* Cambridge: Cambridge University Press, 2000.

Cristellon, Cecilia "Ritratto di una cortigiana del Cinquecento: Caterina de Medici da Verona e le sue vicende (1518–1582)." In *Ritratti. La dimendione individuale nella storia (secoli XV–XX). Studi in onore di Anne Jacobson Schutte,* edited by Robert A. Pierce and Silvana Seidel Menchi. Rome: Edizioni di Storia e Letteratura, 2009.

Cutler, Anthony. "Significant Gifts: Patterns of Exchange in Late Antique, Byzantine, and Early Islamic Diplomacy." *Journal of Medieval and Early Modern Studies* 38, no. 1 (2008): 79–101.

Davis, Natalie Zemon. *The Gift in Sixteenth-Century France*. Madison: University of Wisconsin Press, 2000.

Del Giudice, Luisa. "Armida: Virgo Fingens (The Broken Mirror)." In *Western Gerusalem: University of California Studies on Tasso*, edited by Luisa Del Giudice. New York: Out of London Press, 1984.

Dilmac, Bitül. "Epic Anger in *La Gerusalemme Liberata*: Rinaldo's Irascibility and Tasso's *Allegoria della Gerusalemme*." In *Discourses of Anger in the Early Modern Period*, edited by Karl A. E. Enenkel and Anita Traninger. Boston: Brill, 2015.

Doglio, Maria Luisa. "Letter Writing, 1350–1650." In *A History of Women's Writing in Italy*, edited by Letizia Panizza and Sharon Wood. Cambridge, UK: Cambridge University Press, 2000.

———. "Scrittura e 'offizio di parole' nelle 'Lettere familiari' di Veronica Franco." In *Lettera e donna. Scrittura epistolare tra Quattro e Cinquecento*. Rome: Bulzoni, 1993.

Duindam, Jeroen. *Myths of Power: Norbert Elias and the Early Modern European Court*. Amsterdam: Amsterdam University Press, 1995.

Durling, Robert. "The Epic Ideal." In *The Old World: Discovery and Rebirth*, edited by David Daiches and Anthony Thorlby. London: Aldus Books, 1974.

Dursteler, Eric. "The Bailo in Constantinople: Crisis and Career in Venice's Early Modern Diplomatic Corps." *Mediterranean Historical Review* 16, no. 2 (December 2001): 1–30.

Elias, Norbert. *The Court Society*. New York: Blackwell, 1983.

Erspamer, Francesco. "Il 'pensier debole' di Torquato Tasso." In *La menzogna*, edited by Franco Cardini. Florence: Ponte alle Grazie, 1989.

Faini, Marco. *Standing at the Crossroads: Stories of Doubt in Renaissance Italy*. Cambridge, UK: Legenda, 2023.

Fantoni, Marcello. *Italian Courts and European Culture*. Amsterdam: Amsterdam University Press, 2022.

———. "Le corti e i 'modi' di vestire." In *Storia d'Italia*, Annali 19, *La moda*, edited by Marco Belfanti and Fiorella Giusberti. Turin: Einaudi, 2003.

———, ed. *The Court in Europe*. Rome: Bulzoni, 2012.

Favretti, Elvira. "Rime e Lettere di Veronica Franco." *Giornale storico della letteratura italiana* 163 (1986): 344–382.

Fedele, Dante. "*Ius gentium:* The Metamorphosis of a Legal Concept (Ancient Rome to Early Modern Europe)." In *Empire and Legal Thought: Ideas and Institutions from Antiquity to Modernity*, edited by Edward Cavanagh. Leiden: Brill, 2020.

———. "Uno scritto sull'ambasciatore del secondo Cinquecento: 'Il Messaggiero' di Torquato Tasso." *Il pensiero politico* 51, no. 1 (2018): 113–114.

Feldman, Martha, and Bonnie Gordon, eds. *The Courtesan's Arts: Cross-Cultural Perspectives*. Oxford: Oxford University Press, 2006.

Figliuolo, Bruno. *Il Diplomatico e il trattatista: Ermolao Barbaro ambasciatore della Serenissima e il De Officio Legati*. Naples: Guida, 1999.

Findlen, Paula. "Humanism, Politics and Pornography in Renaissance Italy." In *The Invention of Pornography: Obscenity and the Origins of Modernity, 1500–1800*, edited by Lynn Hunt. New York: Zone Books, 1993.

Fletcher, Catherine. *Diplomacy in Renaissance Rome: The Rise of the Resident Ambassador.* Cambridge: Cambridge University Press, 2015.

Foister, Susan, Ashok Roy, and Martin Wyld, *Making and Meaning in Holbein's 'Ambassadors.'* London: National Gallery of London, 1998.

Formicula, Crescenzo. "Dark Visibility: Lavinia in the *Aeneid.*" *Vergilius* 52 (2006): 76–95.

Foucault, Michel. *Discipline and Punish: The Birth of the Prison.* Translated by Alan Sheridan. New York: Vintage Books, 1995.

Frey, Linda, and Marsha Frey. *The History of Diplomatic Immunity.* Columbus: Ohio State University Press, 1999.

Fubini, Riccardo. "Diplomacy and Government in the Italian City-States of the Fifteenth Century (Florence and Venice)." In *Politics and Diplomacy in Early Modern Italy,* edited by Daniela Frigo, translated by Adrian Belton. Cambridge, UK: Cambridge University Press, 2000.

———. "The Italian League and the Policy of the Balance of Power at the Accession of Lorenzo de' Medici." *Journal of Modern History* 67 (December 1995): S166–S199.

Ghirardo, Diane Yvonne. "The Topography of Prostitution in Renaissance Ferrara." *Journal of the Society of Architectural Historians* 60, no. 4 (2001): 402–431.

Girard, René. *The Scapegoat.* Translated by Yvonne Freccero. Baltimore: Johns Hopkins University Press, 1986.

Gough, Melinda. "Tasso's Enchantress, Tasso's Captive Woman." *Renaissance Quarterly* 54, no. 1 (2001): 523–552.

Grande Dizionario della Lingua Italiana. Prototipo edizione digitale. Turin: UTET Grandi Opere, 2018. https://www.gdli.it/sala-lettura/vol/5?seq=972.

Greenblatt, Stephen. *Renaissance Self-Fashioning: From More to Shakespeare.* Chicago: University of Chicago Press, 1980.

Gullino, Giuseppe. "Trevisan, Domenico," In *Dizionario biografico degli Italiani.* Vol. 96. Rome: Istituto dell'Enciclopedia Italiana, 2019. https://www.treccani.it/enciclopedia/domenico-trevisan_%28Dizionario-Biografico%29/.

Hairston, Julia L. "'*Di sangue illustre & pellegrino*': The Eclipse of the Body in the Lyric of Tullia d'Aragona." In *The Body in Early Modern Italy,* edited by Julia L. Hairston and Walter Stephens. Baltimore: Johns Hopkins University Press, 2010.

———. "Tullia d'Aragona." In *Oxford Bibliographies in Renaissance and Reformation,* edited by Margaret L. King. Oxford: Oxford University Press, 2016.

Hampton, Timothy. "Baroque Diplomacy." In *The Oxford Handbook of the Baroque,* edited by John D. Lyons. Oxford: Oxford University Press, 2019.

———. *Fictions of Embassy: Literature and Diplomacy in Early Modern Europe.* Ithaca, NY: Cornell University Press, 2009.

Heinze, Richard. *Virgil's Epic Technique.* Berkeley: University of California Press, 1994.

Helm, Jennifer. *Poetry and Censorship in Counter-Reformation Italy.* Leiden: Brill, 2015.

Hervey, Mary F. S. *Holbein's "Ambassadors": The Picture and the Men; An Historical Study.* London: George Bell and Sons, 1900.

Horodowich, Elizabeth. "Armchair Travelers and the Venetian Discovery of the New World." *The Sixteenth Century Journal* 36, no. 4 (Winter 2005): 1039–1062.

———. *Language and Statecraft in Early Modern Venice*. New York: Cambridge University Press, 2008.

Howard, Deborah. *The Architectural History of Venice*. New Haven, CT: Yale University Press, 1980; rev. ed., 2002.

———. "The Status of the Oriental Traveler in Renaissance Venice." In *Re-orienting the Renaissance: Cultural Exchanges with the East*, edited by Gerald M. MacLean. New York: Palgrave Macmillan, 2005.

———. *Venice & the East: The Impact of the Islamic World on Venetian Architecture, 1100–1500*. New Haven, CT: Yale University Press, 2000.

Hysell, Jesse J. "Interpreting the Veneto-Mamluk Gift Exchanges of 894–5/1489–90." In *Culture matérielle et contacts diplomatiques entre l'Occident latin, Byzance et l'Orient islamique (XIe–XVIe siècle)*, edited by Frédéric Bauden. Leiden: Brill, 2021.

Jardine, Lisa. *Worldly Goods: A New History of the Renaissance*. New York: W. W. Norton, 1998.

Jardine, Lisa, and Jerry Britton, *Global Interests: Renaissance Art Between East and West*. London: Reaktion, 2000.

Jensen, Katharine Ann. *Writing Love: Letters, Women, and the Novel in France, 1605–1776*. Carbondale: Southern Illinois University Press, 1995.

Jones, Anna Rosalind. "City Women and Their Audiences: Louise Labé and Veronica Franco." In *Rewriting the Renaissance: The Discourses of Sexual Difference in Early Modern Europe*, edited by Margaret W. Ferguson, Maureen Quilligan, and Nancy J. Vickers. Chicago: University of Chicago Press, 1986.

———. "New Songs for the Swallow: Ovid's Philomela in Tullia d'Aragona and Gaspara Stampa." In *Refiguring Woman: Perspectives on Gender and the Italian Renaissance*, edited by Marilyn Migiel and Juliana Schiesari. Ithaca, NY: Cornell University Press, 1991.

———. "The Poetics of Group Identity: Self-Commemoration through Dialogue in Pernette du Guillet and Tullia d'Aragona." In *The Currency of Eros: Women's Love Lyric in Europe, 1540–1620*. Bloomington: Indiana University Press, 1990.

Jones, Ann Rosalind, and Margaret F. Rosenthal. *Veronica Franco: Poems and Selected Letters*. Edited and translated by Ann Rosalind Jones and Margaret F. Rosenthal. Chicago: University of Chicago Press, 1998.

Jones, Ann Rosalind, and Peter Stallybrass. *Renaissance Clothing and the Materials of Memory*. Cambridge: Cambridge University Press, 2000.

Jossa, Stefano. "Da Ariosto a Tasso: la verità della storia e le bugie della poesia." *Studi rinascimentali* 1, no. 2 (2004): 79–92.

———. "The Lies of the Poets: Literature as Fiction in the Italian Renaissance." In *Renaissance Studies in Honor of Joseph Connors*, edited by Machtelt Israëls and Louis A. Waldman. Cambridge, MA: Harvard University Press, 2013.

Kantorowicz, Ernst Hartwig. *The King's Two Bodies; a Study in Mediaeval Political Theology*. Princeton, NJ: Princeton University Press, 1957.

Keller, Vera. "Painted Friends: Political Interest and the Transformation of International Learned Sociability." In *Friendship in the Middle Ages and Early Modern Age: Explora-*

tions of a Fundamental Ethical Discourse, edited by Albrecht Classen and Marilyn Sandidge. Berlin: de Gruyter, 2010.

Kenaan, Hagi. "The 'Unusual' Character of Holbein's *Ambassadors*." *Artibus et Historiae* 23, no. 46 (2002): 61–75.

Kociszewska, Ewa. "Displays of Sugar Sculpture and the Collection of Antiquities in Late Renaissance Venice." *Renaissance Quarterly* 73 (2020): 441–488.

Kolsky, Stephen. *Courts and Courtiers in Renaissance Northern Italy*. Burlington, VT: Ashgate/Variorum, 2003.

Lazzarini, Isabella. *Communication and Conflict: Italian Diplomacy in the Early Renaissance, 1350–1520*. Oxford: Oxford University Press, 2015.

Lewis, Charlton T., and Charles Short. *A Latin Dictionary*. Oxford: Clarendon Press, 1945.

Lindemann, Mary. *Medicine and Society in Early Modern Europe*. Cambridge, UK: Cambridge University Press, 1999.

Lorch, Maristella De P. "The Epicurean in Lorenzo Valla's *On Pleasure*." In *Atoms, Pneuma, and Tranquillity: Epicurean and Stoic Themes in European Thought*, edited by Margaret J. Osler. Cambridge, UK: Cambridge University Press, 1991.

Lucchetta, Francesca. "L''affare Zen' in Levante nel primo cinquecento." *Studi veneziani* 10 (1968): 109–219.

Martin, John Jeffries. *Myths of Renaissance Individualism*. Basingstoke, UK: Palgrave Macmillan, 2004.

———. "The Myth of Renaissance Individualism." In *A Companion to the Worlds of the Renaissance*, edited by Guido Ruggiero. Oxford: Blackwell Publishing, 2002.

Mattingly, Garrett. "The First Resident Embassies: Medieval Italian Origins of Modern Diplomacy." *Speculum* 2, no. 4 (October 1937): 423–439.

———. *Renaissance Diplomacy*. Boston: Houghton Mifflin, 1955.

McCall, Timothy. *Brilliant Bodies: Fashioning Courtly Men in Early Renaissance Italy*. University Park: Pennsylvania State University Press, 2022.

McGough, Laura Jane. "Quarantining Beauty: The French Disease in Early Modern Venice." In *Sins of the Flesh: Responding to Sexual Disease in Early Modern Europe*, edited by Kevin Patrick Siena. Toronto: Centre for Reformation and Renaissance Studies, 2005.

———. "'Raised from the Devil's Jaws': A Convent for Repentant Prostitutes in Venice, 1530–1670." PhD diss., Northwestern University, 1997.

Migiel, Marilyn. *Gender and Genealogy in Tasso's* Gerusalemme Liberata. Lewiston, NY: Edwin Mellen Press, 1993.

———. "Secrets of a Sorceress: Tasso's Armida." *Quaderni d'Italianistica* 8, no. 2 (1987): 149–166.

———. *Veronica Franco in Dialogue*. Toronto: University of Toronto Press, 2022.

Milanesi, Marica. "Ambrosio Contarini." In *Dizionario Biografico Degli Italiani*. Vol. 28.: Rome: Istituto dell'Enciclopedia Italiana, 1983. https://www.treccani.it/enciclopedia/ambrogio-contarini_(Dizionario-Biografico)/.

Moudarres, Andrea. "A Less Perfect Captain: Reconsidering Goffredo in the *Gerusalemme Liberata*." *Forum Italicum* 55, no. 1 (2021): 3–20.

———. *The Enemy in Italian Renaissance Epic: Images of Hostility from Dante to Tasso*. Newark, NJ: University of Delaware Press, 2019.

Moulton, Ian Frederick. *Before Pornography: Erotic Writing in Early Modern England.* Oxford: Oxford University Press, 2000.

Muir, Edward. *Civic Ritual in Renaissance Venice.* Princeton, NJ: Princeton University Press, 1981.

Niccoli, Gabriel. "Autobiography and Fiction in Veronica Franco's Epistolary Narrative." *Canadian Journal of Italian Studies* 16, no. 47 (1993): 129–142.

Ord, Melanie. "Returning from Venice to England: Sir Henry Wotton as Diplomat, Pedagogue, and Italian Cultural Connoisseur." In *Borders and Travelers in Early Modern Europe,* edited by Thomas Betteridge. Burlington, VT: Ashgate, 2007.

Ostrowski, Donald. "City Names of the Western Steppe at the Time of the Mongol Invasion." *Bulletin of the School of Oriental and African Studies* 61, no. 3 (1998): 465–475.

Otis, Leah Lydia. *Prostitution in Medieval Society: The History of an Urban Institution in Languedoc.* Chicago: University of Chicago Press, 1985.

Perocco, Daria. *Viaggiare e raccontare. Narrazione di viaggio ed esperienze di racconto tra Cinque e Seicento.* Alessandria, Italy: Edizioni dell'Orso, 1997.

Pirillo, Diego. *The Refugee-Diplomat: Venice, England, and the Reformation.* Ithaca, NY: Cornell University Press, 2018.

———. "Tasso at the French Embassy: Epic, Diplomacy, and the Law of Nations." In *Authority and Diplomacy from Dante to Shakespeare,* edited by Jason Powell and William T. Rossiter. Farnham, UK: Ashgate, 2013.

Poirier, Guy. "A Contagion at the Source of Discourse on Sexualities: Syphilis during the French Renaissance." In *Imagining Contagion in Early Modern Europe,* edited by Claire L. Carlin. Basingstoke, UK: Palgrave Macmillan, 2005.

Pollock, Griselda. *Differencing the Canon: Feminist Desire and the Writing of Art's Histories.* London: Routledge, 1999.

Portioli, A. "Altre notizie sulla morte di Alberto Maraviglia." *Archivio storico Lombardo* 2 (December 1875): 30–50.

Pubblici, Lorenzo. "Venezia e il Mar d'Azov: alcune considerazioni sulla Tana nel XIV secolo." *Archivio Storico Italiano* 163, no. 3 (605) (2005): 435–483.

Pullan, Brian. *Tolerance, Regulation and Rescue: Dishonoured Women and Abandoned Children in Italy, 1300–1800.* Manchester: Manchester University Press, 2016.

Pyy, Elina. *Women and War in Roman Epic.* Leiden: Brill, 2021.

Quaintance, Courtney. *Textual Masculinity and the Exchange of Women in Renaissance Venice.* Toronto: University of Toronto Press, 2015.

Queller, Donald. "The Development of the Ambassadorial Relazioni." In *Renaissance Venice,* edited by J. R. Hale. Totowa, NJ: Rowman and Littlefield, 1973.

———. *The Office of Ambassador in the Middle Ages.* Princeton, NJ: Princeton University Press, 1967.

———. *The Venetian Patriciate: Reality versus Myth.* Champaign-Urbana: University of Illinois Press, 1986.

Quint, David. "Political Allegory in the *Gerusalemme liberate.*" *Renaissance Quarterly* 43, no. 1 (Spring 1990): 1–29.

Quondam, Amedeo. *Le "Carte messaggiere": Retorica e modelli di comunicazione epistolare. Per un indice dei libri di lettere del Cinquecento.* Rome: Bulzoni, 1981.

———. "'Nato ed allevato in Corte': Torquato Tasso." *LibrosdelaCorte.es* 22 (2021): 399–423. https://doi.org/10.15366/ldc2021.13.22.015.

Ramachandran, Ayesha. "Tasso's Petrarch: The Lyric Means to Epic Ends." *MLN* 122, no. 1 (2007): 186–208.

Ray, Meredith. *Writing Gender in Women's Letter Collections of the Italian Renaissance.* Toronto: University of Toronto Press, 2009.

Refini, Eugenio. "Giuditta, Armida e il velo della seduzione." *Italian Studies* 68, no. 1 (2013): 78–98.

Robin, Diana. "Courtesans Celebrity and Print Culture in Renaissance Venice." In *Italian Women and the City: Essays*, edited by Janet Levarie Smarr and Daria Valentini. Madison, NJ: Fairleigh Dickinson University Press, 2003.

Romussi, Carlo. "La morte di Alberto Maraviglia (1533)." *Archivio storico lombardo* 1 (1874): 249–274.

Rosenthal, Margaret F. *The Honest Courtesan: Veronica Franco, Citizen and Writer in Sixteenth-Century Venice.* Chicago: University of Chicago, 1992.

———. "Veronica Franco's Terze Rime: The Venetian Courtesan's Defense." *Renaissance Quarterly* 42, no. 2 (1989): 227–257.

Rossetti, Edoardo. "Meraviglia, Giovanni Alberto." In *Dizionario Biografico degli Italiani.* Vol. 73. Rome: Istituto della Enciclopedia Italiana, 2009. https://www.treccani.it/enciclopedia/giovanni-alberto-meraviglia_(Dizionario-Biografico)/.

Rozzo, Ugo. *La letteratura italiana negli indici del Cinquecento.* Urbino, Italy: Forum, 2006.

Ruggiero, Guido. *Binding Passions: Tales of Magic, Marriage, and Power at the End of the Renaissance.* New York: Oxford University Press, 1993.

———. *The Boundaries of Eros: Sex Crime and Sexuality in Renaissance Venice.* New York: Oxford University Press, 1985.

———. *The Renaissance in Italy.* Cambridge, UK: Cambridge University Press, 2015.

Russell, Rinaldina. Introduction to *Dialogue on the Infinity of Love.* Chicago: University of Chicago Press, 1997.

Saletti, Beatrice. "Gift Exchanges and Traces of Material Life in Mamluk Diplomacy: First Notes on Embassies from Egypt to Italy and Italian Missions to Cairo (1421–1512)." In *Culture matérielle et contacts diplomatiques entre l'Occident latin, Byzance et l'Orient islamique (XIe–XVIe siècle)*, edited by Frédéric Bauden. Leiden: Brill, 2021.

Sanudo, Marino. *Venice, Città Excelentissima: Selections from the Renaissance Diaries of Marin Sanudo.* Edited by Patricia H. Labalme and Laura Sanguineti White, translated by Linda Carroll. Baltimore: Johns Hopkins University Press, 2008.

Serassi, Pierantonio, ed. *Rime di Domenico Veniero, senatore viniziano.* Bergamo, Italy: Pietro Lancellotto, 1751.

Shemek, Deanna. "'Mi mostrano a dito tutti quanti': Disease, Deixis, and Disfiguration in the *Lamento di una cortigiana Ferrarese.*" In *Medusa's Gaze: Essays on Gender, Literature, and Aesthetics in the Italian Renaissance. In Honor of Robert J. Rodini*, edited by Paul A. Ferrara, Eugenio Giusti, and Jane Tylus. Boca Raton, FL: Bordighera Press, 2004.

Smith, Logan Pearsall. *The Life and Letters of Sir Henry Wotton.* Oxford: Clarendon, 1907.

Snyder, Jon R. *Dissimulation and the Culture of Secrecy in Early Modern Europe*. Berkeley: University of California Press, 2009.

Soranzo, Matteo. "Ermolao Barbaro (The Younger)." *Encyclopedia of Italian Literary Studies*. Edited by Gaetana Marrone and Paolo Puppa. New York: Routledge, 2007.

Sperling, Jutta Gisela. *Convents and the Body Politic in Late Renaissance Venice*. Chicago: University of Chicago, 1999.

Stephens, Walter. "Saint Paul Among the Amazons: Gender and Authority in Gerusalemme Liberata." In *Discourses of Authority in Medieval and Renaissance Literature*, edited by Kevin Brownlee and Walter Stephens. Hanover, NH: Dartmouth College by University Press of New England, 1989.

———. "Trickster, Textor, Architect, Thief: Craft and Comedy in *Gerusalemme Liberata*." In *Renaissance Transactions: Ariosto and Tasso*, edited by Valeria Finucci. Durham, NC: Duke University Press, 1999.

Storey, Tessa. *Carnal Commerce in Counter-Reformation Rome*. Cambridge, UK: Cambridge University Press, 2008.

———. "Courtesan Culture: Manhood, Honor, and Sociability." In *Erotic Cultures of Renaissance Italy*, edited by Sara F. Matthews-Grieco. Burlington, VT: Ashgate, 2010.

Stras, Laurie. "'Onde havrà 'l mond'esempio et vera historia': Musical Echoes of Henri III's Progress through Italy." *Acta Musicologica* 72, no. 1 (2000): 7–41.

Sutton, Robert F. "The Invention of the Female Nude: Zeuxis, Vase-Painting, and the Kneeling Bather." In *Athenian Potters and Painters II*, edited by John H. Oakley and Olga Palagia. Oxford: Oxbow Books, 2009.

Syme, Ronald. "The Casdusii in History and in Fiction." *Journal of Hellenic Studies* 108 (1988): 145.

———. *Lettere di Torquato Tasso*. Edited by Cesare Guasti. Florence: Successori Le Monnier, 1852.

Taylor, Kathryn. "Matters Worthy of Men of State: Ethnography and Diplomatic Reporting in Sixteenth-Century Venice." *The Sixteenth Century Journal* 51, no. 3 (Fall 2020): 741–762.

Todd, Ruth W. "Lavinia Blushed." *Vergilius* 26 (1980): 27–33.

Tucci, Ugo. "Mercanti, Viaggiatori, Pellegrini Nel Quattrocento." In *Storia Della Cultura Veneta*, edited by Girolamo Arnaldi and Manlio Pastore Stocchi. 3 vols. Vicenza: N. Pozza, 1976.

Tylus, Jane. "Tasso's Trees: Epic and Local Culture." In *Epics in the Contemporary World: The Poetics of Community*, edited by Margaret Beissinger, Jane Tylus, and Susanne Wofford. Berkeley: University of California Press, 1999.

Ugolini, Paola. *The Court and Its Critics: Anti-Court Sentiments in Early Modern Italy*. Toronto: University of Toronto Press, 2020.

van Berkel, Maaike. "The People of the Pen: Self-Perceptions of Status and Role in the Administration of Empires and Polities." In *Prince, Pen, and Sword: Eurasian Perspectives*, edited by Maaike van Berkel and Jeroen Duindam. Leiden: Brill, 2018.

Virgil. *Eclogues; Georgics; Aeneid: Books 1–6*. Edited by George P. Goold, translated by H. Rushton Fairclough. Cambridge, MA: Harvard University Press, 1999.

Vocabolario degli Accademici della Crusca, 5th ed. In *Lessicografia della Crusca in Rete*. Florence: Accademia della Crusca, 2000–2004. http://www.lessicografia.it/.

Vuillemin, Pascal. *Une itinérance prophétique. Le voyage en Perse d'Ambrogio Contarini (1474–1477)*. Paris: Classiques Garnier, 2016.

Walton, Izaak. *The Lives of Dr. John Donne, Sir Henry Wotton, Mr. Richard Hooker, Mr. George Herbert*. London: Thomas Newcomb for Richard Marriot, 1670.

Wansbrough, John. "A Mamuk Ambassador to Venice in 913/1507." *Bulletin of the School of Oriental and African Affairs, University of London* 26, no. 3 (1963): 503–530.

Watkins, John. *After Lavinia: A Literary History of Premodern Marriage Diplomacy*. Ithaca, NY: Cornell University Press, 2017.

Weddle, Saundra. "Mobility and Prostitution in Early Modern Venice." *Early Modern Women* 14, no. 1 (Fall 2019): 95–108.

Welch, Ellen. *A Theater of Diplomacy: International Relations and the Performing Arts in Early Modern France*. Philadelphia: University of Pennsylvania Press, 2017.

Wilson, Bronwen. *The World in Venice: Print, the City and Early Modern Identity*. Toronto: University of Toronto Press, 2005.

Wojciehowski, Dolora [now Hannah] Chapelle. "Veronica Franco vs. Maffio Venier: Sex, Death, and Poetry in Cinquecento Venice." *Italica* 83, nos. 3–4 (2006): 367–390.

Wolfe, Jessica. *Humanism, Machinery, and Renaissance Literature*. Cambridge, UK: Cambridge University Press, 2004.

Zamperetti, Sergio. "De Franceschi, Andrea." In *Dizionario biografico degli Italiani*. Vol. 36. Rome: Istituto dell'Enciclopedia Italiana, 1986. https://www.treccani.it/enciclopedia/andrea-de-franceschi_%28Dizionario-Biografico%29/.

Zatti, Sergio. "Dalla parte di Satana: sull'imperialismo cristiano nella *Gerusalemme Liberata*." In *La Rappresentazione dell'altro nei testi del Rinascimento*, edited by Sergio Zatti. Lucca: M. Pacini Fazzi, 1998.

Index

Note: Page numbers in italics refer to figures.

About the Author

Paola De Santo is associate professor of Italian at the University of Georgia in Athens. Her research focuses on early modern Italy, with a particular interest in women writers. Together with Caterina Mongiat Farina, she is editor and translator of Isabella Andreini's *Letters (1607)* for the Other Voice in Early Modern Europe series, and is currently working on an Italian-language critical edition of Andreini's *Lettere*.